ENDORSEMENTS

"George Aldridge was a mentor to me long before I understood the meaning of the term. *What It Takes to Be a Leader* is a superb reflection of the life and career of a gifted, dedicated, humble leader. I benefitted from having him in my life; you will benefit from joining him on his journey in this book."

—*Gen.(R) Martin E. Dempsey, 18th chairman of the Joint Chiefs of Staff and author of* Radical Inclusion *and* No Time for Spectators

"With outstanding leadership skills from over fifty years of experience that make him a scholar/leader, George Aldridge displays in his superb book, *What It Takes to Be a Leader*, the great thinking that not only outlines the challenges but provides us with a pragmatic template on how to fix leadership for the rest of the 21st century and beyond. His research is valuable, his writing is uncomplicated, and his arguments provide solutions."

—*Dr. Bill Ruud, president and professor of management at Marietta College, Marietta, Ohio*

"In *What It Takes to Be a Leader*, George Aldridge provides good, sound guidance rooted in his real-world experience of leading troops. Having assisted George in coaching a CEO through challenging circumstances, I have seen and personally experienced firsthand the growth and development of leaders who take his advice to heart and constructively confront the challenges before them."

—*Anthony Campbell, president and CEO of East Kentucky Power Cooperative*

"*What It Takes to Be a Leader* by George Washington Aldridge provides the reader insight into the deeply ingrained leadership qualities instilled in the author by his father. George lived these values during his own military career and feels passionately about them. This book is a treasure trove of pearls of wisdom from philosophers, statesmen, military leaders, and leaders from many fields of endeavor. It should be required reading at any university offering degrees in leadership."

—C. Dale Elliott, MD, FACC, *founder and president (Retired) of Heart South Cardiovascular Group*

WHAT IT TAKES
TO BE A LEADER
of Character and Competence

George Aldridge

DUNRAVEN BOOKS
Atlanta, Georgia, USA

First Edition: 2025

Printed in the United States

Hardcover ISBN: 979-8-9901331-1-2
Trade Paperback ISBN: 979-8-9901331-0-5
eBook ISBN: 979-8-9901331-2-9

Published by Dunraven Books
Atlanta, Georgia, USA

Book cover and interior design by Glen M. Edelstein

With love and total dedication to my wife, Vicki

*With deep affection and pride to my son and daughter-in-law,
Drew and Christina*

With limitless hopes and dreams for our granddaughter, Edie

CONTENTS

PART THREE: COMPETENCE—WHAT LEADERS DO

PREFACE

A DEFINING MOMENT in my life came on the twenty-first of June, 1990, on a beach in Normandy, France. I was leading a group of fifty very unhappy Army officers through a professional development exercise called a staff ride. The group was unhappy because their unit, the 1st Battalion of the 36th Infantry Regiment, proudly named The Spartans, had just been redesignated as the 5th Battalion of the 18th Infantry Regiment. Soldiers have a strong sense of pride in their unit's history, so when they're forced to give up that unit's loyalty for a new organization, it's a painful experience. Imagine rabid New York City baseball fans being told that their cherished Yankees will now become the Red Birds. I was at the end of my two-year tour in Germany with The Spartans. I decided that I should do my best as its departing battalion commander to attempt to inculcate the same sense of pride in their new unit, the 18th Infantry, as they had in their beloved 36th Infantry.

I knew that changing the minds of my young officers was going to be tough. Still, the task was made slightly easier because the 18th Infantry Regiment had a long and glorious history going back to the Revolutionary War. A significant event in the history of the regiment was June 6, 1944, when the 18th Infantry stormed Omaha Beach on D-Day. So, in my last month of command, I took all my officers and the command sergeant major, fifty in all, on a staff ride to Normandy, France. My plan for the day was to go to Omaha Beach, where the 18th Infantry landed early on D-Day morning. I hoped that by standing on the very same sand where their forebears attacked across the beach on

D-Day, they would walk away from the experience with an increased sense of pride in being a leader in their newly designated regiment.

We jumped off the bus about a mile from where the regiment came ashore and walked along the surf's edge to the spot where the 18th began its assault, which was ironically called Easy Red Beach. From there, the lieutenants and the captains would be walking the same hallowed ground as their 1944 counterparts on that longest day. I reminded them that on D-Day, the 18th Infantry experienced extremely heavy casualties, with hundreds of soldiers killed or wounded on the very ground they currently stood. If you've seen the movie *Saving Private Ryan,* you have a voyeur's sense of what courage it took and the price the soldiers paid to cross that short stretch of sand.

As a group, we trudged across Easy Red Beach for over a hundred yards, then slogged up a steep seventy-five-yard incline to the top of a bluff. For every three steps in the loose sand we climbed, we slid back two. I wanted us to get a feel for the experience of ascending the steep, sandy incline just as historian John McManus described it: "The mere act of movement was exhausting, and not just because of the enemy fire."[1] Even though my officers were in superb physical condition, they were winded when we reached the top of the hill. What they didn't know,

> **We are what we leave behind.**
> —*Jedi Master Yoda*

and the reason I chose to enter from where we did, was that at the top of the crest, unseen from the beach below, was the hallowed ground of the Normandy American Cemetery.

I encouraged my officers to stay together as we slogged up the hill so we would all reach the top of the bluff simultaneously. None of us were prepared for what we saw as we crested the hill. As far as the eye could see were more than 9,000 brilliant white headstones and crosses perfectly aligned in straight rows, all standing at attention on a pristine, flawlessly manicured carpet of emerald green grass. The shock was visceral. We stood for a long moment, taking in the sight, trying to absorb and understand what we were seeing and experiencing: thousands of headstones, each representing a soldier who had made the ultimate sacrifice, each representing a young American soldier no different from the soldiers each of my officers currently led.

Even though I knew the cemetery was at the top of the bluff, seeing the endless field of fallen heroes for the first time was emotionally overwhelming. I was unprepared for the onrush of the kick-in-the-gut emotion I felt at that moment. Looking at my officers, I realized I wasn't alone. I had prepared and rehearsed a detailed lecture espousing the heroism and courage of the 18th infantry leaders and soldiers on that day in 1944 and how we had much to live up to. However, I was so overcome with emotion that every word I had prepared escaped me.

A slice of my own personal history compounded the shock to my senses. My father, who turned twenty years old just five days before D-Day, had landed on that same stretch of Omaha Beach only 100 yards from where I stood. As I lingered in that sea of glistening white headstones, thinking of my dad clawing his way across the beach and up that steep hill forty-seven years earlier, it knocked me for an emotional loop. Standing there, stewing in my emotions, I looked up and saw that my officers were staring at me. They collectively knew that what we had just experienced was something unique and special, and they were looking to me for an explanation, waiting for me to speak. My prepared words escaped me, but I knew I had to say something. What came out of my mouth was unplanned and spontaneous. My words were short and strained, and as I spoke, it seemed like an out-of-body experience.

I motioned for the officers to close in on me. Struggling to hide my feelings, my voice cracked, made worse because it was obvious that many of my officers were also emotionally strained and on the edge. I was fighting to keep my composure but was having a hard time. Doing my best to have a clear and strong voice, I asked:

"If you had been here on D-Day, would you have had the courage to lead your men up this hill? And if you had had the courage, would your men have followed you? Do you deserve to be followed? Your men wouldn't have followed you just because you're a lieutenant or a captain or because you're their platoon leader or company commander. They would have followed you because they trust your character and your competence—*who you are*—not because of your rank or because you're the boss. Do you have what it takes to earn that level of trust?"

Following my few words, we wandered off separately into the ocean of headstones, each of us trying to make sense of our personal feelings. Several personal thoughts burst into my mind. I had been their battalion commander for two years; they knew me, had lived through my strengths and weaknesses, and knew my flaws. As a leader, I always had great concern for the welfare of those I led, but I had never taken a deep dive into my own character to determine if my men were following me because they wanted to or merely because they had no other choice. As I stood amid the sea of fallen heroes' graves, the powerful emotion of the moment forced me to honestly ask myself: *Would I have had the courage to lead my men up that hill? If I had had the courage, would my men have followed me? Do I deserve to be followed? Do my men follow me because they trust my character and competence—who I am—or just because I am their boss? Do I have what it takes?*

That moment on Omaha Beach was my leadership epiphany, the moment where I started a soul-searching, lifelong journey to answer those questions. In that journey, I have learned many lessons and have come to many conclusions about what it takes to be a leader of character and competence. Those lessons apply to every leader, whether on the battlefield, the shop floor, or in the boardroom, the classroom, or the family. As I slide down the backside of life's crescendo, I want to pass on those hard-earned lessons to leaders clawing their way up the front side of that crescendo. That desire to pay it forward inspired me to write this book.

Leadership requires character and competence. Both are necessary, but neither is sufficient alone. My hope is that the following pages will inspire you to start your lifelong journey to do what it takes to become a leader of character and competence, which we so desperately need.

INTRODUCTION

WE ARE IN a leadership crisis, a moment in history when trust in our leaders is rapidly disappearing. This crisis permeates every profession and walk of life, be it politics, government, big business, the judiciary, media, sports, academia, military, or the clergy. This loss of trust is so pervasive that people take it for granted, believing it to be the rule, not the exception. If you haven't noticed this crisis, you're not paying attention. Too many organizations—large and small, public and private—don't get the leadership they need or deserve. We're missing what we want in too many of our leaders, which is mainly trust in their character and confidence in their competence.

On the day I was commissioned as a brand-new second lieutenant, I asked my father, a decorated WWII, Korea, and Vietnam veteran with thirty-four years in uniform, "What do I have to do to be a good leader?" Thinking he would go into one of his long-drawn-out Dad replies, he simply said, "Accomplish your mission, and take care of your men. It's as easy and as hard as that." When I asked what he meant by "it's easy but hard," he replied, "It's easy to know how to be a good leader; just get the job done and take care of those you lead. What makes it hard is actually doing what it takes to get both those things done."

Since that day over fifty years ago, I have come to the sad conclusion that we're in a leadership crisis because not enough people are doing *what it takes* to be a good leader. The leadership theme *de jour* of whether a person is an effective leader versus an ineffective leader is like debating whether a person is honest or almost honest; either you're honest, or you're not. If you're not leading effectively, then you may be managing, supervising, or presiding—but you are *not* leading. Either you're a leader, or you're not. Ask those in your organization two simple questions about their supervisor or manager:

1. Does he make a difference?
2. If she left tomorrow, would anyone care?

In far too many cases, if they have the courage to be honest, their responses will be "no and no." Only a very few people who call themselves leaders make a positive difference to both their organization and its people. And it's not just in the workplace. You don't have to look far to realize there's a pervasive and growing distrust of leaders in every profession and aspect of our lives. Trust in Congress, the executive branch, and politicians in general is at an all-time low. In the last election, many voters complained that they were forced to choose the candidate they "distrusted the least." Trust in business, media, clergy, academia, military, and leaders in general is no better.

By nature, I'm a glass-half-full guy and a rational optimist, so I haven't come to this cynical conclusion easily. For fifty years, I've been looking at leadership through many lenses:

- **Follower:** experiencing the leadership of my bosses
- **Observer:** closely watching the leadership of my peers and followers
- **Student:** studying the leadership of the famous and infamous
- **Adjunct professor:** teaching graduate courses on leadership
- **Consultant:** working with senior leaders

But the leadership lens I've spent the most time peering through and where I've learned the most was as a leader leading organizations small and large. My thirty years of hands-on experience in the Army and twenty years in the corporate world in leadership roles of increasing responsibility and varying environments was a live laboratory to test my leadership skills.

The view through those varying lenses has convinced me that in many organizations, leadership is wanting. As the saying goes, you have to decide whether to "lead, follow, or get out of the way." Too many people are opting for the last two choices. As General Martin Dempsey, the 18th chairman of the Joint Chiefs of Staff, once said, this is "no time for spectators!"[1] I wrote this book to persuade you to be a leader, not a spectator.

This is not a how-to book with simple steps to help you fly up the organizational ladder in order to be the boss, CEO, president, or chief poohbah of your organization. There are many bosses who are not leaders. They may be managing, supervising, presiding, or dictating, but they are not leading. This is a what-it-takes book to be a leader of consequence, one who makes a positive difference to an organization and the lives of the people in it. Knowing *how* to be a leader is easy, but doing what it takes to actually be a leader is hard. That's because it's easy to describe how to be a leader, but most people do not want to do *what it takes*. What it takes to create organizational success and inspire people to be enthusiastically committed to a common goal is not new. There are a lot of old solutions to new problems.[2]

Leadership, as defined in the coming pages, is the ability to create *consistent organizational success and undying follower commitment and loyalty*. Up-front, I want to fully disclose that I do not claim to be one of those leaders. But I have seen them, worked for them, and read about them, and for a brief period in my career, I hope I may have been one of them. If I hadn't written this book, I would have left a debt unpaid to all those leaders who did their best to try to mold me into a leader of consequence. If youth is wasted on the young, then an equally tragic loss is the knowledge and experience wasted because it dies with the old. Given my fifty-plus years of working with leaders and as a leader myself, I want to pay forward the knowledge I learned from the great leaders I had the honor of following and share some of the hard-earned lessons I learned as a leader on my own journey. These words from Mark Twain helped inspire me to write this book:

"While most men learn from their own experience, only wise

men learn from other people's experience."

And it doesn't matter whether you're an aspiring or new leader or a seasoned leader who wants to raise your game. If I can pass on some insights, ideas, or advice that make you a "wiser man" by flattening a few of the road bumps you'll face on your journey, then I've succeeded. Author Douglas Adams once said, "Human beings, who are unique in having the ability to learn from the experience of others, are also remarkable for their apparent disinclination to do so!"[3] For many, our own experience is the only teacher we're willing to pay attention to, but one of the most potent forms of growth is learning from the leaders who have gone before us. I am a great believer that experience is important, but if you can learn from other people's experiences, why not?

Becoming a leader is a never-ending journey of lifelong learning and growth. It's not climbing a mountain with a summit or playing a game with a final score. You're always a work in progress. We should pursue excellence, not perfection, because even if perfection is achieved, it's only fleeting. As the great golfer Jack Nicholas once put it, "There is nothing wrong with a never-ending pursuit of an unattainable goal."

James Mattis, a retired four-star Marine general and the former secretary of defense, addressed the importance of being a lifelong learner in his typical no-nonsense Marine bluntness: "If you haven't read hundreds of books, you are functionally illiterate, and you will be incompetent because your personal experiences alone aren't broad enough to sustain you [as a leader.]" I agree and have peppered the book with leadership lessons learned from real and fictional leaders—famous, not famous, and infamous. Biographies and history are goldmines of practical and pragmatic leadership lessons. Who cannot be inspired by past leaders like Winston Churchill, George Washington, Eleanor Roosevelt, Oskar Schindler, Ernest Shackleton, Margaret Thatcher, Jack Welch, Queen Elizabeth II, and Dwight Eisenhower? However, just as much can be learned by examining the leadership of contemporary leaders. There is a treasure trove of leadership lessons to be absorbed from those in the present-day trenches of business, public service, politics, government, and the military.

I am more of a practitioner than a theorist and gravitate toward people who have led and have been held accountable for their successes and failures. They seem to offer more pragmatic and actionable lessons than those who have spent their lives theorizing. Experience is an honest and, at times, ruthless teacher. But if I have to go to a marriage counselor, I'd prefer one who's married. I'm not saying that the many "experts" who have published books and articles on the subject—yet have not been leaders—do not have something to offer. In this book, you'll find stories or quotes from many of them who have influenced me. However, I must warn you to beware of those pop-psychology prophets who promise easy formulas, quick-fix gimmicks, and psychological tricks that guarantee instant leadership greatness. You should be especially wary of those who try to persuade you to clone or imitate the leadership of others. As you attempt to be a better leader, it's best to follow the advice of Ralph Waldo Emerson: "To be yourself in a world that is constantly trying to make you something else is the greatest achievement." You can't be a copycat. Finding your voice as a leader is much like finding your voice as a writer. You can no more write like Ernest Hemingway than you can lead like Colin Powell. *You can learn from them, but you cannot become them.*

Of course, leadership growth cannot come solely from studying. You don't learn to play the piano by reading a book about it—you learn by playing. Similarly, you learn to lead by leading. Personal growth comes from melding the study of the leadership of others with lessons learned in the crucible of your own practical experiences. We must discover our own leadership style and develop our own leadership voice. The old Irish proverb wisely advises us: "You've got to do your own growing, no matter how tall your daddy is." If you bring commitment, common sense, and the courage to keep an open mind, I'll offer some food for thought on what it takes to be one of those leaders of consequence we so desperately need.

Fifty years ago, when Second Lieutenant George Washington Aldridge III walked into the 3rd Platoon, Charlie Company, 3rd Infantry Regiment barracks and stepped in front of forty-two soldiers, he didn't have a clue what he was getting into—and he didn't have a clue that he didn't have a clue. This book answers the question: What do I know now that I wish I'd known then?

I won't preach or tell you what to do. This is just one man's observation of what it takes to become a leader who reaps the ultimate reward: a legacy of creating organizational excellence while making a profound difference in people's lives. There's no greater sense of accomplishment and achievement than knowing you've done what it takes to create a legacy where people say of you, "I'm better for having known him or her." I hope this book will be a catalyst to get you to think deeply about your leadership, where you are today, and where you want to be in the future. As you read, I want you to slow down, savor, ponder, and reflect on your leadership. Wisdom is the ability to recognize your flaws, weaknesses, and areas where you can do better. Courage is the ability to do something about it.

How to Read This Book

The plan for this book is simple. It has three parts. Part One is a general discussion of today's leadership landscape: a definition of leadership, challenges to becoming a leader or a better leader, methods of influence, commitment versus compliance, organizational culture, and the importance of having a personal leadership philosophy. The book's core are the chapters in Part Two ("Character") and Part Three ("Competence"). Each chapter in these sections presents an aspirational model that addresses the leadership requisites necessary for building trust between leaders and followers. If you don't have a solidified leadership philosophy, I've provided optional exercises at the end of selected chapters for your consideration to either build a philosophy from scratch or refine your existing philosophy. You can also read the book from front to back or jump right to any topic that interests you and read it in a single sitting. After many of the topic chapters, you'll find "Afterthoughts," reflections on the subject beyond the core issue. Here's an example:

Afterthought: Your Leadership Legacy

As a leader, your legacy is those leaders you leave behind. The role of leadership is to produce more leaders, not more followers. Like a parent who has the responsibility to grow the next generation of your family, you have a responsibility to grow the next generation of your organization's leaders. On your journey, as you become more senior and gain more responsibility, your leadership is measured not by what you do as an individual but by your ability to positively influence several levels below you to be the best versions of themselves. Most leaders start their leadership journeys as an individual contributor, then as a leader of individual contributors, then as a leader of leaders of individual contributors, and so on. Those you leave behind at every level of your influence are your leadership legacy. I hope this book will inspire you to focus on your own leadership and be a vehicle for you to use in pay-it-forward leadership by developing the next generation of leaders.

PART ONE

LEADERSHIP

1

BE A LEADER—NOT A SPECTATOR

"There are no bad organizations. There are only bad leaders."
—*Larry Bossidy, author*

EVERYONE THINKS THEY'RE a leader—most are far from it![1] Unfortunately, our current leadership crisis is rapidly worsening because so few men and women are willing to step forward and shoulder the burden to do what it takes to be a leader. The success or failure of any group endeavor can be directly traced to leadership. Most of the complex problems we face in our society, cities and communities, government, businesses, and institutions can be solved with leadership. Without it, organizations stagnate; they lose their way and eventually suffer the consequences.[2]

The difference between poor, mediocre, and great organizations is the difference between poor, mediocre, and great leadership. Many people will passionately argue that there are a multitude of factors aside from leadership that impact organizational success. I disagree. The context of leading may change but the content of leading changes very little.[3] Leadership is the common denominator and the tipping point to an organization's success or failure. It always has been, still is, and always will be.

I don't stand alone in my negative outlook of our current situation. There's a collective pessimism about today's leadership that has been repeatedly validated by the media, think tanks, academia, corporate studies, and polls. A Fordham University study surveyed 450 executives from thirty companies and found that roughly half of all managers don't trust their leaders.[4] Other surveys cite an even more pessimistic outlook on leader trust. A University of Chicago study asked 800 American workers about the quality of their manager's leadership and learned that 4 out of 5 had "only some" or "hardly any" confidence in the people running their corporation.[5] In a Gallup poll of over 100,000 white- and blue-collar workers, 61 percent of the respondents claimed they hadn't received any meaningful leadership in their current jobs.[6]

In the spirit of "trust but verify," I've conducted my own research, although relatively rudimentary and unscientific. To substantiate or refute these cynical perspectives, for the past fifteen years, I've been teaching a graduate leadership course to mid- and senior-level managers. At the start of every course, I ask this question:

Thinking back to all the leaders you've encountered in your lifetime, what percentage have truly made a positive and lasting impact on their organization and truly cared for the people they led?

Averaging the responses of my 2,300-plus past students produces a depressing view of leadership: The students state that only about 10 percent of the leaders they've encountered meet both these criteria! These surveys and my quasi-research beg the question: What does this 1 in 10—the 10 percent—do that makes a positive and lasting impact to both their organization and the people they lead?

The answer is that they do what it takes to build a strong relationship of symbiotic and reciprocal trust between leader and led rather than a parasitic one-way relationship. Both leader and led are giving, and both are getting. Trust in the leaders is powerful enough to inspire their followers to be committed to a joint endeavor and totally engaged in its success. This book presents an aspirational model of what it takes to build that level of trust.

Whether you're an aspiring, new, or seasoned leader, I urge you to start a journey to be one of those few in that 10 percent now! I challenge you to be someone who leads, not just manages, supervises, or presides. Your willingness and ability to grow personally and organizationally are vital to tapping into your inner wells of leadership potential.[7] Becoming a leader is an iterative process, a lifelong journey, and you'll need a detailed plan, not a make-it-up-as-you-go dream. Leadership is not a set of innate or genetic characteristics; it's a lifelong process of self-discovery and improvement.[8]

As with all journeys, you'll likely pick up some scars along the way. Knowing what it takes to be a leader is important, but deciding if you're willing to do what it takes is even more important. This book presents an opportunity to compare where you are as a leader against an aspirational model of ideal leadership. After assessing yourself against that model, if you find that you fall short, it allows you to decide: Am I willing to do what it takes?

Before you start that journey, I want to ensure you know what you're getting yourself into. I warn you: Being a leader isn't for the faint of heart. It's hard work, the criticism is constant, and the problems to be solved are endless and unrelenting. There are obstacles that must be scaled, costs that must be paid, and personal sacrifices that must be made. Here are a few of the uncomfortable truths that await you on the journey:

1. Becoming a leader is a lifelong journey.
2. No one really cares about you but you.
3. You have to be painfully honest with yourself.
4. Like improving anything in life, improving your leadership requires behavior change, and that's hard.
5. Knowing how to be a leader is easy. Doing what it takes is not.

Let's look at each of these truths in detail.

1. Becoming a Leader Is a Lifelong Journey

Becoming a leader isn't a skill that can be learned once and mastered for a lifetime. It's an arduous journey of continuous learning and self-development. Therefore, it shouldn't be a casual business-as-usual decision. It must be a conscious choice and requires a commitment to becoming a lifelong learner. Leadership is the ultimate discipline, and being a good one is a worthy quest of a lifetime.[9] It takes thought, commitment, and energy. Leadership can only be learned if you have the desire to learn it and the self-discipline to do what it takes to achieve it. Unless you commit to actively learning, you're the proverbial horse that refuses to drink even when led to water.

Your leadership ability will evolve over time through personal introspection, human interaction, feedback, life experiences, observations, common sense, and a realistic perspective.[10] The harder you work on your leadership and the more persistent you are in your efforts, the better you can become. If you're looking for gimmicks or quick-fix approaches to becoming a great leader, you're reading the wrong book. Making a positive impact on both your organization and its people is hard. It requires self-reflection, self-discipline, and a willingness to change your outlook or behavior when needed. It's also important to remember that in our journey to becoming a leader, one never arrives at the destination. Becoming the perfect leader is an ideal, not an end-state.

2. Nobody Really Cares About You But You

If I were to ask you, "Quickly, tell me what you're doing *now* to become a better leader?" you'd probably fumble with the answer. Don't feel too bad; most people are in the same boat. That boat may be afloat, but it's aimlessly drifting wherever the prevailing tide takes it. Many executives tell me, "Of course, I have a personal leadership development plan." However, when pressed for details, their thin-gruel plan usually consists of attending a few company-sponsored courses and reading the latest Amazon self-help bestseller. They almost all brag about how they're growing as a leader by learning from their day-to-day experiences. If they have a plan, it's usually vague, poorly defined, and unspecific. In other words, they're making it up as they go along. When I tell them, "You have a dream, not a plan. You're just mindlessly navigating without a map through a checklist of skills someone has told you that you must master!" I usually get one of those "But I'm busy, and I'll get to it when I have time" replies.

Like most people, you've probably put your leadership growth in the hands of someone else who more than likely doesn't care as much about you as you do about yourself. Almost all corporations and organizations pay lip service to developing their managers with cookie-cutter programs that don't address the true essence of leadership. Most of these programs aren't about developing leaders—they're about training managers. These generic programs steer you in the direction they want you to go, which may not be the direction you *need* to go. You must take control of your own future, determine where you want to go, map out your own journey, and head to your desired destination. Becoming a leader isn't easy, just as becoming a doctor or a poet isn't easy.[11]

You have to take personal responsibility and be committed to your own leadership development and growth. Every leader must make the decision to grow or stagnate. It's a conscious decision that must be reaffirmed daily. Don't be naïve and turn a blind eye to the uncomfortable truth that no one will ever be as interested or focused on your life or your career success as you are. Don't let life just come at you; have a plan.

3. You Have to Be Painfully Honest with Yourself

If you're a leader now, you're probably not as good as you think you are. The desire to lead can be like the Sirens' call to Odysseus, simultaneously beckoning and repelling. It sensually beckons to you with its promise of power, perks, fortune, status, a corner office, or rapid professional advancement. However, it comes with high personal and emotional costs, as well as the responsibility for organizational success and meeting the expectations of those you lead. Moreover, it requires you to accept that the weight of leadership that sits on your shoulders is the combined weight of everyone's lives you're responsible for.[12] For many, shouldering the burden required to be a leader is too heavy a responsibility—they see it as a prison robbing them of their freedom. They can't stomach the personal sacrifice, the level of effort, or the degree of commitment required of a leader. As Shakespeare's Henry IV mourned after stealing the crown from Richard II, "Uneasy lies the head that wears the crown."

As a leader, people depend on you. They expect you to deliver success to their organization and prosperity to those you lead. They expect you to willingly accept the responsibility for failure if you don't deliver that success and prosperity. If your organization or endeavor fails, you'll be seen as the reason. You must be painfully honest with yourself when you ask yourself:

Am I willing to accept that weighty responsibility?

Leading requires personal sacrifice. You'll have to give up much of your time and emotional energy. Anytime you give away or give up something, it's natural to ask yourself, "What's in it for me?" There will be times when you'll be forced to choose between what is best for the greater good and what is personally best for you. Ask yourself:

Am I willing to put the needs of others ahead of my own needs?

Leading often requires being unpopular and presenting those you lead and your bosses with uncomfortable truths. Giving bad news and negative feedback is hard—some bitter pills can't be sugared. Putting truth over harmony isn't easy for most people. Ask yourself:

Do I have the stomach to be unpopular when necessary?

If you answered yes to all these questions, then ask yourself one final question.

Why do I want to be a leader?

The following old adage still applies: "You have to decide to lead, follow, or get out of the way." We're in a world of wannabe leaders.[13] Many people want the good things that come with being a leader without considering the burdens and sacrifices that come with the job. They want it all, and they want it now. If your desire to lead is merely for what I call the "Big P's"—Pay, Power, Perks, Prestige, and a Personal Parking Space—then you're doomed for failure. If leading, to you, is a necessary evil to reach the top of your organizational ladder and dealing with people is an irritating but required price to pay to move up that ladder, it won't work. You're a fraud, and you'll be discovered. You cannot preside over an organization and achieve enduring positive results if your primary motivation for leading is self-serving.

4. Improving Your Leadership Requires Changing Your Behavior

To determine what behavior you need to change, you must be brutally honest with yourself, even if it's painful. A vital component of the journey involves a truthful assessment of who you are and what you know. It requires an honest self-reflection of your character and your competence. To those few old dinosaurs

> **"Insanity is doing the same thing over and over again and expecting different results."**
>
> **—Albert Einstein**

who insist that leaders are "born, not made," I say, "Nonsense!" Leadership isn't a mysterious activity.[14] The good news is, regardless of where you are in your life, it's never too late to improve your leadership if you are honest with yourself and have the self-discipline to do what it takes. The leader you are is not the leader you have to be tomorrow. As the leadership guru Ram Charan states, "Companies need you, and this is your time."[15]

That need exists at all levels of our lives, from global corporate CEOs to neighborhood volunteers. We are in a leadership crisis. Will you lead us out of it, follow the herd, or get out of the way? The choice is yours.

5. Knowing How to Be a Leader Is Easy— Doing What It Takes Is Not

As I said, this is not a *how-to* book of simple steps to become a leader. It's a *what-it-takes* book to *be* a leader. Here's the difference: If you want to drive a golf ball off the tee like Tiger Woods, a good golf pro can show you how to grip the club, how to address the ball, and how to start your backswing and follow through just like Tiger. But even if you can do all those things and mirror Tiger's swing when you strike that little white ball, it won't result in a 129-mile-an-hour golf swing that consistently produces drives of more than 300 yards straight down the middle of the fairway. What it takes to get the same results as Tiger is much more than knowing how to grip the club and follow through. What it takes is years of dedication, focused hard work, continual self-improvement, and personal discipline. The same is true when it comes to leadership: There are so few leaders because most people won't or can't do what it takes.

Forewarned Is Forearmed

I've warned you that being a leader isn't for the faint of heart. If you're willing to scale the obstacles, pay the price, and suffer the sacrifices that must be made on the journey—in other words, if you're willing to do what it takes to be a leader—then let's get started!

Summary Points

- If you're not leading "effectively," then you're managing, supervising, or presiding—but you're not leading.
- Few people are willing to do what it takes to be a leader.
- There are no bad organizations; there are only bad leaders.
- Leadership is the common denominator and tipping point to organizational success.
- Leadership potential depends on your willingness and ability to grow personally and organizationally.
- Here are some hard truths about becoming a leader:
  - Becoming a leader is a lifelong journey.
    - Leadership is not innate; it's a lifelong process of self-discovery, continuous learning, and self-development.
  - No one really cares about you but you.
    - Most people don't have an adequate leadership development plan.
    - Almost all leadership development programs train people to be managers, not leaders.
    - Take control of your future; map out your leader development plan.
    - You have to be painfully honest with yourself.
    - You're probably not as good of a leader as you think you are.
    - Becoming a leader comes with a cost: the responsibility for organizational success and meeting the expectations of those you lead.
  - Like improving anything in life, improving your leadership requires behavior change, and that's hard.
    - Improvement requires being honest with yourself, even if it's painful.

- Knowing how to be a leader is easy. Doing what it takes is not.
  - The reason there are so few leaders is that most people don't want to do what it takes.

2
DICTATORS—MAINTAINERS—LEADERS

**"Dictators complain about the wind.
Maintainers hope it will change.
Leaders adjust the sails."**
—George Aldridge

AS ANOTHER MISERABLY bitter night wrapped itself around us, the winds blowing off the mountains peppered us with sheets of rain that bit into our faces. The rain seemed to discover mysterious snake-like ways to slither down our collars and into the creases of our supposedly impenetrable wet-weather gear, making life miserable. As we climbed a thigh-burning hill into the winter sleet, we spotted our destination, a rustic three-sided shelter. The constant rain hadn't given us any opportunity to get dry during our four-day hike, and we'd descended into a dark and gloomy mood. National forest rules prohibited us from having open fires except in those few three-sided huts spaced along the trail, so the shelter was a welcoming sight that instantly lifted our spirits.

For those hikers crazy enough to challenge the mountains in winter, the shelters provided a warm, dry port in the storm. They were a comfy reprieve from the perpetual rain, biting winds, and freezing temperatures that hugged the mountains each evening. At the side of the lean-to was a covered pallet and a wooden sign that read:

Please leave the woodpile as high as you find it
AND
the shelter as clean as you find it.
Thank you

We were wet, cold, ravenous, and bone-tired, so when we saw that what we'd anticipated would be a tall stack of dry firewood was just a tiny pile of soggy leaves and twigs, our shoulders slumped. Darkness had just fallen, so any chance of finding dry firewood was pretty hopeless. Our visions of lounging around a warm campfire in our cozy, dry sleeping bags abruptly turned to the reality of spending another miserable night shivering and smelling like wet dogs.

Inevitably, there will be hikers who come to the lean-tos, burn the entire stack of wood left by the previous backpackers, and leave without replacing the wood they used. These same selfish hikers typically trash the hut and have no regard for the wet, cold, and exhausted travelers who come after them. They consider the firewood and the lean-to as a means to their end—to get warm and dry for the night. They come to the shelter, use it, abuse it, then abandon it. They have a selfish disregard for anybody but themselves. The woodpile, the shelter, and future hikers all suffer and are worse off for their having been there. Thankfully, these hiking reprobates are the exception, not the norm.

Most hikers replace the wood they use and leave the lean-to in the same state they found it: no better—no worse. If there are only a few sticks of firewood when they arrive, they see their obligation as only to follow the words of the sign:

"Please leave the woodpile as high as you find it."

They see no need to add any more firewood than they found.

They've followed the sign's request and have a clear conscience, leaving the lean-to the way they found it. Hikers coming behind them wouldn't even know they'd been there.

Then there are those few hikers who, regardless of how high the woodpile is when they arrive, leave it higher than when they found it. If no wood is on the pallet, they gather enough to warm and dry themselves, and also leave enough for those who come later to do the same. If the lean-to is trashed, they'll clean it before they hike out the following day. These hikers make a positive difference by leaving a higher woodpile and a cleaner lean-to. The grateful hikers who follow them are better off and benefit from them having been there.

My hiking experience is really no different from my leadership experience. Having been in the leadership yoke for more than five decades, I've come to the sad realization that, like the very few hikers who leave the woodpile higher than they found it, only a very few people in management or supervisory positions leave their organizations better than they found them.

Leadership—What Is It?

If you Google the question, "What is leadership?" roughly 850 million results appear. If you do the same for "books on leadership," you get more than five and a half million choices. So many answers, so many books, but so few leaders.

So, where do you start your leadership journey? As the Cheshire Cat told Alice, "If you don't know where you're going, any road will get you there." To get started, we must distill these millions of definitions and books telling us what leadership is down to a single practical definition to ensure you're not taking just "any road." Let's consider the counsel of leadership author John Maxwell, who insists that every leadership journey must start with introspection: "If you want to be successful and reach your leadership potential, you need to embrace asking [yourself] questions."[1] I agree.

The first question to be answered then is: What *is* leadership? It would be naïve to think that we can come up with a definition of leadership on which we all agree. Leadership strikes many people as enigmatic, elusive, and obscure. Virtually anything that can be said about leadership can also be denied or disproved.[2] However, when we distill the many definitions of leadership to its purest form, it's simply the ability to influence people to do what

> **Leadership in its purest form is the ability to influence people to do what you want them to do.**
>
> *George Aldridge*

you want them to do. John Maxwell's Law of Influence states, "The true measure of leadership is influence—nothing more, nothing less.[3]"

Leadership is about translating your individual excellence into group excellence. It's the genius of getting things done through people. Harry Truman once said, "Leadership is getting people to do things they would not ordinarily do if you had not asked them.[4]" Perhaps it's a utility-line foreman influencing his employees to be more safety conscious. Or a CEO of a global trading company attempting to influence his sales representatives to be more culturally aware. It could be a project manager influencing her team to be more attentive to detail.

But it's not just about influencing your team to do things better or differently; it's also about influencing them to grow as people. It could be a coach influencing his star athlete to be more of a team player and less of a ball hog. Perhaps it's a father influencing his son to stay away from drugs, study harder, and be his own man. It could be a teacher who wants to influence her students to embrace challenges beyond their comfort zone in pursuit of personal or professional growth. Leaders inspire others to rise above the norm by influencing them to change their behavior to improve, grow, and succeed.

It's also important to understand that all leaders are influencers, but not all influencers are leaders. Part of the problem in defining leadership is the sad fact that we cavalierly anoint many people as "leaders" who are not. We must debunk the commonly held but false notion that leadership is about title, position, and authority.[5] You may have leadership responsibilities, title, position, and authority, but none of these make you a leader. It just makes you the boss, and just because you're the boss doesn't make you a leader.

People have to *obey* the boss, but they want to *follow* the leader. You may accuse me of being cliché and stating the obvious, but you can't deny that there are scores of titled men and women who wield tremendous influence because they have status, power, and authority but who are not actually leading.

So, if all influencers aren't leading, what are they doing to get people to do what they want? One way to answer this question is to put bosses into three categories: Dictators, Maintainers, and Leaders. All three influence, but they do so very differently. Let me illustrate this point by looking at how each uses influence differently to get people to do what they want them to do.

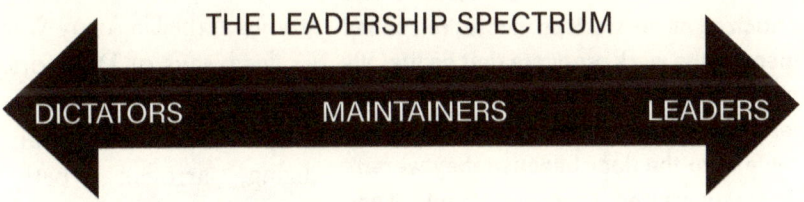

THE LEADERSHIP SPECTRUM

DICTATORS   MAINTAINERS   LEADERS

Dictators—Agents of Disruption

Unfortunately, some organizations have toxic, destructive, demeaning supervisors and managers. They are *Dictators*, those blindly ambitious self-servers who bring misery and havoc to their organization and its inhabitants. These self-made men and women worship their creator and rule their realm with an iron fist. They generate and perpetuate a toxic and fetid atmosphere for everything and everyone in their universe. You can disagree with my choice of the label "Dictator," but you can't argue the sad fact that there are those people in positions of authority and influence whose corrosive behavior breeds organizational discord and a poisonous working environment.

If you've been in the workforce long enough, you've probably worked for or witnessed a "toxic" boss who bullies, belittles, humiliates, or embarrasses subordinates.[6] These bullies are despots who pillage their fiefdoms while inflicting pain and suffering on their employees. They use their positions of authority for egocentric and venal purposes. They view their realm as a means to their self-serving ends. Moreover, they consider those over whom

Pittsburgh Post-Gazette

"You have created a hostile workplace in which you repeatedly denigrate employees, threaten them, and create a state of terror. Your behavior is hostile, erratic, unstable, angry, aggressive and abusive. The office has had 100% turnover in the past year as a result of your leadership. "You were storming around as we walked in, and as we sat down for prep — having just arrived literally moments ago — you started in on an employee and verbally abused him, harassed him, chastised him and criticized all his work products. You called many of the work products that he literally gave up his weekend to produce as 'useless.' You pushed other documents off the table onto the floor because they weren't what you wanted. Then you got angry and demanded we find the documents that you had just thrown on the ground."

they rule as their vehicle to achieve those ends. An article in the *Pittsburgh Post-Gazette* recently described a toxic boss and his negative effects on the team.

There's a difference between being led and being driven. Colonel George Reed, the former director of the command leadership studies at the US Army War College, says of Dictators, "In the most severe cases, their abusive, self-aggrandizing, arrogant, petty, and self-serving behavior make the lives of those they lead a living hell.[7]"

These noxious top dogs see their rank and station as a vehicle to acquire personal gain: fame, power, fortune, ambition, or notoriety. Their interactions with people are impersonal. They use them, abuse them, then abandon or discard them. Employees and teams who have to suffer in this hostile environment become "Organizational Prisoners."

Who can forget or forgive the corporate Enron poohbahs, whose corrupt and toxic leadership led to a corporate genocide that bankrupted a $101 billion company and destroyed the lifetime retirement savings of 14,000 employees? The "too good to be true" mercurial success promised by the Enron C-suiters was just that. When the curtain was pulled back on Enron's "smartest guys in the room," they were seen as blindly ambitious, self-serving, and corrupt. How about the 2008 financial crash that happened when scores of Wall Street executives led their pinstriped battalions to knowingly lie, cheat, and collude the public into buying bad mortgages on homes they knew would most certainly be repossessed?

Too often, the reality is that these despots only depart their organization after they either get what they want or when they eventually get what they deserve. In the first case, once they get what they want from their organization and its serfs, they abandon or desert both. They're like the CEO, who recently, on a Zoom call, told 900 of his employees, "If you are on this call, your employment here is immediately terminated." You may remember that the scores of Wall Street executives orchestrating the 2008 mortgage debacle got rich while those they served got poor. Not one of these pinstriped miscreants served a day in jail or was fined a single dollar.

In the second case, they got what they deserved: Several Enron leaders got prison time but probably a much shorter sentence than the 14,000 people who lost their jobs and decades of retirement life savings would have given them. Selfish acts and blind ambition for fame, fortune, or personal gain have been the demise of many a leader and the bane of many followers. The list isn't short of the organizations that have gone under or failed because they had a Dictator at the helm. Dictators are petty authoritarians who lack any genuine concern for those they lead and are insensitive to the climate of the organization.

> "You can judge the character of a man by how he treats those who can do nothing for him."
> —Goethe, 18th century Philosopher

Dictators Force Obedience

Dictators get people to do what they want them to do, but it's not leadership that causes it; it's forced compliance. This vile form of influence is based on fear and manipulation. They hold some form of psychological chokehold on their employees. They get results by coercing and forcing compliance from their underlings with threats and intimidation, and fear-driven compliance isn't leadership—it's dictatorship. Sure, if you rely solely on the authority of your rank and the power of your position, and depend on threats, intimidation, and fear to get the job done, you can force almost anybody to go through the motions of meeting your demands. However, managers who depend upon demanding obedience and forcing compliance produce short-term and questionable results. Their toxic, disrespectful, and bullying style almost always results in low morale and subpar productivity.[9]

Some Dictators are screamers, and some use a more subtle form of forced compliance—passive aggressiveness. The masters of the latter can be even more toxic than the former. Their passive aggressiveness can seem like death by a thousand cuts to those they rule. They're creating obedience with a residue of resentment.[10]

Dictators breed indignant, indifferent, disloyal followers who never buy into their leadership. Their behavior may achieve temporary compliance, but it will undoubtedly undermine long-term commitment. Ken Blanchard, co-author of *The Power of Ethical Management,* warned that employees who feel they're ill-used and unappreciated as people will find ways to "get even" by taking excess sick leave, pilfering company property, or giving less than their best effort.[11]

So why don't these Organizational Prisoners just quit and walk away? Unfortunately, for often very legitimate reasons, they must endure the toxic environment in which they find themselves. In many cases, they're prisoners of their personal or professional circumstances, wholly dependent on their job for financial, psychological, or other inescapable needs. Their situation may be as simple as the fact that following orders leads to a paycheck, and not following orders will lead to unemployment. They may have no choice but to live with their incessant misery and have accepted their situation with abject resignation. They may be a single parent who can't afford the time or the financial consequences to quit and look for another job. They may be a lifelong employee in a town with only one large employer and no skills to move on to another type of work. There are many reasons people endure toxic leadership. Organizational Prisoners do their jobs because they are *afraid not to*. They stay in their jobs because they cannot escape.

Leadership is about obtaining excellence through people. Dictators leave the organization significantly worse than they found it without considering their responsibility to the people in their organization. Their leadership makes a difference—a destructive difference. They tear down rather than build up. When these toxic Dictators depart an organization, they're long remembered for the damage and misery they inflicted on the company and its employees. They burn all the wood in the pile, then leave. Fortunately, Dictators aren't great in number, but they do exist. Because you're reading this book, I'm comfortable that you're not a Dictator, so let's move on to the next set of influencers.

Maintainers—Agents of the Status Quo

Maintainers are by far the largest group occupying corporate, government, academic, military, not-for-profit, and clergy supervisory and management positions. In most cases, Maintainers are well-meaning. They may try hard to make a positive difference, but despite their best intentions, they don't. Most people in these positions don't set out to be Maintainers, but for various reasons, they've fallen into a perpetual rut of complacency and mediocrity. Why do they lose that youthful enthusiasm they may have once had? Who knows? To paraphrase my favorite band, the Eagles, "Do they get tired, or do they just get lazy?" Many are content with the stasis of inaction and its comfort; they seem to enjoy living in neutral. They have conversations with themselves that go something like this: *This is pretty good. Let's not risk it or jeopardize it. Let's not change anything. Let's maintain.* Why strive for greatness when it's so easy to settle for good? Maintainers are managers of the status quo and see no need to thrive as long as they can survive. They spend their time and energy keeping people from doing their worst rather than inspiring them to do their best.

Maintainers who are good managers are important and necessary for organizational success. Without good management, organizations would flounder and fail. They may be successful at keeping the organization "between the lines" and promoting a workplace aura of contentment and security, but rarely, if ever, do they affect lasting significant positive impact, progress, or change in their company or their employees. They maintain the status quo by effectively managing assets, budgets, and resources, as well as

"All too often, on the long road up, young leaders become 'servants of what is' rather than 'shapers of what might be.' In the long process of learning how the system works, they are rewarded for playing within the intricate structure of existing rules. By the time they reach the top, they are trained prisoners of the structure."

—John Gardner, former secretary of health, education, and welfare

supervising schedules, deadlines, and people—figuratively making the train run on time. The organization and its employees may be no worse for their presence, but like the hikers who only replaced the wood they burned, they're no better for their presence.

It's sad to say, but most US corporations are over-managed and under-led.[12] A Gallup poll identified that of 100,000 workers, 71 percent reported they were disengaged from their workplace.[13] Essentially, they were clock-watchers who "couldn't wait to get home" and admitted to merely complying with the minimum requirements just to get by.[14] They view their work as something to do to just kill time between meals. In this sizable middle world, the Maintainers are like the wolf posing as a sheep, but in this case, they're managers posing as leaders.

These agents of the average don't care to break out of the status quo because they know change implies risk. They have a strong propensity for caution. Their mantra is "Play it safe—don't rock the boat!" For the chronically cautious, the default answer when given the opportunity for change is always "no." They're either ineffective, or worse yet, they don't care. With the "ineffectives," it may be a competency issue. They may not possess the aptitude, talent, or skills needed to do what it takes to move the organization forward or elevate their employees to a higher plane. With those who just don't care, it may be a character issue. The skills may be there, but it's easier and more comfortable to keep moving along in their rut of mediocrity. Due to apathy, arrogance, laziness, or stubbornness, they've become wedded to the calm and comfort of doing things the same way. Change is hard, so why not stay on the safe and easy path of least resistance? Maintainers are a dime a dozen and firmly embrace the great American philosopher Yogi Berra's advice: "I'm in favor of leaving the status quo the way it is."

Leadership requires hard work and a degree of selflessness. Selfishly, Maintainers are content with the self-perpetuating equilibrium of the status quo and aren't willing to expend the effort to suffer the sacrifice to do what it takes to be a leader. They drop to the lowest common denominator by embracing the easiest and the most comfortable choice—the path of least resistance. They feel like they're winning as long as they're not losing. When Maintainers leave the organization, they are soon, if not instantly, forgotten.

Maintainers Buy Compliance

Like Dictators, Maintainers can also get people to do what they want, but that's not leadership. They wield a more benign and lesser degree of coercion than Dictators, but make no mistake, it's still coercion or compulsory compliance. Maintainers achieve results *by buying compliance* from their herd, cleverly manipulating the extrinsic rewards and punishments at their disposal. They're merely managing and maintaining while steering their charges toward mediocrity, complacency, and irrelevance.[15]

When the motivation of those you lead is purely extrinsic, you're purchasing their submission. It's what author Christopher Kolenda calls "legitimized coercion"—the carrot-and-stick approach to achieving follower compliance. Reliance on coercion is a symptom of inadequate leadership.[16] It may not be considered corrosive, but it doesn't achieve willing and enthusiastic buy-in. Employees who work for Maintainers go through the motions of doing their jobs by expending the minimum effort necessary to stay within the lines of what they've determined is an acceptable level of performance to keep them in good stead with their bosses. When employees are indifferently doing what's asked of them, they're not passionate about those tasks and will only make a token effort to complete them.[17] They'll do no more than is required because they feel no emotional attachment or equity to the organization or buy-in to its leaders.[18] They may outwardly and superficially comply with your wishes, but they're much less likely to comply privately and adopt your organization's values, culture, and mission in a sincere and lasting way.[19]

Employees who work for Maintainers do their jobs because they *have to*, not because they *want to*. Compulsory compliance, whether forced by threat or purchased by the promise of reward, is superficial and temporary and only results in the minimum effort to receive the reward or avoid the punishment. Moreover, that minimum effort generally only occurs if the leader is present or has some form of observational leverage over the follower. Noted leadership researcher Peter Senge believes that 90 percent of the time what passes for employee commitment is just compliance.[20] This form of influence, persuasion, or inducement is what leadership theory authority James MacGregor Burns describes as "transactional leadership."[21] The leader and follower make a transaction that looks like this:

"If you (the follower) do what I ask, I (the leader) will reward you. However, if you do not do what I ask, I will either withhold the reward or punish you for not doing what I ask."

The relationship between Maintainers and their followers is based on a transactional, gun-for-hire, quid-pro-quo agreement. Maintainers buy their employees' subservience. Unlike Organizational Prisoners, who have to suffer under the rule of their Dictators, employees who work under Maintainers are "Organizational Mercenaries" who do the minimum to get by to survive in their jobs. They comply with what's expected, but their heart isn't in it. They claim no personal buy-in or ownership in their job or endeavor. As Clarence Francis, a former CEO of General Foods, eloquently expressed, "You can buy a person's time; you can buy his physical presence. But you cannot buy his enthusiasm or loyalty. You cannot buy the devotion of hearts, minds, and souls; these must be earned." In today's vernacular, these type of workers are "quiet quitters," employees who are coasting and doing the minimum to get by. A recent Gallop poll reports the ratio of engaged to actively disengaged workers is at its lowest level in a decade. The sad news is that half the US workforce is allegedly quiet quitting—that is, doing only what's in their job description and no more.[22]

Once the power of reward or punishment is lost, they no longer comply. Organizational Mercenaries are only motivated by personal interests, and they're more concerned with doing what's right for them than what's right for the team.[23] The relationship between a Maintainer and the Mercenary is based on a purely transactional deal. If you ask a Mercenary to go above and beyond the agreed-upon deal, they will but only for a price. Don't expect Mercenaries to exhibit initiative or be proactive; it's not part of the deal. They view their place in the organization merely as a job that has to be survived and endured until they can move to a better opportunity.

Throughout my consulting life, I've heard many versions of the Organizational Mercenary's mantra:

- "As soon as I find another job, I'm gone."
- "It's only a job."
- "I'm waiting the boss out; luckily, he'll be gone soon."
- "Only three more years until I retire, and then I'm out of here."

In many cases, Mercenaries are good employees starving for positive leadership. However, under their current management, their only commitment is to their professional and personal survival. They simply react to their boss's demands, but they never do anything proactive when it comes to the needs of their job, the task, or the organization.

Leaders—Agents of Change

There are too few men and women in supervisory positions who are *Leaders*. As Leaders, they build long-term intrinsic value in the organization and meaningful prosperity for those they manage or supervise. Leaders are rare, and as with all things rare, they are precious. Whereas Dictators suck the life out of an organization and Mercenaries slowly kill an organization, Leaders breathe life into an organization.

By no stretch of the imagination can I claim to be one of those rare and precious few. But I have seen them, and I have been led by them. What makes them different is their ability to positively change organizations and improve people's lives. Leaders create an environment and culture where people willingly and enthusiastically want to follow them. They seem to possess an almost imperceptible power to win the absolute trust of everyone they encounter.

Leaders understand that before people "want to follow you," they must have boundless trust in your character and competence.[24] The key to earning that trust is by convincing them that you have their best interests at heart by ceaselessly demonstrating that you genuinely care about them through your actions, behavior, and decisions. Nothing yields higher dividends in terms of team cohesion, employee satisfaction, and organizational momentum than advancing the best interests of the people who work for you.[25] If you do that, they'll be more productive, show more initiative, and be more committed to your endeavor. The idea that followers must have a genuine sense that their leaders care about them isn't new. Xenophon, a 4th century BC philosopher, argued that everything a Leader does must demonstrate to his followers that he constantly thinks of their welfare and works for their benefit.[26]

Truly caring shouldn't be misinterpreted as coddling, stroking, or gratuitous praising. As the novelist David Foster Wallace wrote in his 2000 *Rolling Stone* article, "Leaders are people who help us overcome the limitations of our own laziness and selfishness and weakness and fear and get us to do better, harder things than we can get ourselves to do on our own."[27]

On the flip side, caring sometimes means tough love. When a Leader is more demanding, that doesn't equate to less caring. Either through persuasion, example, or tough love, Leaders inspire a group to pursue the objectives held by or shared by the leader and his followers.[28] They skillfully balance that delicate and fragile equation of mission and people, balancing sustained organizational success with taking care of their employees.

Leaders Are Impact Players

The harder the task and the greater the change an organization requires, the more you need a Leader. What distinguishes Leaders from Maintainers is that Maintainers cling to the comfort of normal while Leaders live in a place that doesn't know normal. Maintainers say, "It may be possible, but it's too difficult," whereas Leaders say, "It may be difficult, but it's possible."

Those few players in the sports world who inspire extraordinary performance from their teammates are called "impact players." The significant positive influence that impact players have on their team's performance is not unlike the positive influence that Leaders have on their organization and its employees. Dictators also have a significant impact on their team, but that impact is negative and harmful. They're the ball hogs who focus on their own stats rather than the team's collective effort and winning percentage. They're the trash-talkers who blame the quarterback when they miss a pass and whose off-field behavior brings discredit to the sport and their team. Maintainers aren't game-changers. They're bench warmers and utility players who are necessary to the team, but you don't necessarily depend on them to inspire their teammates to higher levels of play. Leaders, like impact players, compete on the same field and are confronted with the same opposing team as their Dictator and Maintainer peers. Yet at the end of the day, their positive impact is significant and long-lasting. You want a Leader as the quarterback when you're in the red zone. Similar to impact players in the sports world, Leaders are a special breed. Their presence is felt in a profound way as they take the game to a higher level and inspire their teammates to fight above their weight.

Impact players and Leaders alike inspire extraordinary performance from their teammates and employees while earning their respect and loyalty. They both prove that one person can positively change the culture and environment in which they operate.[29] They bring a distinguishable vibe, a feel, and a texture to the team or organization that's different from what other people bring. They inject a sense of spirit, esprit, and soul into the team that didn't exist before they were there. Leaders are the David Beckhams, Tom Bradys, Stephen Currys, Wayne Gretzkys, and Michael Jordans of the leadership universe. They're the future leadership hall of famers of the business, government, and civic organization worlds. Impact players not only want to play—they want to play to win, and they inspire their teammates to want to play to win as well. Similarly, Leaders don't want to just survive—they want to thrive. Whereas Maintainers will sit back and let things unfold, Leaders interject themselves into the situation. They bust the status quo by inspiring people to look higher and achieve those things that lead to winning. They solve problems, build high-performing teams, make sense out of confusion, and overcome adversity.

Leadership isn't about popularity, position, pay, prestige, rank, or title. It's about results. It's about positively achieving two critical measures of leadership success: 1) sustainable organizational success and prosperity and 2) employee commitment and satisfaction. Leaders build successful organizations by developing a team of people who are committed to the business and engaged in its prosperity. Leadership, as we describe it, is rare, but you should aspire to achieve it.

The true leadership litmus test in the military is: Would you want this person leading you in combat? The leadership litmus test in the private sector is: Would you follow this leader to another company? Leaders leave the organization better than they found it, and the people in the organization are better for them having been there.

Leaders Inspire Commitment

The journey I urge you to take steers you toward becoming a Leader, someone who inspires your team to commit to your leadership rather than merely going through a ho-hum pretense of complying with your orders. True leadership cannot be awarded, appointed, or assigned—it only comes from influence because following is a voluntary act. Without influence, you have no followers. So, you must convince people that you're worth following. If they won't follow you, you're not leading. If they're only complying, you're merely presiding. The end game for all leaders is to inspire Organizational Mercenaries to become "Organizational Patriots."

So, how do you achieve long-term organizational success and inspire those you lead to commit to both the business and you? Said another way, how do you inspire enthusiastic employee engagement by marrying their needs and interests with your organization's goals? It's achieved by influencing and positively transforming your followers' attitudes, beliefs, and values, leading them toward commitment. Commitment implies that your followers want the organization to succeed. But inspiring commitment is difficult and takes more than extrinsic rewards. You want employees to buy into and be engaged with your organization's mission and vision. You want them to feel they have a shared responsibility for its success and are contributing toward that. You want them to go above and beyond the minimum requirements of just getting by. Just as we don't want employees who never do what they are told, we also don't want employees who do *only* what they're told. We want committed and engaged employees who use initiative to proactively do what's best for the common good of the organization. We want employees who possess the initiative to solve problems in the absence of orders, direction, and supervision. By taking care of those you lead, you greatly enhance the probability of leading a business of Organizational Patriots.

Committed Shareholders

Bill Belichick, the head coach of the six-time Super Bowl Champion New England Patriots, is a master of inspiring commitment from his players. He inspires all his players to feel as if they're shareholders of the team. He works hard to create a strong team identification manifested by a culture where the values and, ultimately, the success of the Patriots belong to every player. Each player is a shareholder and, in that role, is an enthusiastic ambassador for the team—a team of Patriots, figuratively as well as literally.[30] When organizational identification is strong, job satisfaction and performance are higher. It produces higher employee retention, which can deepen trust and enhance any team's collaborative effectiveness.[31] Employees do the right things because they want to, not because they have to.

Coach Belichick's powerful influence is akin to what James MacGregor Burns calls "transformational leadership."[32] It's about engaging followers and inspiring them to buy into a shared belief system, a collective passion, or a group goal where their performance reflects their shared beliefs, values, needs, wants, and aspirations. Those you lead must recognize that you have the organization's success at the top of your priority list and that you genuinely care for them. Add to that a convincing sense that you're a vehicle to their personal goals, aspirations, success, and well-being, and you'll find yourself transforming your team of Mercenaries into Patriots. When they see that you've invested in them, they'll enthusiastically follow you and be more committed to your shared endeavor.

Organizational Mercenaries say, "I do my job because if I don't, I might get fired." Organizational Patriots say, "I do my job because if I don't, I'll be letting my team, my boss, and my company down." It's a symbiotic relationship based on mutual trust between the leader and the led. The behavior of Mercenaries is determined first by the "deal," then by how closely they're supervised. When they feel comfortable enough to back off the organizational standard because they believe no one will know or care, they will. Patriots, on the other hand, commit to the organization's goals and are high-performing whether supervised or not. They're working for a purpose that's higher than merely wanting extrinsic rewards or fearing punishment. Their sense of equity in the organization is manifested by an attitude of "Not only is this my workplace, but it's a place I have pride in." Patriots see themselves as shareholders and embrace a sense of responsibility for the success of their organization. They're fully engaged, proactively taking on tasks that benefit the organization, even if they don't fall into their job description or purview. They have a sense of ownership in the success of the company. They feel like they're working *with* you, not *for* you.

> **"Leaders instill a sense of ownership, because no one washes a rental car."**
> —*Lawrence Summers, former secretary of the treasury*

Becoming a transformational leader who inspires Mercenaries to become Patriots is extremely tough but achievable. It's the deeds of the followers, not the words of the leader, that's the telling indicator of transformational leadership. As leaders, we must constantly evaluate our words and deeds, asking ourselves, *"Is my leadership transactional or transformational? Am I maintaining or leading?"*

Demand Far Exceeds Supply

I'm often asked, What's the percentage of Dictators, Maintainers, and Leaders? As the philosopher and balladeer Bob Seger opines, "I wish I didn't know now what I didn't know then."[33] I yearn for that youthful optimism I once enjoyed, as naïve as it was. But I can't,

> **"I have learned that real leadership is a rare and precious commodity and requires qualities that many people might possess piecemeal in varying degrees, but few exhibit in total."**
> —*Robert Gates, former secretary of defense, to the 2011 US Naval Academy graduates*

because I *do* know now what I didn't know then. As I find myself growing older, I prefer to label what some may call "grumpy-old-man cynicism" as "wisdom and hard-earned skepticism" gained through my many years in the leadership crucible.

In his book, *12 Rules of Life*, Jordan Peterson makes the critical point that there's an unequal distribution of talent in human societies.[34] Only a finite number of people have the talent to create positive change in any given field. For example, just a small percentage of the thousands of working scientists produce new and valuable science. Only a very tiny proportion of people who might call themselves musicians record the music we listen to. Of the thousands of people working in the technology industry, it's just a small fraction who make society-changing breakthroughs. And of the millions of books published each year, only a few hundred authors sell the books we most often buy and read.

Like Peterson, I believe there's an unequal distribution of talented leaders in the world. There are only a finite number of people who inspire commitment, and transformational leaders are rare. Based on our definition of Maintainers and Leaders, if I were to ask you to list the Maintainers you've experienced or known, you could probably run off a pretty long list. However, if I were to ask you to do the same for Leaders, I bet your list would be considerably shorter.

When I'm pushed to answer this same question, I am forced to uncase my cynical colors. Based on decades of personal experience, study, and my quasi-scientific surveys as an adjunct professor, my answer is 10 percent are Dictators, 80 percent are Maintainers, and 10 percent are Leaders. You may assume that I have an acidic view of the world. Quite the contrary: I'm a rational optimist who believes that despite a significant shortage of Leaders with desire and self-discipline, most people can become one, whether they're a Dictator or a Maintainer to start. Let me explain: A person can be a Maintainer but can become a Leader with only a slight improvement. It should be our aspiration to be a Leader 100 percent of the time, but the reality is, you can drift back and forth between Leader and Maintainer, depending on the situation, job, or where you are in your life. Having said that, most Dictators stay Dictators until they're bulldozed by some personal or professional catastrophe that forces them into accepting the reality that they must change to survive.

The art of leadership is achieving organizational success through those you lead—inspiring people to produce sustained high performance while loving their jobs for the work itself. A leader's task is to get work done through other people.[35] That's the type of leadership you seldom see and the kind that I've experienced and witnessed only a few times in my professional and personal life. Yet it's the leadership we should all aspire to achieve.

From this point forward, when I use the term "leader," I'm referring to the supervisors, managers, and others who achieve sustained organizational success and inspire employees to be willingly committed and enthusiastically engaged. Remember, commitment cannot be compelled, only inspired.

Where Are You? Where Do You Want to Be?

Would you describe yourself as a Dictator, a Maintainer, or a Leader? Be honest with yourself. Do you place yourself in the thin air of the 10 percent—a Leader? If you answered yes, are you sure?" The uncomfortable truth is, you're probably not. Whether you agree or disagree, read on and repeatedly ask yourself where you stand as you travel through this book. And even if you're the "real deal"—one of the few Leaders—your potential for further leadership growth and development is always there. Whether you're a Dictator, Maintainer, or Leader, this book is a call for you to be a better leader than you are today.

For the rest of the book, we'll be addressing what it takes to become a Leader. If you're a Dictator who has the mettle to self-confess to being a Dictator and want to become a Leader, I applaud your honesty and admire your courage. Most Dictators never see the man in the mirror for who he truly is until they're forced to do so. It usually comes in the form of a significant-enough jolt to make them realize that leadership change is necessary for their survival. Like Step One in Alcoholics Anonymous, you have to admit, *I am a Dictator*! Taking that first step is the toughest. If you're a self-professed Maintainer, once again, I applaud your honesty. If you genuinely want to improve your ability to lead, improve organizational success, and inspire commitment from your charges with hard work, *you can*! It just takes an open mind, undaunted determination, honest self-reflection, and the acceptance that it will take some sacrifice and selflessness.

Summary Points

On Leadership

- Leaders influence people to do things they wouldn't ordinarily do.
- Leaders motivate people/employees to improve, grow, and succeed.
- All leaders are influencers, but not all influencers are leaders.
- Just because you're the boss doesn't make you a leader.

Dictators

- Agents of disruption.
- Focused on personal success and employee obedience.
- Focused on short-term wins over long-term successes.
- Influence by using fear, intimidation, and manipulation to force obedience.
- Organizations and employees are worse for their presence.
- Those who work for Dictators are Organizational Prisoners who:
    - Are fearful employees and followers.
    - Do only what they're ordered to do.
    - Are disengaged in their work and indifferent to its purpose.
    - Require constant supervision.
    - Do their job only because they're afraid not to (fear-driven).
- Organizational Prisoners' relationship with the boss is based on fear.

Maintainers

- Agents of the status quo
- Focused on personal survival and employee compliance.
- Focused on the present and playing it safe.
- Influence by using extrinsic rewards and buying compliance.
- Organizations and employees are no better or worse for their presence.
- Those who work for Maintainers are Organizational Mercenaries who:
  - Do only what they're required to do, i.e. give token effort.
  - Have minimum engagement and are unenthusiastic about their work.
  - Require constant supervision and demonstrate no initiative.
  - Do their job because they have to (survival-driven).
- Organizational Mercenaries' relationship with the boss is based on extrinsic rewards.

Leaders

- Agents of positive change.
- Focused on organizational success and follower commitment.
- Focused on long-term organizational and employee welfare and success.
- Influence by inspiring employee buy-in and engagement.
- Organizations and employees are better for their presence.
- Those who work for Leaders are Organizational Patriots who:
  - Are committed employees/followers.
  - Go above and beyond what's required.

- Are engaged and enthusiastic about their work.
- Require little or no supervision and demonstrate initiative.
- Do their job because they want to (pride-driven).
- Organizational Patriots' relationship with the boss is based on symbiotic trust.

3

THE VALUE OF COMMITMENT

"The true test of leadership is not what happens when you are there but what happens when you are not there."

—Ken Blanchard, author of **The Leadership Pill**

MY FIRST CIVILIAN job after leaving the Army was with The Coca-Cola Company in Atlanta. A few days after starting my new job, I found myself in a deep conversation with one of Coke's senior executives. As he was coaching me on the intricacies of Coke's culture, he commented:

> "George, I hope you understand that leading here at Coke will be very different from what you were used to in the Army. Leadership in the military is about giving orders and getting instant, unquestioned obedience. You'll find it much harder here; you can't just give orders and expect results."

His remark took me aback, and I realized I couldn't let it pass. I responded:

> "Bill, there may be a common misperception that just because you order soldiers to do what you want them to do, they'll follow orders willingly, enthusiastically, and

without question.[1] However, that perception of military leadership couldn't be further from the truth. Today's service men and women, like Coke employees, are intelligent, dedicated, and hard-working, and they expect much from their leaders. They don't suffer fools gladly, and they certainly don't suffer foolish leadership gladly. Just like here, simply because you occupy the corner office doesn't automatically earn your employees' loyalty, respect, or high performance. Sure, if you rely on the authority of your rank, in most cases, you can get soldiers to do what you want them to do. But if you want your troops to have the level of commitment and engagement necessary for success, it takes more than barking orders. You must prove that you're up to the task at hand, you have their best interests at heart, and you care for them. In other words, they have to trust your character and have confidence in your competence."

The executive dropped his chin, sighed, and with a wry sideways smile, said:

"George, you are naïve. You'll quickly learn that leading is much more complicated here than what you experienced when you were in the Army."

I walked away from the conversation, and for a moment, I felt almost apologetic for my time in the Army and what I thought I'd learned about leadership. I questioned myself: *Am I indeed naïve and out of touch?* My self-doubt was short-lived. What it takes to inspire your followers to willingly and enthusiastically follow you is universal and timeless. It's the same whether they're employees, soldiers, teammates, or volunteers. The well-meaning but misguided executive believed military leadership was about barking orders and getting *instant, unquestioned obedience.*

In any context, to inspire all-in commitment in those you lead, you must earn their trust by demonstrating strong character and adequate professional competence. In golf, the coveted combination is long and straight. In leadership, the coveted combination is character and competence. Too many leaders work hard on one at the expense of the other. Both are necessary, but neither is sufficient alone to inspire a level of trust that leads to commitment from those you lead. We'll look at character and competence more closely and see how they impact the commitment of those we lead. However, let's first look in the mirror.

Compliance or Commitment

No reasonable person would argue that a Dictator's toxic behavior is acceptable leadership. However, some will argue that there are circumstances when being a Maintainer is acceptable. These advocates of the status quo will adamantly bicker, "An employee's commitment isn't necessary as long as they do what they're told." They're bullish in their belief that leadership is simply about setting clear expectations and getting your employees to comply. They embrace the idea that as long as those compliant efforts meet the needs of your endeavor, commitment is unimportant.

I admit there are situations where this may work. Mediocrity could be sufficient in a static business environment where no forward movement is required. Perhaps being a Maintainer is OK when just keeping the ship on a straight and steady course is your only goal. If your team's success doesn't depend on engaged employees using individual initiative, ingenuity, creativity, or proactive problem-solving, then maintaining the status quo may be sufficient. Or if you're comfortable with an environment where employees do what's asked, even if it's without enthusiasm, passion, or emotion, being a Maintainer may be a good fit.

If you're a Maintainer, your business relationship with your employees is purely transactional. It's predicated on the granting and withholding of extrinsic rewards, which are always short-lived motivators. You have a clear expectation of what you want your employees to do (X work for Y compensation); they give you that and nothing more. Your employees have a clear and narrow expectation of what you'll give them for what they do (Y compensation for X work); they get that and nothing more. If you're happy with that arrangement and level of engagement, a lack of employee commitment may be tolerable.

The practical reality of today's dynamic environment is that very few organizations can afford to remain static or stationary and also remain relevant. Change and uncertainty demand the ability to adapt to prosper and even survive. Companies manned with disengaged "me-first" workforces are characterized by organizational mediocrity and lethargic employees who just go through the motions of doing their jobs. To use the popular vernacular, in a volatile, unpredictable, changing, and ambiguous (VUCA) world, leaders don't have the luxury of being content with disengaged and indifferent employees. Sustained high performance cannot be achieved without engaged and committed employees who buy into those leading. Leadership success must be consistent, not a one-hit wonder. In the military, that means repeatedly accomplishing the mission. In the private sector, that means repeatedly getting the job done, meeting the plan, making the numbers, completing the project, accomplishing goals and objectives, and making the corporate vision a reality. If your troops or employees aren't behind you, committed to you and your leadership, you may find yourself alone when tough times come.

> **"If you're ridin' ahead of the herd, take a look back every now and then to make sure it's still there!"**
>
> —*Texas Bix Bender, author of* *'Don't Squat With Yer Spurs On!*

To Comply or Commit, That Is the Question

Every day, we make decisions about whether to commit to something or merely go through the motions of complying. Let's look at some examples. Like most drivers, when you're on the highway, you probably drive at a speed you're comfortable with that's above the legal limit. Urban legend has it that you're not going to get pulled over as long as you're not driving more than ten miles per hour over the speed limit. Even then, when I see the local police or state patrol, I rapidly *comply* with the law by yanking my foot off the gas pedal and decelerating to the posted speed.

Unobserved, I do what I think I can get away with and don't obey the law until I see that I might be in danger of getting a ticket. I've been using this formula of selective compliance my entire driving life, and so far, so good.

Whenever I get in a car, however, I immediately fasten my seatbelt. I bought into this law because I know it's in my best interest to follow it whether I'm under a state patrolman's watchful eye or not. I have fully *committed* to obeying that law because I've internalized the behavior of doing what's in my best interest; fastening my seatbelt has become an automatic part of my life. Commitment is an employee's internalization of the organization's practices, behaviors, and values, inculcated so powerfully that it becomes an instinctive part of their life. They're committed because they have the passionate conviction that they have a role in the success of their organization. It is *their choice* to merely comply or fully commit.

Here's another example: You don't want your children to stay away from drugs only when they think they'll get caught. You want them to internalize that taking drugs can be terribly harmful to themselves and others, and by the way, it's against the law. You also want them to know and deeply care that it will disappoint you. You want your kids to *commit* to being drug-free and not merely comply with your wishes when they feel like they may get caught. In the same vein, you don't want employees to do the right thing only when they have a supervisor looking over their shoulder. You want them wearing safety gear all the time or focusing on customers all the time. You want your employees to *commit* to the norms and culture you bring to them through your leadership on a consistent and sustained basis. With both your employees and your children, you don't just want them to do the right thing; you want them to *want* to do the right thing.

In his huge bestseller, *Good to Great*, author Jim Collins quantifies consistent and sustained success as meeting the metrics, measures, and criteria of the company's goals and objectives for extended periods.[2] As Collins asserts, long-term focused leadership consistently accomplishes the organization's *raison d'être*. Success is measured by how well the organization consistently meets its goals and metrics: bottom line, higher sales, project completion, increased customer satisfaction, fewer accidents, less turnover, improved morale, or any other indicator of success. Leaders who meet Collins' definition of success—getting the job done without running the organization and its employees into the ground—are few.

What does getting the job done on a habitual and consistent basis really mean? It can mean many things: surpassing past and current success, building new organizations that are efficient and successful, inspiring ordinary people to extraordinary performance, bringing about change, creating something that didn't exist, or turning ideas into action. In extreme conditions and times of crisis, it can mean merely surviving in a VUCA environment. Leaders must guide the organization to consistent and sustained success and that success is dependent on committed and engaged employees or followers.

Commitment Leads to Engagement—Engagement Leads to Success

Leaders are expected to deliver. But leadership isn't measured by the personality or the words of the boss; it's measured by the success of the organization. It's not about popularity—it's about results. Bill Gates was a successful leader because he brought personal computing to the average Jack and Jill. Dwight Eisenhower was a successful general because he led the US to victory in WWII. Former Starbucks CEO Howard Schultz was a successful leader because he changed the culture of how Americans drink coffee. Martin Luther King was a successful leader because he inspired change in laws and attitudes.

There are leaders in every organization and at every level who have a reputation for consistently producing successful results. They have a history of getting employees committed and engaged in the tough projects, earning them a reputation for leadership success. If you look closely at the leadership of Gates, Ike, Schultz, MLK, and those in your organization who've earned a reputation for success, you'll find that they were masters of inspiring a spirit of commitment from those they led, instilling within their followers a deep desire to be engaged in achieving the success of their company, the dream, the team, or the endeavor. They also seem to easily earn committed loyalty and respect while inspiring excellence from their people.

Sustaining high performance without engaged employees or followers is almost impossible. Depending on the source, you'll find that anywhere from 63 to 70 percent of American workers aren't fully engaged in their jobs.[3] That means that only about a third of workers are engaged. To further dishearten you, these studies state that 18 percent of workers are fully disengaged at work, and 9 percent to 5 percent are actively sabotaging their employer's businesses.[4] These are the quiet quitters. Thousands of other studies have verified the importance of the correlation between engagement and performance.

Organizational Patriots perform at a higher level than Organizational Mercenaries. It's almost impossible to be a high-performing organization when less than a fourth of your employees engage in your endeavor. Even in the Army, units judged to be less than 70 percent strength are deemed combat-ineffective. When most of your employees merely comply with the minimum requirements, sustainable success is unlikely. You obtain excellence with Patriots who are committed to your endeavor and who will be proactively engaged on its behalf to achieve success. Commitment leads to engagement, and engagement leads to success.

Inspiring Mercenaries to be Patriots

Inspiring Organizational Mercenaries to become Organizational Patriots is easy to say but incredibly hard to do. If you're in a position of authority and you tell someone to do something, in most cases and under normal circumstances, that employee will do what they're told. Because they depend on that job for their livelihood, they'll do what's required for their personal survival and professional self-preservation. But how do you motivate the individuals you lead to *commit* to your leadership rather than merely *comply* with your orders? To make it even harder, how do you move beyond individual commitment to collective and organizational commitment? Collective commitment in the military is called *esprit de corps*. The more common term for collective commitment in the private sector is "cohesion." The focus of the rest of this book will be on what it takes to achieve a level of trust that will inspire those you lead to be willingly committed and enthusiastically engaged.

Summary Points

- Leaders and their organizational success are measured by results.
- Few organizations with merely compliant employees will remain relevant.
- Consistent organizational success requires committed and engaged employees.
- Two-thirds of US workers are not fully engaged at work (Organizational Mercenaries).
- Committed employees are fully engaged (Organizational Patriots).
- To inspire all-in commitment, leaders must earn the trust of their followers.
- That trust is only given to leaders who demonstrate character and competence.
- Both character and competence are necessary, but neither is sufficient alone.

4

THE LEADERSHIP EQUATION

"Nobody cares how much you know until they know
how much you care."

—*Teddy Roosevelt*

ON THE FIRST day of a graduate leadership course that I've been teaching for the past fifteen years, I ask the students to answer two questions:

1. What is leadership? Define it by completing the following sentence: Leadership is (*fill in the blank*).
2. Describe the person or leader who has had the most influence in making you the person and leader you are today.

Like Google's million definitions of leadership, I've heard innumerable responses to my questions, running the gamut from the ridiculous to the profound. However, there's been a consistently recurring theme in the responses to both questions. When asked, "What is leadership?" people invariably describe the things leaders *do*—their skills and competence. They describe leadership using action verbs: "Leadership is . . . motivating, organizing, communicating, directing, providing vision, making decisions, building teams, setting direction, creating culture, and taking charge." It's not sur-

Leadership is _____.

- Motivating people to accomplish something.
- The ability to organize people to complete a task.
- The art of directing people to succeed.
- Providing organizational direction and vision.
- Making the right decisions.
- Building teams.
- Setting the direction for the company.
- Creating a positive organizational culture.
- Taking charge of a situation.

prising that of the $366 billion spent annually in the US on leadership development and training, almost all those dollars are spent on teaching skills and competencies—what leaders must *do*.[1]

Those development programs almost always fall into the category of how-to courses. Peruse the many corporate leadership training brochures and read any business school syllabus, and you'll find an endless list of skills that company consultants or college professors have determined you must master to be a successful leader. These how-to courses focus on what skills to learn, what habits to develop, how to capitalize on your leadership strengths, and how to overcome and improve your leadership weaknesses.

Competence—what you *do* as a leader—is essential for success. To create a prosperous organization and inspire positive change, or even if you just want to survive as a leader, you must master the professional competencies necessary to make that desire for prosperity, change, or survival a reality. Those you lead expect you to know your business. You must consistently demonstrate that you have the competency, skill, and professional knowledge to lead your organization and guide your charges to prosperity. Employees don't want to just survive. They want to thrive, and they'll hold you accountable for leading them to that prosperity. Without the requisite professional competence, you won't succeed as a leader. If you're not up to the task because you lack the necessary professional skills to succeed, the most you can ever achieve is forced or purchased compliance.

Granted, professional know-how is essential for leadership success, but don't fall into the trap, as many do, of believing that all you have to do to achieve professional success is master a Swiss Army knife array of career skills. Many capable people in leadership positions are competent, credentialed, skilled, degreed, and experienced in all aspects of what a leader does. However, not all are leading—they just think they are. Competence alone is not the essence of leadership—it's only the beginning. Professional and subject matter expertise are threshold requirements for earning the trust and confidence of those you lead. Competence is necessary but insufficient to inspire your Organizational Mercenaries to become Organizational Patriots.

After asking "What is leadership?" I follow up with the second question: "Describe the person or leader who has had the most influence in making you the person and leader you are today."

It might surprise you that people's answers to this question differ dramatically from their responses to my first question, What is leadership? They don't roll off a checklist of skills their role models possess, but rather, they describe the person from an emotional perspective. They passionately describe the *character* of the men or women who influenced their core values and shaped their worldview. They paint a picture of who those leaders *are*, not what they *do*. They define their character, not their competencies. They almost always use emotive language to describe the qualities of that person's character: "She was trustworthy, generous, confident, ethical, and courageous. She deeply cared for

Describe your most influential Leader:

- I trusted him with my life; he was trustworthy.
- She made me realize I could be and do better than I thought.
- He never talked down to people; rather, he built you up.
- He had confidence; everyone trusted him.
- He had ethics and integrity.
- She inspired pride and enthusiasm in the organization.
- He had the courage to hold everyone accountable to the same standard—no favorites.
- He taught me everything I know about___.
- She was a servant leader.

me and brought out my best self." They tell expressive and moving stories about the people who molded them into who they are. "I trusted him." "He built me up." "He was a servant leader." "They were and still are my role models." They respond as the poet Maya Angelou predicted:

> *"People will forget what you said. People will forget what you did. But people will never forget how you made them feel."*

When I ask, "Who are these people who have had such a powerful influence and impact on your life?" without hesitation, they reply, "My parents, coaches, teachers, teammates, spouses, clergy, work associates, or bosses." Of the thousands of responses I've received to these two simple questions, only a tiny handful of answers have deviated from this pattern.

The Tipping Point

The key to successful leadership is the ability to positively change human behavior. However, most of the popular leadership literature and institutional leadership training either ignores, flippantly mentions, or subtly side-steps the importance of character—who you *are* as a leader. Instead, they focus on your competence—what you *do* as a leader.

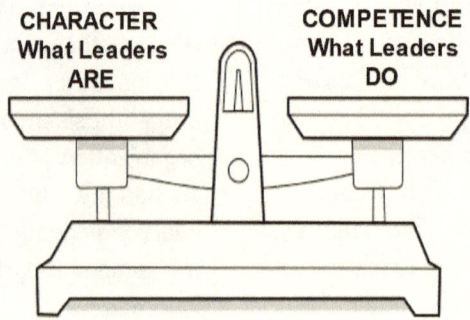

Your character is the tipping point that gives you influence powerful enough to positively change people's behavior. It's your character that influences those you lead to share the same level of commitment for success as you have for your collective endeavor. It's your character that influences them to willingly and enthusiastically engage in a shared belief system that makes the organization better. It's your character that influences your Mercenaries to become your Patriots. Converting Mercenaries to Patriots is, first and foremost, about who you are. Depending on title, rank, position, and authority will not get it done. As I said earlier, just because you're their boss doesn't mean you're their leader. That title of leader is bestowed upon you by those you lead. Following is a voluntary act. You must be the leader who people want to follow because of who you are before what you do comes into play.

Mastering what you do is a complex and arduous journey. But mastering who you *are* is considerably more difficult. It's often much more painful but profoundly more critical. Until you know and have mastered who you are, you're in a pipe dream if you think you're doing more than merely presiding over your charges. The first person you have to lead is yourself. This isn't something new. As the 5th century Greek historian Herodotus advised, "Your character is your fate."[2] So, let's dig deeper into the essence of "character": What is it, and why does it have such a profound effect and impact on your ability to lead?

The Road to Character

In David Brooks' excellent book, *The Road to Character,*[3] he metaphorically addresses "competence and character" in what he refers to as "resume virtues and eulogy virtues." Your "resume virtues" are what you list on your LinkedIn page. They're your professional competencies—the skills you bring to the job market, your professional expertise, your talent.[4] They're the virtues you display as a *professional,* what you *do.*

Your "eulogy virtues" define your character—what people will say about you when you're gone, whether you're honest, brave, kind, or humble. They're the virtues you display as a *person,* who you *are*. I would never suggest, and I believe that Brooks would agree, that character alone will bring you leadership success. Character without competence is a recipe for failure. Even failing honorably and virtuously is still failing. Mother Theresa possessed impeccable character, but I suspect she wouldn't have been a successful Amazon CEO. Likewise, a professionally competent leader who doesn't possess character is a formula for mediocrity or disaster. As the fictional Captain Jack Aubrey in the great book and movie *Master and Commander* advises his midshipmen, "It takes a great deal more than mere seamanship to be a captain of a ship!"[5] Jerry Sandusky was a gifted football strategist and the coach of the perpetually winning Penn State football team. No one would question his professional competence. But his lack of character caused irrevocable harm to the lives of many young men and the reputation of a highly respected university.

Trust Achieves Leadership Success

To be anointed "leader," those you lead must have trust in both your character and your competence. Trust in both is necessary to earn the willing commitment and enthusiastic engagement of those you lead. Neither is sufficient without the other.

Trust is the keystone that keeps the leadership pillars of character and competence upright. Pulling trust from a leader-follower relationship is like pulling the keystone from a Roman arch; all will come tumbling down around you. Without trust, any attempts to inspire commitment are futile. Archimedes bragged, "Give me a lever long enough, and I can move the world." Like that lever, give a leader enough trust, and he can move the world. The level of trust you earn as a leader is directly proportional to the level of commitment your followers will possess. So, what does it take to be trusted enough to inspire total commitment rather than mere ho-hum compliance? What is the relationship between leadership and character and competence, and specifically, how do they impact your ability to lead? Bear with me for a few minutes as I answer these important questions.

In his book, *7 Habits of Highly Effective People*, Stephen Covey advises, "When considering any new endeavor, you should

Begin with the End in Mind."[6] You can't know what you want until you've envisioned it. Let's do just that: Start with the end—*leadership*—and work your way back to *character* and *competence* in this relationship.

Leadership – What is it?

Let's take Covey's wise advice and describe what we want our leadership to look like. For this exercise, let's say you want to be:

> A leader who creates sustained organizational success with the ability to inspire or persuade those I lead to be willingly committed and enthusiastically engaged in our common endeavor.

What does it take to achieve the goal of being a leader of a prosperous organization staffed with Organizational Patriots? What it takes is influence—influence strong enough to inspire, persuade, or motivate people to internalize a desire to do something above and beyond what they would ordinarily do, where they embrace the mission and goals of your organization as their own and have a sense of equity in its success. As John Maxwell says in his book, *The 21 Irrefutable Laws of Influence*, "The true measure of leadership is influence—nothing more, nothing less." Leadership isn't a position or title; it's a condition of permission given by followers once they buy into the leader.[7] Leadership can't be awarded, appointed, or assigned—it comes only from influence.[8] So, what does it take to persuade your followers to embrace your organization's mission as their own and feel equity in its success?" The answer is that it takes influence powerful enough to positively change people's character or behavior.

Influence → Leadership

It's as simple and as complicated as that. The verb "influence" means to move someone by persuasion or example, motivating them to move in a new direction. Dictators and Maintainers influence through forced and bought compliance. Leaders, on the other hand, possess a level of influence compelling enough to motivate their followers to willingly and enthusiastically perform at a higher level. They complete challenging tasks, win wars, work harder, pay more attention to customer needs, and generally punch above their weight.

True leadership can't be awarded, appointed, or assigned—it comes only from influence.[9] Leaders influence not only what people do but who they are. Leaders, unlike Maintainers, affect a person's behavior, moral fiber, and worldview. It's about influencing ordinary people to do extraordinary things. It's about influencing ordinary people to become extraordinary people. It's about arousing in people an eagerness to *do* better. It's about arousing in people a desire to *be* better. It's about changing value systems, unleashing human potential, stimulating personal growth, and inspiring a shared vision. It's about motivating people to commit to doing better or being better.

It's so easy to say but so hard to do. Changing behavior and attitudes is hard. The more difficult the task, the more influence is required. The stronger the attitude to be changed, the more influence is needed. Massive accomplishments require massive influence. Influence is an emotional connection, a human dynamic.[10] When a leader has strong influence over her charges, it can be an incredibly powerful tool for good but also for bad. So, what does it take to achieve that level of influence and persuasion? The answer is that it takes symbiotic and reciprocal trust between leader and led.

Trust → Influence → Leadership

As I noted in the introduction to this book, we're in the midst of a leadership crisis because we're in the middle of a *trust* crisis. America's trust in its leaders and institutions has been falling for decades. In the 2022 *Harvard Business Review Global Survey*, only 49 percent of full-time workers responded that they had a "great deal of trust" in those working above them.[11] Vast numbers of Americans no longer seem to have trust in their leaders in their important social and civil institutions.[12]

In a 2023 Gallup Poll across fourteen key institutions, including government, big business, the media, education, science and medicine, technology, financial institutions, religious institutions, law enforcement, the military, and others, the average proportion of Americans who said they had "a great deal or quite a lot of confidence [trust]" in them was 27 percent. This is the lowest number ever recorded. In the 1970s, when Gallup started measuring this number, it was close to 50 percent.[13]

This loss of trust isn't just a problem; it's a *crisis*. Trust is the basis of any meaningful relationship. It's the gift that keeps on giving. America finds itself as a nation in which large numbers of its citizens profoundly mistrust the leaders and institutions that govern them.[14] Researchers have discovered that the level of trust followers have in their leaders determines the amount of influence they're willing to accept from that leader.[15] There are a few hard-and-fast rules, but this is one: Without trust, you're not leading, you're merely presiding.

Let's go back to the question I've been asking my students for fifteen years, "Describe the person or leader who has had the most influence in making you the person and the leader you are today."

Trust Is the Basis of Every Relationship

Leader–Follower
Parent–Child
Wife–Husband
Employer–Employee
Doctor–Patient
Teacher–Student
Merchant–Customer
Officer–Soldier
Friend–Friend
Clergy–Parishioner
Coach–Player
Police–Public
Government–Citizens
Politician–Voter

"Every failed relationship is ultimately because of an actual or perceived breach of trust."
—*Christopher Kolenda, author of*
Leadership: The Warrior's Art

What was the common denominator in their replies? It was trust. They deemed the most influential people in their lives as trustworthy enough to positively impact their behavior and affect their lives.

The single most important element in influencing commitment

is trust. Influence powerful enough to change people's behavior is derived from, and proportional to, the level of trust they have in you. If a person is easy to trust, they're easy to follow. The stronger their trust in you, the stronger your influence is and the more you can ask of them. To quote General Martin Dempsey:

> *"Trust is undeniably the most profound leadership imperative.*
> *It must be earned and then earned again."*[16]

Do not mistakenly assume, as many do, that just because you're not distrusted that you are trusted. Followers don't buy in and commit to your vision, organizational goals, objectives, or dreams. They buy in and commit to *you*. To bring Harry Truman back into the conversation, when he said, "Leadership is influencing a group of people to do things they ordinarily would not do," he went on to say, "...without being asked, and like it." President Eisenhower added, "Leadership is influencing people to want what you want," which is another way of saying committing to what you want. This trust is part of James MacGregor Burns' "transformational leadership"—influencing those you lead to internalize what you want as their own, inculcating your desires as their desires. Symbiotic trust between you and those you lead creates a sense of collective ownership in your vision, decisions, and desires. It triggers deep emotions of connectedness. There is a close relationship between truth and trust. Just tell the truth. What higher praise can a leader hear from her followers than "I trust you?" There is none.

It takes trust to inspire deep and sustained follower commitment over passive ho-hum compliance. When trust is high in a leader, followers will willingly do more difficult and arduous things when asked. Very high-trust followers will do things before being asked or without being asked. They will demonstrate initiative and be proactive rather than reactive. They'll do the right thing because it is the right thing to do, not just because they have to do it or, worse yet, just because they're afraid not to. Influencing low-trust followers by forcing compliance is temporary. In trusting relationships, followers trust that the leader will do what's best for the organization and them. They know their leader cares for and about them. A follower's trust in their leader is the most important factor in the success of any organization.[17] The higher the stakes, the tougher the task; the more you need your followers to be committed and engaged, the more trust is required. You have to earn and build trust *before* the crisis—before you have to ask the followers to go above and beyond.

If you're like me, you don't give your trust easily. Ask yourself the question, "Why do I trust people?" In most cases, when we get a new boss, we consciously or subconsciously ask ourselves, "Is this person worthy of my trust?" The tipping point to inspire your Mercenaries to become Patriots is when they're convinced that you care about them and have a genuine concern for their well-being, and that you're a vehicle for their success, goals, and aspirations. But the burden of proof is up to you. You have to prove to them, time and time again, that trusting you is the right thing to do. The awarding of trust from followers to leaders is a voluntary act; it cannot be demanded, mandated, or dictated. It is a conscious decision.

A *Harvard Business Review* survey found that while 58 percent of people trust strangers, only 42 percent trust their own boss.[18] You can't simply declare yourself a leader; that title is awarded to you by the people whose trust you've earned. It has to be apparent that they're getting something better by following you than by not following you.[19] If your employees trust you, they'll follow you anywhere. Without trust, as Miami Heat President Pat Riley once said, "Everyone will gear down just enough to get by." Organizations, like teams, can't survive by just getting by. Once you've won their trust, you have to sustain it by earning it again and again. What does it take to earn a level of trust that motivates those you want to lead to be willingly committed to your joint endeavor? The answer is that it takes a day-to-day demonstration that both your character and competence are worthy of trust.

[Character + Competence] → Trust → Influence → Leadership

Neither is sufficient without the other. First comes trust in your character, then trust in your competence. Follower trust is the *sine qua non* of leadership and is necessary to create committed followers. It's worth saying again: Neither is sufficient without the other. It's the fusion of the two that stimulates trust in those you lead. However, character is the first among equals. Character and competence overlap: the heart and the head, motive and skill, intent and technique, moral strength and intellectual horsepower.[20] Pursuing one to the exclusion of the other is a recipe for failure.

The essence of leadership isn't just about making a difference in ourselves but making a difference in those we lead. Before leading others, we must know who we are and what we stand for. To repeat Aristotle's advice: Know thyself.-

In the coming chapters, you'll have the opportunity to take stock of various attributes of your character and competence. This is an opportunity for self-reflection and personal growth, which should be a constant exercise on any leadership journey. Let's start by looking at the importance of a personal leadership philosophy in the next chapter.

Summary Points

[Character + Competence] → Trust → Influence → Leadership

- Leadership is influence powerful enough to inspire followers to fully commit and enthusiastically. engage in a common endeavor, producing sustained organizational success.
- Influence is the capacity to affect someone's character or behavior.
- Leaders influence not only what people *do* but who they *are*.
- What it takes to achieve a high level of influence from followers is their total trust in you.
- What it takes to earn that total trust is the day-to-day demonstration of both character and competence by someone deemed by followers to be worthy of their trust.

- Trust is the most profound leadership imperative. It must be earned, then earned again and again.
- Trust is the keystone that keeps the leadership pillars of character and competence upright.
- Character and competence are necessary for leadership success, but neither is sufficient alone.

5

YOUR LEADERSHIP PHILOSOPHY

"If a man does not know what port he is steering for, no wind is favorable to him."

—Seneca, ancient Roman philosopher

MY LEADERSHIP PHILOSOPHY grew from the seed planted during my first year at North Georgia College (NGC). NGC was a small military college tucked away in the foothills of the Blue Ridge Mountains. The military program at NGC was strict, 24/7, and unforgiving, and it did a great job of taming young men who needed taming. The most important lesson I learned at NGC was that before you can be a good leader, you must be a good follower. It took my entire freshman year to learn that lesson. That year, I earned the dubious distinction of being the freshman with the most demerits. That meant every weekend was spent working off my demerits rather than enjoying free time. My cadet leaders made me understand that I had to prove I could be a follower before I could earn the honor of being a leader.

The seeds planted at NGC continued to grow during my formative years in the Army, starting on the day I was commissioned a second lieutenant and took an oath of office. I raised my right hand and swore, "I will faithfully discharge the duties of the office on which I am about to enter." Faithfully discharging the duties of my office included keeping the promises I made in that oath by obeying a code of conduct and living by an unambiguous set of Army values. I knew it was my duty to follow those rules and live by them, and if I didn't, I would be letting my fellow soldiers and my country down. I also knew that if I didn't follow those rules, there would be consequences—disgrace and humiliation. The oath, the code, and the values were my talisman whenever I was confronted with tough leadership decisions or questions of character. They provided the answers; no forethought was necessary. Each was a guide on how to conduct myself as a leader when faced with dilemmas of doing the "hard right" over the "expedient easy." They clearly laid out the standards of behavior and core principles expected of me as a leader. They were the building blocks of my leadership philosophy, which grew with experience, continued over time, and helped me defeat my worst impulses in favor of my best instincts.

As my leadership philosophy matured, it helped take the mystery out of how I wanted to lead. It pre-determined what was right and wrong, giving me a mental rehearsal of how I would respond to challenging leadership situations. It made decisions a choice, not a chance. When I came face-to-face with a tough choice, I would ask myself, *Am I going to live by my principles, or am I going to ignore them?* Predetermining what I had deemed right and wrong and knowing I was accountable for my actions steered me in the right direction.

The 2 AM Phone Call

Early in my Army career, I worked for a boss who treated people unequally by showing blatant favoritism. His behavior had a huge negative impact on morale and teamwork. Even though I was one of his "favorites," I found his treatment of those not in his inner circle repugnant. As a result, I promised myself that I would always treat everyone fairly and equally as a leader. Quite simply, one principle of my leadership philosophy would be "No favoritism, not once, not ever, period."

Years later, as a battalion commander, I was faced with the decision: Am I going to live by my philosophy, or am I going to ignore it? At the time, the Army in Europe was experiencing a high number of soldiers who were involved in fatal traffic accidents because of drunk driving. I gathered my battalion of 900 soldiers and issued an edict: "Anyone found driving under the influence will face appropriate military punishment." Shortly after I made the threat of punishment for a DUI, I received a call one morning around 2 am. It was from the battalion duty officer who said, "Sir, I have a soldier who was just stopped at the post's front gate for a random breathalyzer and failed." Normally, I wouldn't have been advised of such an incident. Instead, the soldier's company commander would have received the late-night call and informed me of the situation with his soldier the next day. I asked the duty officer, "Why are you calling me and not the soldier's company commander?" He hesitated, then nervously replied: "Sir, it's your driver, Staff Sergeant Smith." After a short pause, the duty officer continued: "I asked the MP officer at the gate, who's a friend of mine, that since it was a random check and Sergeant Smith was just barely over the legal limit, would he keep it out of the duty log? He agreed." I thanked the lieutenant and told him I would take care of it in the morning.

At the time, the appropriate military punishment for a DUI was what's called an "Article 15." Punishment under this article typically consisted of a reduction of the soldier's rank and a fine of several hundred dollars. But for a staff sergeant (SSG), a career soldier, it meant much more—the probable end of a career. SSG Smith had been my driver for over twelve months; we were as close as a lieutenant colonel and a staff sergeant could be. We had been through much together. Technically, since the results weren't listed on the post duty log, I could have kept this incident off the books and taken care of it without having to officially punish SSG Smith. My pre-determined leadership philosophy addressing favoritism was clearly stated: No favoritism, not once, not ever, period. I knew what the right thing to do was, now I had to decide: Was I going to live by my principles, or was I going to ignore them? Leadership is hard because you have to hard things. My leadership philosophy was clear; I just had to decide whether to *follow it, ignore it, or abandon it.* I knew what I stood for—now, I just had to stand for it. As painful and gut-wrenching as it was, I stayed true to my core values by administering Article 15 to SSG Smith.

Building Your Leadership Philosophy

The only way most of us get any sense of how we're doing as leaders is either from our boss's periodic performance review or from some generic assessment administered in a leadership development program. The problem with both is, more often than not, the feedback is poorly delivered, over-complimentary, and lacks specificity. A Gallup poll found that only 14 percent of employees strongly agree that the performance reviews they receive inspire them to improve.[1] Depending on cookie-cutter training programs to hone your leadership skills means you'll have to rely on broad-brushed, generalized instruction that's focused on management practices, subtly avoiding the hard aspects of your character. These generic programs aren't tailored to your individual needs.

You've probably participated in some version of these training regimes. They usually start with a personality assessment: Myers-Briggs, 360, MMPI, CPI, or some other one-size-fits-all tool. The assessment is usually followed by structured group training sessions promoting the latest leadership flavor of the day: Management by Objectives, Covey's Habits, Six Sigma, Total Quality Management, Lean Thinking, or Reengineering. The fad *de jour* assesses your leadership strengths and weaknesses, then goes through a standardized exercise to determine how to best leverage your strengths and mitigate or improve your weaknesses. The exposed strengths and weaknesses are almost always focused on skills and competencies but rarely, if ever, address the more important aspect of your leadership: your character.

My experience with these exercises is that they are thin gruel.[2] At the risk of being labeled a leadership development heretic, I contend that this approach may be well-meaning and, in some cases, offer minor benefits. Still, almost all fall short of developing leaders. In the best of these, we leave the training event with short-lived enthusiasm and a nonspecific recipe to improve a few generic professional skills or competencies. We walk away without any long-lasting, meaningful impact on transforming ourselves as a leader. In most cases, they're superficial, inaccurate, and too shal-

> **"One of the problems with standard leadership courses is that they focus exclusively on skill and produce managers rather than leaders, when they produce anything at all."**
> *—Warren Bennis, author of*
> **On Becoming a Leader**

low a dive into who we really are as leaders. Don't depend on some all-purpose training program to hone or kick-start your leadership skills. It's worth repeating: No one really cares about you but you!

The Wake-Up Call—A Kick in the Gut!

It's one of life's unfortunate truths, but most of us coast along relatively oblivious of how we're doing as leaders until we get a wake-up call, that proverbial kick in the gut. For many, it takes what author Warren Bennis calls a "crucible event," a personal or professional setback, crisis, or catastrophe that brings us to our knees, to convince us that maybe we've been asleep at the wheel.[3] The relative comfort of "If it ain't broke, don't fix it" guides us until "it breaks" and we're forced to "fix it" to survive. Philosophy professor and author Edith Hall wrote, "Many people, perhaps the majority, live intuitively, and often unreflectively on autopilot."[4] Unfortunately, most people not only live but lead intuitively, and often unreflectively, on autopilot. Our reluctance to look closely at our reflection in the mirror is, in most cases, because we believe "It ain't broke" and, in extreme cases, because we're afraid of what we might see.

Rarely do we voluntarily fan the flames to expose our souls to ourselves. We get into a success rut. We may not be as successful as we can be or as we'd like, but we're not *unsuccessful*. We get stuck in the Maintainer's comfort zone by reminding ourselves, *If all is going OK, even if it's not great, why rock the boat?* That motivation to take a deep introspective peek into our leadership abilities often comes only when we get that kick in the gut, an unforeseen life-altering event that derails us so drastically that it forces us to recognize that we must change how we lead or we will perish. I've heard it many times and personally experienced it once. The kick in the gut makes those who experience it ask, *What happened? Why was I let go? Why wasn't I promoted? How did I get in this fix? How could I get downsized, rightsized, restructured, furloughed, fired!?* Of course, we may become a professional casualty through no fault of our own. It could be industry failure, corporate down-sizing, COVID-19, or just some uncontrollable act of bad luck.

For many, a sudden derailment is the end of their leadership journey. The rolls of those who've failed, then quit, are long. The secret to getting ahead is getting started. With the will and the grit to carry on, you take that first step to build or rebuild. It requires an honest and sometimes painful self-examination. You have to identify, acknowledge, and accept ownership of those aspects of your character that may have caused that kick-in-the-gut experi-ence, and that takes strength of character. Character is based on decisions—on *your* decisions.[5]

Don't Be an Icarus

I strongly urge you not to wait for that out-of-the-blue kick in the gut, that painful personal or professional crucible event, to take a good hard look at that person staring back at you in the mirror. Gird your leadership loins now. Don't wait until you're dying of thirst to dig a well. As a young man, I was either deaf or immune to the advice of those wise men and women who'd gone before me. I had to learn my lessons by experience, even if it was the hard way.

Like Icarus' father, Daedalus, who told him not to fly too close to the sun because the wax binding the feathers to his wings would melt, I had parents, teachers, coaches, mentors, and bosses who repeatedly tried to warn me to stay away from the sun. But, alas, like Icarus and many other young leaders, I had to experience that crash into the sea before I paid attention. Over the years and many dips in the ocean later, I finally tried to become one of Mark Twain's "wise" men. It took several muggings by reality to force me to pay attention to the advice of those who cared for me. I finally learned to listen and learn from others. Now, I can read about Washington and Churchill's experiences, listen to the wise counsel of my mentors, and use their lessons and advice in making better decisions about my life and my leadership. The past is never past; it may be forgotten, but its influence endures.[6] It took me a long time to embrace what Otto von Bismarck, the WWI Prussian chancellor, once suggested: "Any fool can learn from his mistakes—the wise man learns from the mistakes of others."

Who Do You Want to Be as a Leader?

It's not enough to be aware of our weaknesses and flaws. We have to do something about them and change our behavior. To have a weakness or flaw and not know it is a lack of self-awareness. To know you have a weakness or flaw and do nothing about it is arrogance, stupidity, or both. It's like being aware that you're farsighted and hoping it will disappear. But your blurred vision won't correct itself or go away unless you do something about it—until you get glasses.

Too often, leaders go through the gut-wrenching, soul-searching process of deciding what they stand for and making promises to themselves, but when called upon to live up to those promises, they stumble. Your character is revealed by how you deal with temptation, whether you win the struggle between impulse and conscience.[7] Often, the slip of our leadership from honest to dishonest, moral to amoral or immoral, selfless to selfish, or courageous to cowardly is slow and subtle. If our convictions are shallow, we're much more apt to make poor choices, either denying or ignoring the consequences of our actions to ourselves and those we lead. We have these delusional conversations with ourselves to justify or rationalize behavior with which we are intuitively and instinctively uncomfortable: *The ends justify the means. No one but me will notice. I'll do it just this one time. This is no big deal—everybody else does it.*

This insidious, subtle self-denial can quickly and almost unperceptively turn into situational integrity. Small compromises of integrity on Monday lead to bigger compromises on Tuesday. Before you know it, unethical behavior is the norm, and you don't notice it anymore. When we only stay true to our core values on a situational or convenient basis, we exercise those values less and less. They begin to disappear from our character, and who we want

> **"Comin' as close to the truth as a man can come without actually gettin' there is comin' pretty close, but it still ain't the truth."**
> —*Texas Bix Bender, author of* Don't Squat With Yer Spurs On!

to become gives way to who we are. We may have a moral compass, but occasionally, we let the needle wobble a little bit. It's like when Ernest Hemingway was asked, "How did you go bankrupt?" He replied, "Gradually. Then suddenly." How big a lie do you have to tell to be a liar? How much do you have to steal to be a thief? How many times do you have to do what's best for yourself over what's best for those you lead before you're selfish? It's through your deeds, not your words, that your followers determine your character—who you really are.

Who you really are is what author Bill George refers to as a leader's "True North."[8] Your True North is your leadership philosophy, "your most deeply held beliefs, your values, the principles you intend to lead by." It allows you to consistently operate on a foundation based on values and principles that you have clearly defined for yourself. As James Kouzes and Barry Posner point out in their book, *The Leadership Challenge,*

> **"Leaders who have a clear leadership philosophy are nearly 30 percent more likely to be trusted by their constituents than those unclear about their leadership philosophy."**
> —*James Kouzes and Barry Posner, authors of* The Leadership Challenge

"The trust of those you lead is greatly improved if you have a clear understanding of your leadership values and principles."[9] It's easy to say to yourself, "I intend to lead an organization whose culture is characterized by operational excellence and crewed with high-performing, committed, and engaged employees." That doesn't just happen. Good intentions are insufficient.[10] You must have the self-awareness to decide who you want to be as a leader, then you must have the self-discipline to do what it takes to become that leader.

You decide your own character.[11] Your leadership philosophy reflects your character, the rules, and the values you lead by. It determines the culture of your organization. When those you lead look at you, what do they see—a person and leader of character, or something else? The leadership philosophy you build today is your foundation for success when facing difficult times tomorrow. It's deciding and preparing in advance for how you'll react and respond to ethical and character decisions before you find them staring you in the face. No one has addressed this better than George Washington during his farewell address at the end of his second term as president in 1796:

"All humankind is guided by rules. The only question is: What are the rules we choose to live by?"

Growing Your Leadership Philosophy Is a Lifelong Journey

No organization does a better job than the military of instilling in their leaders a sense of right and wrong, a philosophy focused on the greater good over self. Each of the services uses oaths, codes, and mottos to guide their leaders through tough and stressful times. When an Army lieutenant comes to a crossroads and must choose between right or wrong, she can look for strength and guidance in the principles of "Duty, Honor, Country." Likewise, Marines look to *Semper Fidelis* (Always Faithful), and Airmen lean on "Service Above Self." Those leaders in uniform don't view these maxims as superficial recruiting slogans or public relations hyperbole. They embrace them as a way of life, rules by which to live and lead. Of course, there are always a few who don't buy into this ethos. But I'm happy to report that they are few in number and usually don't last long in uniform. Most men and women in uniform passionately internalize the spirit of their service's culture and continue to embrace that spirit even when the uniform comes off.

There's a much-told story about a young man in WWI that reflects his heartfelt devotion to his service:

An American lady who was visiting a WWI French hospital sees a wounded soldier who looked quite different from the bearded French soldiers. She went to his bedside; "Oh," she said, "surely you are an American!" "No ma'am," he casually answered, "I'm a Marine."

If you don't believe me and think it's all organizational propaganda and trite slogans, the next time you run into a Marine or former Marine, tell him you think *Semper Fi* is bunk. Warning: Do it from a distance and with backup!

Growing as a leader is a constant journey with no deadline; it's a lifelong trajectory. My leadership philosophy matured at each rung of my professional ladder with experience, constant observation of other leaders, and self-study. When I became a Ranger, I was

What Is a Leadership Philosophy?

"It's preparing yourself for what may come."
—*Epictetus, Greek slave-turned-philosopher in his Discourses*

expected to follow the Ranger Creed. When faced with tempting opportunities to do what was best for me but at the team's expense, there was the answer in the creed: "Never shall I fail my comrades." When I became a member of the great 36th Infantry Regiment, my leadership was expected to be one of "Deeds Not Words." The battalion's motto constantly reminded me that my leadership was about what I did, not what I said. When I became a brigade commander in the 1st Infantry Division, I was expected to embrace a code of "No Mission Too Difficult. No Sacrifice Too Great. Duty First!" When faced with "What should I do?" dilemmas, it's amazing how many can be solved with "Just do your duty!" You can never do more than your duty.

The concept of organizational philosophies and codes of conduct isn't the exclusive domain of the military. Granted, the level of intensity that civilian organizations put into codes and philosophies isn't at the same level as the military, but most have formal and informal rules and cultural norms. Whereas military officers swear an oath to lead with integrity, private-sector leaders *choose* to lead a life of integrity. Many vocations, such as doctors, attorneys, and engineers, also use codes of conduct or covenants to inculcate culturally expected norms into their profession. Like a physicians' commitment based on the Hippocratic Oath, "First, do no harm," these organizations have their members affirm to a professional philosophy that reflects the specific norms of their profession.

Some corporations also use various forms of codes of conduct, mission statements, core values, credos, and operating principals. Among these are many well-known companies: Coca-Cola, Facebook, Ford, General Motors, Google, Hershey, IBM, Ikea, Johnosn & Johnson, Microsoft, Nokia, PepsiCo, Proctor & Gamble, and Starbucks. They span various industries, but all outline the ethical, legal, and cultural rules or norms they expect their employees to embrace and live by. Even those organizations without formal codes usually have some form of informal, often unspoken but expected, cultural codes and norms they want their employees to follow.

What Is Your Leadership Philosophy?

Whether your organization has a formal code or not, when you assume the role of leader, you must define your personal leadership philosophy. To do so, we must overcome the prejudices and biases we have about ourselves, and that's hard. We have to reach within ourselves and have the self-awareness to decide who we are and how we'll lead. We have to decide what we stand for as a leader. At the very least, a leader must have a foundation of character to distinguish right from wrong and have the moral courage to do what's right[12]

Once you've defined your personal leadership philosphy, that self-image gives you residual strength of character and banks psychological fortitude, so when you need it, it's there for you. Internalizing a concept of what we stand for allows us to recognize our innate, selfish desires and override them. Those who've established a character of internal strength have always carried the day against those of lesser character.[13] They've decided what they stand for, and when called upon, they stand for it. When tempted by a flirtation from the dark side, they rebuke it without hesitation. Now let's consider the idea of deciding what you stand for.

Simply wanting to be a leader and being willing to do what it takes to be one are two different things. To paraphrase my old boss, friend, and mentor Bob Carroll in his book, *Building Your Leadership Legacy*, "Knowing and understanding the importance of character as a leader is a far cry from living and leading with character."[14] If there's a gap between the leader you are today and the leader you aspire to be in the future, your philosophy should reflect who you aspire to be. You can call it what you want—your leadership philosophy, code of conduct, mission statement, values, talisman, road map, etc. Still, whatever you call it, it should reflect your character—those core

My Leadership _____

- Philosophy
- Code of conduct
- North star
- Covenant
- Mission
- Road map
- Scorecard
- Promise
- Values

values and principles that define who you are or aspire to be as a leader. It answers the question, Who am I as a leader?

Building your character is like erecting a Lego structure; each building block contributes to the quality and strength of your character. Specific building blocks of character that contribute to reciprocal trust between you and those you lead include integrity, honesty, humility, resilience, courage, and self-confidence. They form a solid foundation of who you are as a leader. That foundation is your leadership contract or covenant with yourself, defining what rules you'll lead by. It's your moral compass that steers your decision-making and actions in the direction of your pre-determined values and beliefs. It's your North Star.

Once you make that contract with yourself, then you must be faithful to it. You've established what you stand for as a leader; now you have to stand for it. At twenty years old, Ben Franklin created a system to develop his character. He made a contract with himself that consisted of thirteen virtues he needed to follow to be a man of great character. He graded himself on each virtue daily.[15] I'm not advocating that you need to be as obsessive as old Ben, but your

"First tell yourself what kind of person [leader] you want to be, then do what you have to do to be that person [leader]."

—Epictetus, Greek slave-turned-philosopher in his Discourses

leadership philosophy must be specific enough so that when you're faced with leadership dilemmas, it guides you to a decision point. It's that foundation that empowers you to operate from a position of strength. Proclaiming your values isn't enough; you must live by them. You make choices that are deliberate, intentional, and reflective of your values and priorities. Your choices are clear: Will I follow, ignore, or abandon those promises I made to myself?

Your Reputation Is Your Brand

As you demonstrate your character over time, you establish a reputation—your personal brand. Your character is who you are; your reputation is what others think of you. Leaders live and die by their reputations.[16] A "good" reputation is a fragile thing. It can take years to earn, but it can be lost in an instant. It's almost impossible to talk your way out of something that you behaved your way into. Once you've touched the proverbial unprincipled tar baby, your hands are forever stained. You can spend the rest of your life trying to pay for what you said or did in ten seconds. With character violations, trust is irretrievable and reputation unrecoverable. Like it or not, your reputation follows you like your shadow.

Recently, there's been a tsunami of supposed leaders of character who've fallen from grace after years of ostensibly honorable behavior. Any past good they had done has been quickly forgotten, and they're now forever remembered for their misdeeds. These high-profile leaders have fallen from grace not for lack of professional competence but because their character flaws were publicly exposed. If they had a personal code or a moral compass, their clouded moral judgment led them to violate that code with some contorted or post-hoc justifications for their behavior.[17] Temptation sang a siren song, and they were too weak to resist.

Some would contend there's been a global-warming-like phenomenon in which the character of our leaders is melting. I would argue that we've always had the same percentage of so-called paragons of good whose honorable character was merely a veneer sheathing their lack of integrity, but in the pre-digitized days, they were either undiscovered or unpublicized because it was easier to hide. There are no safe places to hide from iPhone cameras or social media today.

Most derailed leaders fell from grace after ignoring the needle on their moral compass. But let's not get ahead of ourselves: Before we can live and lead with character, let's come to a common understanding of what it is.

Shortly, I'll ask you to codify your leadership philosophy in writing, but we have some work to do first. A leadership philosophy is a reflection of a leader's character. Let's look at what it takes to have the character to inspire trust from those we lead.

Who Do You See in the Mirror?

Over his lifetime, Vincent van Gogh painted around three dozen self-portraits. He would sit in front of a mirror with his brushes and paint the reflection he saw onto a canvas. In each of his paintings, he captured himself differently. In the early years, he aspired to portray himself as handsome and confident or self-assured, gentle, and worldly. Later in life, he painted himself as tortured, worried, and thoughtful. And in his most famous self-portrait, the one without his ear, he depicted himself as confused and disturbed. In every painting, he wanted the world to see him as he saw himself. He used the act of painting self-portraits as an opportunity for introspection and a method to develop his skills as an artist.

Developing your character as a leader requires Van Gogh-like introspection. You want to capture who you are on a mental canvas. Visualize yourself as an artist sitting in front of a blank canvas. You're looking in a mirror, and you have a fist full of brushes in one hand and an extensive palate of colored paints in the other, except you're painting a self-portrait of your character, not your face. Like van Gogh, you want to portray your character as you want the world—your family, your friends, your peers, your employees, and your employers—to see you. It goes back to that conversation with yourself: What do I stand for? What are my non-negotiables? What are my core values and principles? Who am I as a person? Who am I as a leader?

Your answers to these questions define your character. They provide the picture of yourself you want the world to see, the list of your eulogy virtues that you have etched on the walls of your skull. Perhaps you want your self-portrait to show the world that you're honest, trustworthy, caring, determined, self-confident, and courageous. Whatever you choose, ask yourself: *Does the world see me the same way I see myself? Is there a difference between my idealized self and my perceived self?* The uncomfortable truth is, the answer may be no.

How Do People See You?

Let's look at another artist's self-portrait, Picasso. Like van Gogh, he was fond of painting himself. Picasso referred to his self-portraits as the window into his soul. But there's no similarity between how Picasso saw himself (right photo) and how the world saw him (left photo). Some leaders have the same problem. The world sees them differently than how they want to be seen or how they think they're seen. Your leadership challenge is to be the "real deal," where your view of your character is a mirror image of that seen by those you lead.

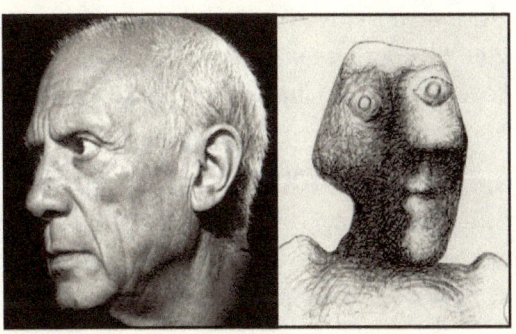

One of the things I do in my consulting life is to guide senior executives through an introspective process of self-evaluating their leadership. During these exercises, I ask the executives to describe various aspects of their character: integrity, trustworthiness, authenticity, moral courage, selflessness, passion, and resilience. Then I ask their employees to rate their boss of those same attributes. It's shocking to see just how vast the gulf is between their perceptions of their character compared to those of their employees, peers, and bosses.[18] In extreme cases, they see a Norman Rockwell portrait, while their employees see a Jackson Pollock or Salvatore Dali. A large percentage of leaders who participate in this exercise consistently express a much higher opinion of their character than that held by those who rated them. They also overestimate the regard their employees have for them. These executives blissfully go through their daily routines, assuming that those they work with see them the same way they see themselves.

I'm not alone in finding these shortcomings in leaders' self-perceptions. Rasmussen, a Houston outsourcing firm, reported that of the 1,854 managers they surveyed, 92 percent said they were doing an excellent job, yet only 67 percent of their workers agreed while 10 percent said they were doing a bad job.

The journey to authentic leadership begins with understanding yourself.[19] It's amazing the number of people who don't understand themselves. They see themselves as leaders when, in fact, their employees view them as Dictators or Maintainers. Many have become complacent, forget to pay attention, take what they have for granted, and turn a blind eye to important things.[20] Every time they turn that blind eye to something everyone knows is wrong, they lose a measure of trust. They've forgotten, or never considered, that a leader's character is determined by the eye of the beholder—those they lead. Character is built, not given.[21]

Do Those You Lead See You as You See Yourself?

Getting to a resounding yes to this question is simple in principle but extremely hard in practice. What's important to leadership success is how others see you, not how you see yourself. Your character is internal and is only revealed by your behavior. Being deemed trustworthy doesn't happen because you *think* you're trustworthy; it only comes when your followers have decided you *are* trustworthy.

"I always wanted to be somebody, but I should have been more specific."
—Lily Tomlin, comedienne

What does it take to ensure our self-image is the same as the one seen by those we lead? Let's return to the self-portrait analogy. Every stroke of van Gogh's brush painted a clearer picture of his image. With a few brush strokes, his eyes appeared; a few more strokes, and you could see his mouth. Eventually, his brushstrokes provided a clear picture of how van Gogh wanted you to see him. They produced a self-image made up of many strokes that were seen as a clear picture of who he was.

The picture you paint of your character should emerge much like van Gogh's portrait of himself, but rather than one stroke at a time, your picture is painted one *action* at a time. Your daily actions and behavior are the brushstrokes that reveal your character—who you are as a leader. Your canvas is the world in which you live and work. Your brushes and paints are your words and deeds.

The belief that your character is demonstrated by your deeds, not by your words, isn't a new idea. Aristotle insisted that the only way we can assess a person's character is by watching that person doing and saying things.[22] Every brush stroke is an act that either depicts or distorts the picture you want to paint. Everything you do adds more detail to the picture of who you are as a leader; each act either builds trust or erodes it. Each time your deeds are revealed to align with your words, you paint a picture of integrity and trustworthiness. Each time you praise your team rather than take credit yourself, you paint a picture of humility and selflessness. Each time you stand up for the harder right rather than taking a path of professional or personal expediency, you portray a picture of moral courage. Each time you follow through on a promise, big or small, you show the world that you can be depended upon. Every word you say and every action you take paints a clearer picture on the canvas of your character, revealing to the world who you are as a person and a leader. Your behavior is your character translated into action, the outward demonstration and validation of the quality of your character. You can't see integrity, honesty, or trustworthiness; you can only see the behavior that demonstrates those values. You can't see good intentions; you can only see them when they are exhibited and become a reality.

When conducting these introspective self-portraits, we must ask ourselves: *Is who I say I am as a leader the same as I actually am as a leader?* We often find we're not the people we thought we were or we hoped to be. If those you lead see your character differently than you see yourself, it's time to look closer at the person you see in the mirror. It's time to conduct an audit of your leadership philosophy. Does it need revision, or are you violating those promises you made to yourself?

When you assume the role of leader, everything you say and do is viewed through a magnifying glass by those you lead. Your every word and deed will be weighed to see if you're worthy of trust. If you promise that "I am and will be honest, trustworthy, humble, and selfless, and I will work hard to make us successful," then you can expect that those you lead will listen, watch, and wait to see if you'll be true to that promise. Your every word and deed are judged, consciously or subconsciously, by everyone in the organization against a standard of integrity. They'll look at your leadership to determine if it builds trust or erodes it. Your words are merely a scorecard by which your deeds are graded. Be ready for them to judge every action you take and to ask themselves these questions:

- "Is his moral compass pointing in the right direction?" (integrity)
- "Is he genuine and authentic?" (authenticity)
- "Is she self-serving. Does she have my best interests at heart?" (selflessness)
- "Can she be trusted to do what she says she is going to do?" (trustworthiness)
- "Does he have the grit to lead us through tough times?" (resilience)

If you Google "character attributes," you'll get over 136 million results, each of which cites a long list of attributes the author has deemed important. However, soldiers are different from high school teachers, power-line foremen, corporate CEOs, and project managers, and embracing these endless lists of attributes is impossible. As you plot the course of your leadership journey, you must tailor a catalog of character attributes that make sense to you—those that fit your life, your core values, and your individual professional and personal requirements and goals. Only *you* can define who you are as a leader.

Trust Builders

Over the years, I've seen a consistent set of character attributes that exceptional leaders possess. Moreover, these are the same aspects of character that Dictators and Maintainers lack or ignore. What this set of attributes has in common is that they build trust, inspire commitment, and influence those you lead to become Organizational Patriots. We all know people who are kind, polite, reliable, and optimistic, but we wouldn't trust them any further than we could throw them. The character traits that I recommend you brush onto your canvas are those that are essential for the trust component of the leadership equation. I can't guarantee that you'll be a successful leader if you pos-

Character Attributes

- Integrity
- Compassion
- Selflessness
- Fairness
- Passion
- Loyalty
- Humility
- Humor
- Kindness
- Respectfulness
- Forgiveness
- Authenticity
- Courageousness
- Grit
- Generosity
- Resilience
- Politeness
- Optimism
- Reliability
- Politeness
- Optimism
- Conscientiousness
- Self-awareness
- Self-discipline
- Self-confidence
- And many more

sess these attributes, but I can guarantee that without them, you'll never win the trust of those you lead. I don't make many emphatic statements, but this is one of them. We'll come back to this shortly.

Self-awareness Buttressed by Self-discipline

Developing your leadership philosophy starts with *self-aware-ness*, recognizing the aspects of your character that build trust and, more importantly, those aspects of your character that erode trust. Many imposters posing as leaders have little appetite for self-reflection or developing self-awareness.[23] We have to know our Achilles' heel. Without self-awareness, you're doomed to be a lifelong Maintainer.

Once you've mustered the intestinal fortitude to acknowledge those areas needing improvement, you have to call on your *self-discipline* to do what it takes to follow through and do something about them. Character development is like learning a new habit; it must be adopted, reinforced, and practiced.[24] Aristotle considered character a habit—the sum of our daily choices of right over wrong, not something implanted by nature.[25] Sometimes, it may require doing something new, revising some existing behavior, or stopping something you're doing now. In the most extreme cases, it may require that you drastically change your behavior. In other cases, it may be a minor directional nudge; you stay on the same path but tweak some minor behaviors or aspects of your character. Or it may be that you're perfectly happy with where you are today and choose to continue on the same path.

SELF-AWARENESS

"An MRI for the soul."
—*David Axelrod, former chief strategist to President Barak Obama*

We'll take that look in the mirror shortly, but let's not put the cart before the horse. Before you decide who you want to be as a leader, you must decide what kind of organization you want to lead. Who you are as a leader will determine the ethos of your organization. So, let's answer the question, What do you want the culture of your team to be?

Summary Points

- The trust of those you lead is greatly improved if you have a clear understanding of your own leadership values and principles.[26]
- Leader development is also character development.
- Your leadership philosophy is a reflection of your character.
- Growing your leadership philosophy is a lifelong journey.
- Your reputation as a leader is your brand.
- Many leaders see themselves differently than their employees see them.
- Every leaders' words and deeds are observed and judged by their followers.
- All leadership philosophies start with self-awareness.
- The character that matters is not the character we profess but the character we practice.

6

YOUR ORGANIZATION'S CULTURE

"If you don't know where you're going, you might not get there."
—Yogi Berra, former New York Yankees player and manager

ONE OF THE most frustrating times in my professional life was when I worked for a leader who was incapable of instilling a sense of mission or purpose in our company. Because he didn't clearly define our organization's objectives, expectations, and values, we had difficulty achieving our business goals, and morale was poor. He was a Maintainer who stumbled through his and our daily lives without a compass. Our organization's direction was dictated by expediency and survival. Unlike Maintainers, leaders have a direction and a personal vision for where they want to lead. They know what culture they want to instill in their organization.

If you're not the architect of your organization's culture, someone else will be. All leaders must ask themselves:

What type of organization do I want to lead?

To answer that question, let's again trust author Stephen Covey's advice: "Begin with the end in mind." Before you start "leading," you must determine what kind of organization you want to lead. Ask yourself, What do I want the *culture* of my organization to be? Only when you can clearly describe the culture of the organization you want to lead can you craft a leadership philosophy to do what it takes to get you there. I asked you to consider the culture of the organization you want to lead because, too often, we run off deciding to be a leader without determining where we want to lead. Any road will get you there if you don't know where you're going. You don't go to Home Depot and start buying materials to build a new tool shed before you determine whether you want one made of wood or brick.

An organization's *culture* is defined as the collective beliefs and convictions of all concerned—how they act, how they treat one another, and what they value. It's the company's DNA. It reflects the organization's character, and that character is established by its leader. As stated at the start of this chapter, if the leader fails to set the organization's culture, someone else will. It's important to decide the type of culture you want to build because it makes a significant difference in how you lead. Are you content with an organization that maintains the status quo with satisfied and compliant employees, or do you want to lead the business to a better place with employees who are strongly engaged and willingly committed to your endeavor? Building an organizational culture goes far beyond posting lofty slogans or hanging pictures on the wall of people rowing in the same direction.

Maintainers either accept the organization's culture that existed when they took its reins or let the employees determine the culture. Like a vacuum where the Maintainer surrenders the initiative to her followers, a culture will emerge in empty places. Subcultures will manufacture their own cultures that meet their self-interests, taking the opportunity to create their own fiefdoms and cliques and incite organizational-identity confusion. That puts the responsibility on the leader to set the culture for the organization.[1] Just as a person's character can be immoral, amoral, or moral, an organization's culture can be negative, neutral, or positive. The culture of any team, company, or group is a mirror image of its leader's character, ethics, behavior, and standards of performance.[2]

"No Problem" or "My Pleasure"?

Let's look at my favorite fast-food chain to see a great example of how a strong leader has shaped the organization's culture. I'm not a big fan of fast food, but when time or circumstances force me to grab a quick bite, I always look for the closest Chick-fil-A. Going into one of their restaurants is a far more extensive experience than just buying a chicken sandwich. The minute you walk into one of their stores, you sense a vibe unique from any other fast-food eatery. You see and feel a dining environment that puts other fast-food joints to shame. It's not just that their sandwiches are great, but it's apparent that the stores are modern and spotlessly clean and run with military-like precision. What really makes the place special is the obvious commitment of their

> **"Excellent companies seem to have developed cultures that have incorporated the values and practices of their leaders, and thus, those shared values survive for decades, often even after the passing of the original guru. The real role of the leader is to manage the values of the organization."**
>
> —*Thomas Peters and Robert Waterman Jr., authors of* In Search of Excellence

employees to something bigger than just selling a chicken sandwich. They act differently, and they treat you differently. They exude positivity. Every employee's cheerful demeanor comes across as authentic and sincere, with no hollow panache or fake sincerity. You're treated with respect and patience, and you're certain they want to please you as a customer. "Please" and "Thank you" are commonly uttered by employees. They usually ask if you need anything even before you ask, and when you say "Thank you" for the refilling of your Coke Zero or giving you more ketchup, you'll hear "Of course, my pleasure," and you're convinced it really *is* their pleasure.

On those few occasions when I'm reluctantly forced to eat at other fast-food places, the response I usually get when asking for help is a nonchalant "No problem," even though they act like it *is* a problem. I always have the urge to shout, "Of course, it's not a problem. It's your job!!" Unfortunately, this inattentive and often resentful attitude toward customers across the service industry has become the norm rather than the exception. We expect it, therefore, we get it. The challenge today is that organizations recruit and hire a higher percentage of employees who arrive with no moral compass and who do not self-govern.[3] Add to the recruiting pool problem the painful fact that most potential hires don't have the social skills required to interact with customers effectively.

A Strong Culture Leads to Organizational Success

Chick-fil-A has somehow solved this challenge. Over the years, I've visited several dozen of their restaurants during my cross-country travels. The experience is the same in every instance: consistently great food, an engaged workforce, and the ubiquitous "My pleasure" attitude. So, how does Chick-fil-A, in over 2,600 separate locations spread across the country, create an organizational culture that cascades down to and is embraced by its more than 40,000 employees? How do they take young people from the same pool of workers as the rest of the service industry and inspire them to embrace a culture of sincere politeness, civility, and self-governance, and imbed in them social skills that are the envy of the entire service industry?

To answer that question, consider what Thomas Peters and Robert Waterman Jr., authors of *In Search of Excellence,* found in their exhaustive research on what makes companies successful: "The leader sets the character and spirit of the enterprise, its culture."[4] Chick-fil-A's culture didn't just happen; it reflects its founder, S. Truett Cathy. Cathy was a role model for Robert Greenleaf's concept of a "Servant Leader," a leader who subordinates self-interest to the needs of those being led.[5] He created a corporate culture within Chick-fil-A that reflected his servant-leader character, values, and strongly held Christian beliefs. Chick-fil-A's corporate culture is one of product excellence, superior customer service, and genuine concern for the well-being of its employees. The company's values are an expression of Cathy's character—it's his leadership legacy. Cathy's expectations for perpetual excellence have survived for 50 years because he instilled that ethos of excellence in those leaders who came behind him. They are his living legacy. They have the same cultural DNA. Andrew T. Cathy, Truett's grandson and the company's current CEO, continues to propagate that culture today.

The culture created by Truett Cathy has resulted in incredible business success, which continues to generate fanatically loyal customers and deeply dedicated employees. Even though the restaurants are closed on Sundays, Chick-fil-A has led the fast-food industry year after year in average sales per restaurant. Despite being open only six days a week for decades, the company has outperformed their competitors in sales per restaurant, with total corporate sales of over $21 billion in 2023. The proof is that Chick-fil-A, since 2015, has been the top-rated fast-food restaurant on the American Customer Service Index.

The Free-Range Culture

Truett Cathy knew what type of organization he wanted to lead, then tailored his leadership to achieve that culture. His legacy is Chick-fil-A's long-term survival and success. An organization's culture reflects its character, and that character *should be* established by its leader. I say "should be" because some senior managers believe in what I call a "free-range" organization. They believe an organization's culture should be established by its employees, not its management. In a flat, self-governing, free-range culture, you don't have to be a leader who charts the course; you can be a Maintainer and sit back and shepherd your Mercenaries. Like the farming concept of free range, all fences are torn down, and team members can roam as they please. Acting as shepherds, Maintainers watch over their compliant flock and point them in the general direction of where they want their herd to go. Using reward and punishment as their rod and staff, they cajole their flock to comply with their desires.

For Maintainers, what has worked in the past is fine. All Maintainers have to do is not screw up, shepherd their Organizational Mercenaries in the right field, and avoid risk, change, conflict, friction, and any problems that would negatively affect their flock. If an occasional wolf threatens the flock, they may have to stand up and fight it, but once the threat is gone, they can return to business as usual.

If you don't make a conscious decision about what kind of culture you want to create in your organization, then someone else will, and you'll just be along for the ride. The leader has the responsibility to point the organization in the right direction, establish the culture, and accept responsibility for success or failure.

The free-range advocates intensely and vehemently disagree with this point of view. Their narrative contends that the members of the team should establish the organization's culture rather than have a single "leader" forcing a culture on those in the organization. The proponents of this free-range philosophy, who oppose the proposition that leaders create the group's culture, strongly believe developing an organization's culture must be a bottom-up effort. They promote increasing individual freedom, establishing fewer (if any) rules, and protecting personal independence over collective considerations. Advocates of no-rules cultural environments declare that organizations must tear down hierarchical structures and add safe spaces, trigger warnings, bias response teams, and conflict-free zones, as well as ban all microaggressions and eliminate every physical or mental barrier that inhibits personal expression.

Beyond the organizational structure, they espouse a culture where leaders are responsible for accepting everyone's ideas, ensuring all decisions are made collaboratively, and making sure that every member's input is woven into the final fabric of every decision and plan. They claim that this collective culture leads to effective operations and good decisions by avoiding the pitfalls of "group think" or the domination of a single overpowering personality. In a free-range organizational culture, they contend that leaders must create an environment that's considerate, avoids conflict, never bruises an individual's feelings, and creates an atmosphere where everyone is a winner and no one is a loser. They insist that regardless of the outcome, no one is responsible if failure is the result. Some will accuse me of being overly dramatic in my description of a free-range organization, but I argue that I am not.

Where There Are No Rules, Chaos Reigns

Sports are governed by rules, and these rules can't be violated regardless of the players' desires. You can't foot fault in tennis, double dribble in basketball, or jump off-sides in football. The rules control the players' behavior so the games don't devolve into chaos. Just like sports, life is governed by rules. Rules manage people's behavior so that business, government, and life in general don't descend into chaos.

Maybe in theory, and perhaps even in some limited environments, these cultural fads *de jour*, managed by committees with loose, vague cultural norms, may succeed, but in reality, most group endeavors must have rules. Of course, I don't mean a culture of onerous restrictions that shackle our followers with management levels tiered to the sky. What I suggest is growing a culture of rules and norms that quell chaos, create predictability, and provide clear professional and personal expectations to the team. As I strongly argued earlier, the Dictators who cage their employees and rule their organizations through micromanagement and manipulation are doomed to failure. I also strongly argue that the Maintainers who create "free-range, *laissez-faire*" organizational cultures, in the best cases, are mediocrities and, in the worst cases, are doomed to failure. As Bobby Jindal, the former governor of Louisiana, once said, organizations would "devolve into a modern-day Tower of Babel without norms and rules."[6]

An organization's culture is established by the leader, who must point it in the right direction, set clear and understandable rules and expectations, and lead it in that direction. But before we can lead in a direction and set rules and expectations, we have to decide where we want to go and what organizational culture we want to instill in those we lead. Said another way, we have to establish a personal leadership philosophy that will determine the culture of our organization. Leaders who set high standards of performance and values create a culture that brings out the best in people. Establishing and maintaining those high standards and creating a healthy and productive culture sometimes requires confrontation and controversy, not merely compromise and consensus.

Building a Leadership Philosophy—Optional but Encouraged

The following two parts of this book are the most important. In these sections, you'll be challenged to think deeply about who you are now as a leader and who you want to be as a leader in the future. It's the vital work of building your leadership philosophy. (If you already have a leadership philosophy, read on to get another perspective to consider.)

In each chapter, I'll guide you through a discussion of the characteristics that build trust between leader and led, then describe what it takes to build a level of trust to inspire your Organizational Mercenaries to become Organizational Patriots. After each chapter, you'll be guided through an exercise to help you focus on the aspect of your personal leadership philosophy that's related to the topic in that chapter. Whether you participate in the exercises or just move on in the book is your choice. However, I highly recommend you complete the exercises where you recognize you may need to improve. You're more likely to hold yourself accountable when you write something down—if you document a promise to yourself, it becomes a contract. It's also tougher to break your written promises than to conveniently forget the causal mental discussions you had with yourself. Good intentions are insufficient—a written vow will remind you of what you promised yourself. You can participate in all the exercises, a selected few, or none of them. Each exercise has three steps. I have given you some space to write notes after each of the exercises. If you do not have enough space to write you thoughts, I recommend you start a journal or notebook to store your self-evaluation comments and leadership philosophy and plan.

Step One: Look in the Mirror

Becoming a leader is a lifelong journey. All journeys should start with determining where you are, then deciding where you want to go. Step One is a self-awareness audit. It will pose questions about specific leadership attributes, asking you where

> **"First say to yourself what you want to be and then do what it takes to be that."**
> —*Epictetus, Greek slave-turned-philosopher in* **The Enchiridion**

you are now versus where you want to be in the future. The process of learning about yourself on an in-depth level requires hard work. The more time and effort you put into building your leadership philosophy, the more valuable this exercise will be to your leadership growth. Take a good, hard look in the mirror, and be as honest with yourself as your courage will allow. If you can move the needle from good to great or from OK to better, you've grown as a leader.

As you go through the questions, ask yourself:

- Am I living and measuring up to my full potential as a leader?
- Am I living up to what my employers and employees expect and deserve from me?
- What am I doing as a leader that I should not be doing?
- What am I doing that I should continue to do?

As the saying goes, the road to hell is paved with good intentions. You want to build a leadership philosophy that leverages and complements your strengths. But sometimes, you must confront the reality that you must change things about your leadership. Some refuse to do so or put questions like these on the back burner because they're overwhelmed by day-to-day life. Don't fall into that trap. If some of the questions make you uncomfortable, good! Now's the time to be honest with yourself.

Step Two: My Leadership Philosophy

Following each "Look in the Mirror," you'll be asked to describe your leadership philosophy regarding that attribute. The author of *True North* Bill George explains, "It is a process of examining your character, then providing an aspirational model" of what you want to be. Remember what we said earlier: Your leadership philosophy is a reflection of your character, the rules and values you choose to lead by. Your philosophy may be one or two lines or a manifesto, depending on your values and perspective of where you are today. Take time to step aside from the daily grind and thoughtfully consider what you stand for. Listen closely to your in-

ternal critic. Write it down, sit on it for a day or so, re-read it, and adjust where necessary. I've provided some examples in each case.

Step Three: My Action Plan

Once you've penned a leadership philosophy that lays out who you want to be as a leader, you must have the self-discipline to do what it takes to achieve it. We often give ourselves advice that we ignore. It's easy for us to say, "I will do better at showing appreciation to my employees," but we need to take tangible actions to make that intention a reality. In this step, you'll define some tangible behaviors and specific actions that will move you in the direction of where you want to be. Don't think of each attribute individually but rather as a sum of the parts, with each trait a thread in the tapestry of your leadership. With the exception of integrity, you can possess lesser degrees of the other attributes and still be successful as a leader. Let's get started!

Summary Points

- Leaders must determine what culture they want for their organization.
- An organization's culture is defined as the collective beliefs and convictions of all concerned.
- An organization's culture reflects its character, and the leader determines that character.
- If the leader fails to set the culture, someone else will. Subcultures will manufacture their own cultures that meet their self-interested needs, creating fiefdoms, cliques, and overall confusion of organizational identity.
- A strong culture leads to organizational success.
- Organizational success is a two-way street that depends on the leader and the led, but the leader has the weightier responsibility.
- The leader sets the culture of a company, team, or organization. He or she must point it in the right direction, set clear and understandable rules and expectations, and then lead it in the right direction.
- The culture of the organization will reflect a leader's personal leadership philosophy.

PART TWO

CHARACTER
WHAT LEADERS ARE

7

THE POWER OF CHARACTER

"Circumstances do not make a man's character, they reveal it."
—Epictetus, Greek slave-turned-philosopher

MUCH TO THE chagrin of many of my colleagues, I argue against the idea of "effective leadership." Here's why. Effective leadership, as defined by many, is "the process of influence by which an individual induces a group to pursue the objectives held by the leader." Historian Andrew Roberts reminds us that, although the most common understanding of "leadership" connotes inherent goodness, leadership is, in fact, completely morally neutral, as capable of leading mankind to the abyss as to the sunlit uplands. Another perspective from Machiavelli is that "the only truly bad leadership is weak leadership." With these definitions, Idi Amin, Pablo Escobar, Muammar Gaddafi, Adolf Hitler, Saddam Hussein, Jim Jones, Benito Mussolini, and Vladimir Putin could all be considered effective leaders. All unified a group of people toward a common goal, and they influenced their followers "to pursue the objectives held by the leader." The perfect storm of personal charisma, social environment, the psychological and physical needs of their followers, and other influencing factors made them "effective leaders." But while they may have been effective, they lacked the moral and ethical values that our society holds our leaders accountable to—commonly referred to as "character."

The character of a leader reflects their moral and ethical behavior, decisions, and perspective. Character is the single most crucial factor that followers look to when they decide whether to trust their leaders. Ultimately, we judge our leaders by their moral and ethical character. The difference between the Dictators we revile and the Leaders we praise is their individual levels of character. Leadership is *always* about character. It's the price of admission, the basis for everything else.[2] As we flounder in our leadership crisis, we don't need more experts; we need more men and women of uncompromising character. Leadership development is character development, and character development is a lifelong pursuit. Talented and skilled people who possess even the highest levels of competence but lack character will quickly abandon ship when they sail into their first heavy sea. A Dictator or Maintainer can exercise great judgment, make sound decisions, solve the most complex problems, and communicate superbly. But if they don't possess character, they'll fall into the trap of merely presiding, not leading. The writer Timothy Clark has studied the relationship between character and competence. He states, "Great leaders are first built from the inside, and then comes competence."[3] Character inspires people to trust you enough to commit to your leadership. Talent may win games, but character wins championships. Nobody said it better than Army General Mathew Ridgway:

> "Character is the bedrock on which the whole edifice of leadership rests. It is the prime element for which every profession, every corporation, every industry searches in evaluating a member of its organization. With it, the full worth of an individual can be developed. Without it, at worst—failure or disaster.
> At best—mediocrity."

If character is so all-important, what is it? Its definition is clear and concise. Your character is an amalgam of your mental and ethical traits, attributes, and qualities, commonly referred to as your "personal characteristics." It's a collection of David Brooks' "eulogy virtues," those attributes that people use when defining who you are. They know you for the distinguishing characteristics of your character. Your character is the storehouse of those attributes that build trust in your leadership.

Leadership that produces committed and loyal followers is first based on your character and only then by your competence. It's worth saying again: Competence without character leads to organizational mediocrity or disaster. Of course, that begs the question: Is character innate, or is it developed? Asked another way, Are people with strong character, yet lacking in competence, doomed to fail as leaders? The answer is, "It depends." Let's look at an example of a leader whose lack of competence bordered on incompetence, but because of his strong character and self-discipline, he became a leader of great consequence.

The Incredible Revolutionary

He was a man of many flaws. His cold, forbidding manner, mercurial temperament, and chronic aloofness prevented him from developing any close personal relationships or cultivating even a single truly intimate friend. His insecurities ran deep and were manifested by irritability, moodiness, night terrors, occasional waves of panic, and a periodic inability to focus on his duties. Bouts of indecision and crippling moments of despair caused him to doubt himself at key decision points in his life. He had a colossal temper and struggled for a lifetime to control his emotions. His intense shyness and acute sensitivity to criticism deeply bruised his pride and eroded his self-confidence. He considered himself unworthy of almost every leadership position that was thrust upon him.

As a military leader, he committed major strategic blunders, losing many more battles than he won, with only two victories in an eight-year war—more losses than any victorious general in modern history.[4] In many ways, he could have been considered the least intelligent, educated, sophisticated, or politically savvy of all our founding fathers. Ben Franklin was far more thoughtful, Alexander Hamilton was more brilliant, John Adams was better educated, Thomas Jefferson was more intellectually sophisticated,

James Madison was more politically astute, and Patrick Henry was a more powerful orator. Yet each and all of these prominent figures acknowledged that he was their unquestionable senior.[5]

So how did this shy, aloof, insecure, indecisive, emotionally volatile man become America's most respected and revered leader—the Father of Our Country? For all his shortcomings, George Washington was a man of supreme character. As the Continental Army commander and our first president, his moral compass steered America toward greatness. When his fellow founding fathers were writing, orating, and espousing their virtues while giving their opinions on how to defeat the British, he was doing it. He was demonstrating his character through his actions and deeds, not his words. He possessed in full measure every vital quality of character that defines indispensable leadership.

"I hope I shall possess firmness and virtue enough to maintain what I consider the most enviable of all titles, the character of an honest man."

His success in inspiring and persuasively influencing American patriots to endure and persist through eight years of war was a direct result of the powerful levels of undying trust he earned. When he asked, they willingly and repeatedly gave. They gave even when their enlistments and obligations ended because they trusted him. He earned that trust by demonstrating his character time and time again. He proved that they were not foolish to follow him, even though the cause seemed never-ending and unwinnable. One of Washington's favorite and most effective generals, Henry Knox, said to him during the dark days of Valley Forge, "The people of America look up to you as their father, and into your hands, they entrust their all, fully confident that every exertion on your part is for their security and happiness."[6] How many leaders can earn that depth of trust and commitment from those they lead? Washington demonstrated his character by leading with integrity, selflessness, resilience, humility, courage, self-awareness, and self discipline.

INTEGRITY

Washington's reputation for honesty is firmly entrenched in American culture. It grew from Mason Weems's 1806 children's book where young George admits to his father, "I cannot tell a lie; I cut it down [the cherry tree] with my hatchet." Weems, a Presbyterian minister and a college professor, wanted to present Washington as a perfect role model for the virtues of character and honesty to children. The cherry tree incident never happened, but the parable grew into legend and is forever a part of the fiber of our American cultural heritage. The story may be a myth, but Washington's legacy of integrity is not. Washington understood that becoming a leader is a journey, and he spent a lifetime reflecting on his integrity and relentlessly attempting to lead a life of virtuous character. Every word he spoke and every decision he made passed through his filter of integrity. He possessed a transcendent ability to learn from living. "Errors," he wrote, "once discovered, are more than half amended."[7]

SELFLESSNESS

Washington understood that earning the undying trust of those he led required selflessness and often painful personal sacrifice. Over and over, Washington showed that he was willing to sacrifice his own happiness for the good of others.[8] As the commander of the Continental Army, he demonstrated unremitting selflessness by suffering the same hardships and deprivations as his soldiers. Consistently sharing the same dangers as his soldiers and leading from the front in battle greatly endeared him to every soldier in the Army. The fashion of the time was for senior officers to return to their homes each winter while their soldiers bore the hardships and deprivations of a winter bivouac. Selflessly, Washington refused to abandon his army and vowed to "share in the hardship and partake of every inconvenience" as his men.[9] During the entire eight and a half years of the war, he only spent eight nights at Mount Vernon.[10]

The most famous of the winter encampments, Valley Forge, is the stuff of legend and a typical example of Washington's selfless leadership. The Continental Army's suffering at this point of the war was unimaginable. Whole regiments were without clothes or equipment. The Army's long marches could be traced by following the blood-stained snow of barefoot soldiers. The soldiers slept in the open and on the ground for months without tents or blankets. Shivering, barely clad soldiers endured week upon week of monotonous and meager rations, ice-cold winds, deep snow, virulent disease, soot-choked huts, and exhausting tedium, with only the steadying hand of General George Washington to offer hope.[11] When the ragtag army got to Valley Forge, they lived in flimsy and leaky tents until they could complete building small 14-by-16-foot huts to hold a dozen men each. Their only food was an unpalatable fire cake, a barely digestible concoction of flour and water baked over an open fire on a stone. Washington slept in a tent and refused to move into a farmhouse until his men could move into their huts. He lived in the same squalid conditions and suffered through the same unappetizing food as his men. The men could feel Washington's sincere concern for them.[12] As things worsened, the more they looked to him for inspiration, solutions, and hope. He pleaded with his officers to lead by example and share their men's hardships, saying, "It ought to be the pride of an officer to share the fatigue as well as danger to which his men are exposed."[13]

RESILIENCE

Washington not only demonstrated his selflessness by sharing and suffering the same physical hardships and depravations as his soldiers. He did so by enduring, without complaint, the unrelenting psychological hardships of staying focused in an environment of false promises, distrust, second-guessing, and disloyalty. He soldiered through countless situations where many lesser men abandoned the revolutionary cause because they didn't have the depth of character to sacrifice their personal comfort or the grit to withstand the perpetual frustration of fighting a seemingly endless and unwinnable war. He tasted failure many times without becoming a failure.

He had legitimate reasons to doubt the trust in those he was obligated to obey, as well as reasonable cause to question the trust of those who supposedly were fellow patriots. His bosses, the Continental Congress, regularly didn't keep their word, pledging Congressional support they knew they could not or would not deliver, promising soldiers' pay that rarely came, and repeatedly vowing falsely to send equipment and supplies to his beleaguered Continental Army. As well as having to tolerate and regularly find ways to compensate for Congress' broken promises and empty assurances, Washington nobly and unselfishly endured the ever-present and unfair criticism and second-guessing of his leadership. One powerful and congressionally well-connected fellow officer, General Thomas Mifflin, attempted to humiliate him into resigning during the grim winter of Valley Forge. He smeared Washington as a self-serving egotist, besmirched his military ability, and did his best to persuade Congress to fire him.

> "He was a different kind of general fighting a different kind of war. His fortitude in keeping the army intact was a major accomplishment. Washington was resilient in the face of every setback and courageous in the face of every danger. He was that rare general who was great between battles and not just during them. The extraordinary wearisome, nerve-racking frustration he put up with for nearly nine years is hard to express. He labored under terrible strain that would have destroyed a lesser man. Few people with any choice would have persisted in this impossible, self-sacrificing situation for so long."
>
> —*Ron Chernow, author of* **Washington: A Life**

Regardless of how often he was lied to, ridiculed, second-guessed, and humiliated, Washington refused to be "beaten into submission by the world around him."[14] Besieged by critics, heart-sick at the shabby state of his troops, and angry at Congressional neglect, Washington refused to abandon his army.[15] He stayed the course selflessly, leading with strength of character. He demonstrated his integrity by staying focused on his mission and his men. He defeated every urge to be cowered by setbacks, distrust, and the petty jealousies of his peers. One-third of the country was against the revolution, one-third were for it, and the other third were waiting to see which way the wind blew before they decided. All this might have been enough to induce a commander of lesser character to throw up his hands and return home to the peace and comfort of Mount Vernon and his wife and family. Washington, needless to say, was not that man.[16] Without Washington's personal resilience, determination, passion for the cause, and mental toughness, America would not be the country it is today.

HUMILITY

Examples of Washington's modesty are too numerous to mention, but two historically momentous events that changed the course of American history reveal a leader of profound humility. First was his refusal to be anointed the American king after he led the Continental Army to victory. George III, the despot ruler of England who lost the American colonies after eight long years of war, asked the visiting American portrait artist Benjamin West, "What position will Washington take after winning the war? Will he choose to be head of the army, or will he choose to be the head of state?" When West replied that Washington's sole ambition was to return to farming, the thunderstruck king declared, "If he does that, he will be the greatest man in the world."[17] He did, and he was.

The second testament to Washington's humility was his refusal to serve a third term as president when many begged him to do so. In the first case, Washington was strongly pressured to assume the role of American king, and in the second case, he was urged to be president for life. In both instances, he became an American Cincinnatus, declining the role of an American Caesar by returning to the role of citizen and farmer.

Ron Chernow describes Washington's selflessness and humility best in his excellent biography, *Washington: A Life*: "Few people with any choice would have persisted in this impossible, self-sacrificing situation for so long."[18] Many did not. Scores of sunshine patriots revealed their true character as the dark days of the Revolutionary War dragged on with seemingly no end and as victory seemed more and more doubtful. Benedict Arnold was the most famous summer soldier to quickly bend in the winds of despair when confronted with disappointment and frustration, forsaking his character and his country for selfish reasons. His infamous act of treason was born of resentment toward Congress and Washington for not awarding him the accolades and promotions he felt he was entitled. When he didn't receive the recognition he strongly believed he deserved, he revealed his true character and sold his soul to the enemy. As the commander of an important American fortification, Arnold's unbridled ambition and insatiable appetite for advancement motivated him to plot the defeat of the essential American stronghold, West Point, by handing over the Fort's defensive plans to the enemy. His plot and conspiracy were discovered, and his treasonous act was thwarted. However, America's most famous turncoat, who betrayed his good friend Washington and his country's trust, escaped and fought the rest of the war in a British Redcoat. Although Washington endured many times the frustrations, strain, and setbacks as Arnold, he persevered with integrity, selflessness, humility, and courage.

COURAGE

Washington's physical courage in the face of every danger and his moral courage to overcome failures and disappointment while not losing hope and maintaining enthusiasm was remarkable. Very few of us will have to test our physical courage, at least not to the extent that Washington was tested. But anyone who steps into a leadership position can expect—and better be ready—to have their moral courage tested.

Physical courage. Ron Chernow says of Washington's bravery: "Few if any of us will be called upon to demonstrate the same level of physical courage as Washington. He took little care of himself in battle, insisting on animating his troops by the sheer force of his example."[19] His physical courage often bordered on recklessness and frightened his aides and fellow soldiers. An aide once pleaded with him, "Sire; please take cover; artillery is falling closer, and enemy's bullets are hitting close by!" Washington replied to his aide, "Take cover if you wish," as he continued to stand his ground. Too often, the overwhelming and better British Army won the day and forced the Continental Army to conduct a hasty strategic withdrawal across unruly rivers or bodies of water. In every dangerous "strategic withdrawal," a polite name for retreat, Washington's would be the last set of boots to step into the last boat to leave the enemy shore. His physical courage was legendary among his men and was a defining force that inspired them to commit to his leadership and their cause.

Moral courage. As legendary and impressive as Washington's physical courage, in many ways, it paled in comparison to his moral courage, which was repeatedly tested throughout the war and his presidency. His leadership presence was known and felt by every soldier in the Army and every citizen in the country. His most powerful demonstration of moral courage was accepting the Continental Congress' invitation to lead the American Army. He was a successful and wealthy plantation owner who could have easily weathered the war's storms without getting involved. But rather than take the easy way forward, he accepted the invitation

"The punishment for high treason is a slow and hideous death. It will begin with the accused being tied to a horse and dragged to the gallows. He will then be hanged by the neck but cut down before he dies so that he remains alive for what comes next, which is the slicing open of his abdomen and the burning of his intestines as they dangle outside his body. Only then will his head be cut off. His corpse will then be cut up into four parts. But the punishment will not end there. All lands and monies will be confiscated, and if his wife should also be accused of treason for conspiring with her husband, she will be burned alive."

—*Bill O'Reilly, co-author of* **Killing England**

to lead the Continental Army when, at the time, many, if not most, thought the fight unwinnable. As the new commander in chief, he was expected to raise, train, feed, clothe, and equip an army and defeat the British regulars, widely considered the world's greatest fighting force.[20] By accepting the leadership of the Army, he was well aware of the penalty for failure—he would be tried for high treason by the British. As Bill O'Reilly describes in his book *Killing England*, most men, considering the slim odds of victory weighed against the brutal penalty for failure, would have run away from the invitation to lead and quickly returned to the safety of Mount Vernon. I've often wondered if George consulted Martha on this before he accepted the generalship.

SELF-AWARENESS

How did the Father of Our Country overcome the chronic self-doubt, deep sense of inadequacy, and many personal flaws that plagued him in his youth to become the most revered leader in American history? As with all leadership journeys, Washington began with the daunting task of self-reflection and understanding himself. He spent a lifetime honing and harnessing every aspect of his character that affected his leadership ability. It didn't come easily to him. Through sheer willpower to acknowledge and overcome his leadership flaws, he became the leader he knew he needed to be.

Constant self-reflection and resolute acknowledgment of his flaws moved Washington to reign in the volcanic temper of his youth. He was also inspired to conduct rigorous self-study to overcome his academic insecurities, which motivated him to adopt tactical audacity and strategic adaptability to make up for his military shortcomings. George Washington grew during the Revolutionary years, but he never lost his self-awareness of his flaws.[21] "He wrestled with demons of discouragement"[22] and insecurity all his life but always came to the realization of what he stood for, and then he stood for it. During Washington's leadership journey from young man to seasoned leader, he experienced many life-altering events and devastating disappointments that forced him to stop and reconsider who he was as a leader. These events compelled him to dig deeply into his ego to discover what weaknesses were holding him back and, perhaps more importantly, to determine what flaws in his leadership character led to distrust. These experiences that forced Washington to take a hard look at his leadership were crucible events: personal or professional setbacks, failures, or crises that force you to conduct introspective self-assessment, reconsider your leadership, and fix what needs fixing. Washington was driven by circumstances to do just that on several occasions.

From each failure and disappointment thrown at him, he emerged stronger and better able to lead. As the preeminent Washington biographer, James Flexner, says of Washington's growth as a leader, "At times he swerves off the track, but always he swings back again, further ahead on the road to greatness."[23] At each of these significant crucible events, Washington conducted self-reflection and determined which aspects of his leadership he had to change to become a better leader.

SELF-DISCIPLINE

Washington made up his mind to do whatever it took to make up for his weaknesses of character and overcome his flaws of temperament and disposition. He understood Einstein's admonition 200 years before Albert said it: "Insanity is doing the same thing over and over again and expecting different results." Washington publicly professed, "I hope I shall possess firmness and virtue enough to maintain what I consider the most enviable of all titles, the character of an honest man."

Washington was a master of acknowledging what he had learned about himself. Still, more importantly, he had the self-discipline to transform those lessons into the necessary behavioral adjustments required to be a better leader. He understood that he had to change his behavior to improve his leadership, which eroded trust and confidence in him as a leader. More important than understanding he had to change, he had the self-discipline to do it.

Discipline is what we need most in our lives but want the least. It's the difference between potential and achievement.[24]

Of course, you or I will never be called upon to lead in dire circumstances like our first president. Few men have. But even in business, leaders at every level will need to tap into the same aspects of character and inner strength as Washington—handing out pink slips, missing forecasts, facing new competition, and failing projects. To succeed as a leader, you must be as committed as he was to determine the aspects of your character that build trust, and more importantly, but much more difficult, you must acknowledge and repair those aspects of your character that lead to distrust. Washington's qualities of character that personify great leadership are the same qualities all leaders should strive for.

What Can We Learn from the Father of Our Country?

Studying George Washington is a master class on what it takes to build trust in your followers. He understood that leadership was about character. It revolves around living in accordance with key ethical and moral values: integrity, humility, resilience, and courage. Those aspects of his character ran through his veins as naturally and effortlessly as his blood. However, perhaps the greatest lesson we can learn from George Washington is his courage to recognize what it takes to overcome his personal flaws through self-reflection and self-discipline. When forced by crucible events or guided by gut instinct, Washington had the self-awareness to realize he had to be painfully honest with himself and acknowledge and accept responsibility for his flaws or suffer the consequences. Then, he had the self-discipline to do something about it. Everyone has flaws—no one is ever rid of them all.[25] Leaders in every profession and at all levels, at some time or another, will have to dip deeply into their reserves of character and tap into their inner strength. Washington, like all of us, had flaws, but he was wise enough to understand that to succeed as a leader, he had to acknowledge and control them, and he did.

A Leadership Philosophy Reminder

As I mentioned earlier, if you don't have a solidified leader-ship philosophy, I've provided exercises at the end of the coming chapters for your consideration to either build your philosophy from scratch or refine your existing philosophy. You can skip these exercises or participate in as many as you see fit.

These exercises are an opportunity to conduct a self-aware-ness audit, acknowledge those aspects of your character that affect your ability to win your followers' trust, then practice your self-discipline and do something about it. My only advice is that if you participate, be brutally honest with yourself—no one is watching.

8

INTEGRITY

"The supreme quality of leadership is unquestionably integrity.
Without it, no real success is possible, no matter whether it is on
a section gang, a football field, in an army, or in an office."
—*Dwight D. Eisenhower*

INTEGRITY BUILDS TRUST. Regardless of how abundant a leader's other qualities of character are, without integrity, they're irrelevant. As Warren Buffett, the Oracle of Omaha, put it, "In looking for leaders, you look for three qualities: integrity, intelligence, and energy, and if they don't have the first, the other two will kill you." Integrity must be as central to your makeup as the blood in your veins. With few exceptions, a leader can overcome minor lapses of selflessness, resilience, humility, or courage without suffering a fatal loss of their employees' trust. However, even a slight or momentary lapse in integrity can be catastrophic. You may survive it professionally, but once the trust of your followers is lost, it can never be fully recovered.

Integrity:

"Is doing the right thing, even when
no one is watching."
—*C.S. Lewis, author*

"Is not doing the wrong
thing, even when you know
you can get away with it."
—*George Aldridge*

Your integrity reveals the content and quality of your character, either building trust or eroding it. Integrity-based leadership, how you behave and act as a leader, is the daily manifestation of your character. Consistent trust-building leadership is what inspires willing engagement from those you lead and thus motivates them to join the ranks of your organization's stalwart Patriots. It stirs them to enthusiastically commit to your endeavor rather than to indifferently, reluctantly, or resentfully comply with its tasks. The level of commitment you're rewarded from those you lead is directly proportional to the level of trust they have in you. When your integrity convinces those you lead that they can trust your character, they'll go to the ends of the earth for you.

To earn a level of trust that inspires Mercenaries to become Patriots, you must clearly demonstrate your integrity again and again. Those you lead won't trust you just because they're supposed to. Before they give you that valuable gift of their trust, they must experience tangible evidence that proves you deserve it. Their trust should be valued as a gift that's not easily earned but easily lost. They must see that you're not only an *ethical* leader but an *authentic* one. Regardless of what you declare about your integrity, people want to be shown. They watch every move you make and judge the consistency between your words and your deeds. They need to feel secure that you have their best interests at heart and care about them and what they do. They want to be comfortable that you're serving the cause or endeavor you share with them more than just serving yourself. The strength of a leader's integrity often determines the fate of the entire organization. As I said earlier about character, understanding the importance of having integrity as a leader is a far cry from deciding to live and lead with integrity.[1] Let's look at several essential components of integrity and consider how each affects our ability to build trust powerful enough to inspire willing commitment and engagement.

How Does a Leader Demonstrate and Display Integrity?

Integrity is much more complicated and extends far beyond the commonly held rules of simply not lying, cheating, stealing, or tolerating those who do. There are many components of your integrity, but three aspects are essential for winning the trust of your employees. It's like the proverbial three-legged stool: If one of these legs is missing, you're sitting on the floor. The first leg is your *honesty*, your ethical and moral compass. The second leg is your *authenticity*, the picture you paint of yourself for the world to see. Are you genuine? The last leg is your *selflessness*, your motives for leading. Without all three legs of the stool, there is no trust.

The New Boss Test

There are three intuitive tests that people put their new bosses through before they deem them trustworthy. Try to recall the last time you started working for a new manager or supervisor. I suspect you consciously or subconsciously put him through these tests. First, you asked yourself, *Does he have a moral compass that points in the same direction as mine?* The second question you ask is, *Is she the real deal, authentic, genuine, sincere?* And the third question I know you asked yourself in some variation is, *Does he have my best interests at heart? Will his own self-interests outweigh what's best for our organization and me? Am I smart to follow this guy? Does he care about me?"* Let's consider each of these questions.

TEST 1- Honesty: Does his moral compass point in the right direction?

A leader's honesty is revealed by his behavior. It's a zero-sum game—he's either ethical or unethical, honest or dishonest. People expect their leaders and bosses to be ethical. They take for granted that their leader won't lie, cheat, or steal. It's a given. Your ethical behavior isn't measured on a sliding scale. You can't be more-or-less ethical; either you are or you aren't. And if you aren't, then you'll never be trusted. If you've earned trust in the past but suddenly make an ethical misstep, that trust will disappear like the air in a popped balloon.

At some point in our leadership lives, we have had or will have the opportunity to lie, cheat, or steal. As we face the pressures and seductions that come with leadership, how we react to them is a test and demonstration of our integrity. It reveals our character. No person is entirely without temptation. Your integrity, reflected by your character, determines how you react to those temptations. Climbing the professional ladder comes with growing responsibilities, an increased span of influence, and more people impacted by your leadership. This broadening leadership scope also comes with new opportunities, temptations, and seductions, but it also comes with increased scrutiny.

Opportunity—The Devil Made Me Do It!

Let's look at opportunity first. Moving up the organizational ladder comes with increasingly enticing opportunities that may tempt you to step across the ethical fault line for personal and professional gain. Many leaders don't think about how they'll react to the allure of those temptations until the enticements present themselves. Some have adopted a loose personal code of conduct, promising themselves that they won't wander into unethical territory. Most work hard to stay as true to their promise as humanly possible. However, they only cavalierly consider that they won't lie, cheat, or steal. Leaders who don't firmly erect their own leadership philosophy, their code, on an integrity-based foundation of a strong character are much more susceptible to being seduced by a false sense of invulnerability, a feeling of being above the rules. The famous line attributed to Honest Abe Lincoln is, "If you want to test a man's character, give him power." Ambition, personal and professional advancement, the need for recognition, and a fear of failure are powerful enticements to any leader. We must acknowledge the existence of what Northwestern University management professor Maryam Kouchaki calls "moral humility—the recognition that we all have the capacity to transgress if we're not vigilant and that the human mind is skilled at justifying questionable behavior when enticed by its benefits."[2]

A recent survey by EduBirdie, a professional writer's service, found that 73 percent of C-level executives have admitted to professional dishonesty.[3] They were presented with an opportunity to cross the line into unethical territory, and they took it. There are scores of examples, recent and historical, where leaders who were viewed for decades as paragons of integrity have run amok and fallen from grace, succumbing to the seductive wails of ambition, greed, lust, and egoism. Most of those leaders who ethically derailed clearly understood the difference between right and wrong. Many even evangelically embraced and espoused the expected character virtues of their profession, but they didn't live by those virtues. Somewhere, they lost their way. The temptations for personal plea-sure, gain, or recognition were so intense that they couldn't resist. Knowingly, they bent in the wind of temptation. They failed to realize that their original rationale for not doing something wrong was not based on personal values but on a lack of opportunity.[4] It was a flaw in their character waiting for an opportunity.

There are those who will argue that a leader's integrity isn't proven until they've been tested with an opportunity to lie, cheat, steal, or commit some lesser misdeed. Anyone can say they have integrity; it's another thing to show you have it. The question I ask myself every time I hear of yet another counterfeit exemplar of integrity who has tumbled from grace is, *Did they ever possess integrity in the first place, or did they jump at their first real op-portunity for personal or professional gain?* I've concluded that many of these leaders have never seriously considered what they stand for. They didn't ethically derail—they were never on solid ethical tracks in the first place. Either they didn't embrace a per-sonal leadership philosophy, or it was so weak that it allowed their conscience, their inner jury, some wiggle room to justify crossing the ethical fault line. It wasn't their moral compass that kept them between the lines—it was the lack of opportunity.

Honesty is binary. You cannot be half or almost honest. How big a lie do you have to tell to be a liar? How much do you have to fudge to be a cheater? How heavy a purse do you have to heist to be a thief? The unfortunate fact is that many leaders (you pick a percentage) don't possess the integrity and core values that many of us take for granted. Most leaders can recover from a mistake of competence unless it's catastrophic to the organization. Few, if any, leaders can recover from a lapse of character. We may have years of saint-like behavior with one slip of integrity, but unfortunately, we're all remembered for our last, worst act. As the old saying goes, it takes time and effort to work your way up to the penthouse "but only one violation of your integrity to get kicked down to the outhouse." A mistake of competence will be forgiven. A mistake of character will not. Your character is like a Ming vase, highly prized, yet fragile and easily broken.

When tempted to go to the dark side of integrity, leaders who haven't established a strong leadership philosophy conduct what can be called a payoff-versus-risk cost-benefit analysis. In short, they ask themselves, *Is the payoff for doing this unethical act worth the risk I'll take of getting caught?* Over the years, I've been shocked by how many leaders I've witnessed who miscalculated that analysis and decided to fudge the system because they thought no one would notice. While working at Coca-Cola, one of the company's account teams was trying to sell a new beverage to one of our customers. The customer was initially skeptical about the product but eventually agreed to conduct a field test at its restaurants in a large midwestern city. For the first few weeks of the test, sales of the beverage were considerably lower than had been predicted by the sales team. Then, suddenly, it became the hottest drink in all the test restaurants. The account manager, a rising star, attributed the increase in sales to the popularity of the drink. Unbeknownst to anyone but him, the increase in sales was because his team had distributed hundreds of free drink coupons to all the local high schools. When the customer learned of the ruse, they immediately stopped the test and took the product out of their stores. The account manager tried to rationalize distributing the free coupons as a "marketing" strategy. The customer didn't see it that way; they saw it as fudging the sales numbers. The account manager was so ambitious to be seen as successful that he took the risk of fudging the system to make himself look good. His lack of a strong leadership philosophy based on honesty marred the reputation of a great company and cost him his job.

Scrutiny—Leading in the Age of the "Digital Echo"

General George Patton once said, "The higher up the flagpole you go, the more people see your ass." Crudely put but true. The higher up the organizational ladder you climb, the more intense the scrutiny of your integrity. As General Martin Dempsey points out in his excellent book *Radical Inclusion*, we're all subject to what he calls the "digital echo."[5] He warns us that social media has enabled anyone with a cell phone to be a Cecil B. DeMille, posting negative or positive statements or observations on the conduct of our leadership performance, whether they're true or not. The fact is, you can run, but you can't hide. People have always lied; it's just harder to get away with it now. This underscores the fact that leaders must not only live and breathe an ethical existence but also avoid even the slightest appearance of ethical impropriety. Like Caesar told his wife, Pompeia, "You must be beyond reproach and above suspicion." A conscience built on strong values will whisper good advice when you're faced with murky issues of right or wrong. When you hear that good advice, don't ignore it. A clear conscience is a beautiful thing to possess.

Like it or not, as a leader, you're always on stage, and everything about you will be fair game for comment, criticism, and interpretation or misinterpretation. Every aspect of your personal and professional life will be inspected, dissected, and judged.[6] Your words and deeds will be subject to microscopic examination, constantly tracked and measured. Those that bend in the winds of impropriety will ethically derail. As Caesar said, "They have cast the die." Those who steadfastly stand by their pre-determined core values will demonstrate the kind of character we all aspire to. It often takes a steel spine and steadfast resolve to resist these temptations. Your leadership *will* be tested. *Be ready!* For that reason, it's important to choose your rules to lead by now so when those inevitable temptations try to seduce you, you'll be prepared. If you anticipate the temptations and plan for their arrival, your actions will be a moral reflex. Remember, it wasn't raining when Noah built the Ark. Integrity is everything.

TEST 2 -Authenticity: Is she the real deal?

Once your charges have determined that your moral and ethical compass is pointed in the right direction, their next test of your trustworthiness will be to make up their minds whether you're the real deal. They'll ask themselves, *Is she authentic and genuine?* In other words, is what they see really you, or are you just playing a part? A leader must be able to convey to her followers that what they see is what they get. It's simple. People trust authentic leaders and don't trust inauthentic ones—the frauds, the fakes, and the hypocrites. Are you authentic, or do you come across as photoshopped? Do you have authentic relationships? Do you practice what you preach? If your sincerity is seen as contrived, you're doomed. You want them to believe you, but more importantly, you want them to believe *in* you. Everything you say and do *must be trusted* as authentic, genuine, and sincere. We keep coming back to this whole *trust* thing, don't we?

In a world so focused on the superficial, it's not that easy to know if our leaders are the real deal or merely playing a part. We've become disenchanted with imitation leaders who come across as plastic, photoshopped, shallow, glad-handing, false, and fake. When these counterfeit leaders who masquerade as paragons of authenticity are forced by circumstances to unmask and reveal their true selves, they're shown to be disingenuous, insincere, misleading, and duplicitous. As Rob Goffee, author of *Why Should Anyone Be Lead by You?*, puts it, "People want to be led by someone real."[7] They're starved for even a minimal level of authenticity and genuineness in their leaders. There's been a lot of ink spilled defining "authenticity," but it boils down to recognizing who you are and presenting to the world a self-portrait that's consistent with your real self. To convince others you *are* authentic, you must *be* authentic.

Even though many try, you cannot fake it until you make it.[8] The old comedic curmudgeon George Burns once said about honesty: "If you can fake it, you've got it made." But faking it doesn't work for long—frauds will be discovered. (More on that in a few pages.) Persuading those you lead that you're the real deal requires possession of palpable genuineness, sincerity, and a total absence of pretension. If you lack that aura of being the real deal, you lack the power to persuade. You cannot be seen as finessing your way through life and playing a part that isn't you.[9] Leaders who are viewed as insincere, self-absorbed, and inauthentic will never gain the trust of their followers. You know the type: self-made men who worship their creator and walk down lover's lane holding their own hand. One of the most significant causes of misery for employees is the feeling

that the person they work for isn't interested in who they are and what goes on in their lives, personally or professionally.[10] Authentic leaders have a personal alchemy that enables them to connect with their people personally and make them feel genuinely valued and respected.

As James Kouzes and Barry Posner Jr. state in their seminal work on leading, *The Truth About Leadership*, it turns out that the believability of a leader determines whether people will willingly give of their time, talent, experience, intelligence, creativity, and support.[11] Dale Carnegie's theme in one of the all-time business bestsellers, *How to Win Friends and Influence People,* is "You don't want to listen to cheap, insincere flattery, but you do crave sincere [authentic] appreciation."[12] Employees determine your authenticity by your behavior and your actions. It may be basic, but it's so unfortunate that many Maintainers just don't get it.

Being authentic isn't just about what you are but also about what you're not. Rick Atkins in his book, *The Day of Battle*, describes the authenticity of Teddy Roosevelt Jr., the oldest son of President Teddy Roosevelt, who was poshumously awarded the Medal of Honor for his heroic D-Day leadership as "anti-bluffing, anti-faker, anti-coward."[13] *That* is true authentic leadership.

Leadership is a long journey into your soul.[14] We should heed the advice of the Pythia, the Oracle of Delphi: "Know thy self." How we present ourselves, not just as bosses, supervisors, and managers but as people, determines how we're perceived—real or fake. You can't fake honesty, genuineness, and sincerity. If you lack the vital component of sincerity, you lack the final power to persuade.[15] Without the power to persuade and influence, you're not leading. I recently read about Robert Gates, the former secretary of defense:

> "He provides them [those he leads] respect, motivation, job satisfaction, upward mobility, personal dignity, esteem, and finally the confidence that, as a leader, he genuinely cares about them collectively and as individuals." [16]

That's authentic leadership personified.

TEST 3—Selflessness: Does he have my best interests at heart?

The third leg of the integrity stool is convincing those you lead that you're not in it just for yourself. Like authenticity, there's been much ink spilled on the subject of selfless leadership. In his excellent book, *The Second Mountain*, David Brooks writes that for decades, we have "normalized selfishness" and that the only real human motives are the self-interested ones: the desire for money, status, and power.

Leaders who are seen as unselfish, however, reap genuine commitment rather than pro forma compliance from their employees.[17] You'll never earn the trust of those you lead if you give them the impression that your motives for leading are solely self-serving. Just as true, if you've earned their trust, it will be lost the instant they sense that you're focused on your own success at their expense. What's more, if your employees are unsure whether your motivations for leading are selfless or self-serving, they'll more than likely assume the latter. So, you must prove your unselfishness, or they'll assume you are otherwise.

The author who stands out as the most evangelical proponent of Service Above Self is Robert Greenleaf, a retired AT&T executive. He coined the term and wrote the bestseller of the same name, *Servant Leadership*. In that book, he argues that to inspire commitment from your charges, you must put the interests of your endeavor and those in it ahead of your own self-interests.[18] Self-LESS-ness versus Sel-FISH-ness has been a choice for leaders since the beginning of time. Followers quickly discern if their leader is more interested in self-promotion than their welfare and interests. The last thing you want is for those you lead to perceive that you're in it purely for yourself. People want servant leaders.

> "The servant-leader is servant first. The test of servant-leadership is this: Do those served grow as persons? Do they, while being served, become healthier, wiser, freer, more likely themselves to become servants? Will they benefit from my leadership?"
> —*Robert K. Greenleaf,* author of Servant Leadership

Truett Cathy is the personification of a corporate leader who believed, lived, and led as a servant leader. He literally followed the old challenging axiom "Put your money where your mouth is." The decision to close his restaurants on Sundays is a demonstration of true selflessness. Selflessness often requires sacrifice, giving something up for the greater good. Who knows how much revenue Chick-fil-A loses by being closed on Sundays? Mr. Cathy didn't care!

Like Greenleaf, I'm a disciple of the philosophy that to be a leader, you must unselfishly fulfill your obligations to your organization and your charges. Only then can you positively transform organizations and inspire commitment from your people. Selflessness is characterized by convincing your followers that your motivation for leading includes a strong desire for the success of your mutual endeavor and an authentic and sincere focus on their best interests. Selflessness is also characterized by your realization that at times, doing the right thing for those you lead may be at the expense of your own personal gain or ambition. Let's consider the "at your expense" question.

The Constant Battle with Yourself

Years ago, when attending the National War College, I listened to a lecture where an admiral made this statement:

> "Many have succumbed to the myth that morality [integrity] comes naturally, but the truth is that natural human instinct is to put yourself first. Putting your soldiers, sailors, airmen, and Marines ahead of your own self-interest and ambition will not be easy. You will face a *constant battle* with your instincts to lead selflessly."

His warning applies to all leaders, not just those in uniform. Let's be honest: Being a servant leader is not easy; in fact, at times, it can be tough. When it comes at a personal or professional cost, doing the more difficult right over the politically correct, professionally beneficial, or personally less onerous wrong can be difficult. Doing what you know you *should* do when it conflicts with doing what you *want* to do is never easy. It's what differentiates *selfless* leadership from *selfish* leadership. Let's discuss the two extremes of the self-interest spectrum.

THE SELF-INTEREST SPECTRUM

SELFISH   SELFLESS

<u>SELFISH</u>—Losing the constant battle

It's hard to ignore people in positions of responsibility and authority who lose that general's "constant battle." They lose it because they don't have a personal leadership philosophy or a code, or if they do, they don't follow it or care about those they lead. We have all witnessed leaders who are more interested in their trappings of power and personal advancement than in the welfare of their employees. They're too focused on satisfying their own needs to be concerned about the needs of others. They're more concerned about becoming a legend than leaving a legacy. They may publicly tout loudly and often say, "Employees are our most important asset," but their actions show otherwise.

SELFLESS—Winning the constant battle

When I heard the admiral's comment years ago, I both agreed and disagreed with him. I *agree* that we must make a conscious decision to lead unselfishly. When being unselfish is personally or professionally costly, it's tempting to follow your natural human instinct. However, I *disagree* that you have to "constantly battle your instincts."

Those who dwell on the right side of the spectrum are predisposed to selflessness. They are servant leaders. For whatever reason, either innate or learned or because some crucible experience has moved them to focus on others more than themselves, these people are more inclined to lead selflessly. This selflessness has

> **"Integrity is not an act but a habit, what we repeatedly do."**
> —*Aristotle*

been called many things: altruism, the do-unto-others attitude, the love of your fellow man's outlook, the *noblesse oblige*, the kindness gene, and so on. These are leaders who derive joy from seeing their organization prosper and those they lead flourish. They relish their pride in knowing they've contributed to the success of others. Those leaders on the right side of the spectrum who watch their employees not just survive, but thrive, experience an indescribable but palpable sense of gratification, fulfillment, and personal satisfaction. It's what defeats that constant battle with your selfish instincts. Just because that sense of satisfaction is difficult to describe doesn't mean it doesn't exist. Even though I'm not fluent in Italian and don't even know what the lyrics mean, I get teary-eyed every time I hear Luciano Pavarotti sing *Nessun Dorma*. It just has that effect on me. I can't describe it, but it exists.

Do I Have to Be a Selfless Monk to be a Leader?

It's fair to ask, *Do I lack integrity if I have ambitions for professional and personal success?* The real question behind this question is, Can I be ambitious and still be a selfless leader? The answer is yes. Your employees or those you lead want the comfort of having a leader they can trust. They want leaders who are ethical and authentic and who have their best interests high on the list of their priorities. Those you lead look at the first two legs of the integrity stool, honesty and authenticity, as zero-sum equations. If they don't see you as *honest,* then you're seen as unethical and dishonest. If they don't see you as the real deal, authentic, then you're viewed as shallow and disingenuous. But it's not zero-sum when it comes to self-interest. Just because you have ambition and want to succeed doesn't make you selfish. Those you lead don't expect you to become a cloistered monk who takes a vow of total selflessness. They don't expect you to be devoid of personal goals and professional aspirations. They understand that unselfish leadership and ambition aren't mutually exclusive.

We all possess a level of self-interest. There's nothing wrong with a leader being ambitious and desiring to better herself. The key to developing as an authentic leader is not eschewing your extrinsic motivations but balancing them with intrinsic motivations that provide fulfillment.[19] The litmus test for unhealthy ambition is when it's perceived as poisonous because it comes at the expense of the greater good of the organization or its employees. Controlled ambition is healthy and normal, whereas blind ambition is unhealthy and dangerous. You cannot put your ego and personal ambition above the interests of those you're leading. Anything seen as the glorification of yourself at the expense of the team will be seen as selfish.

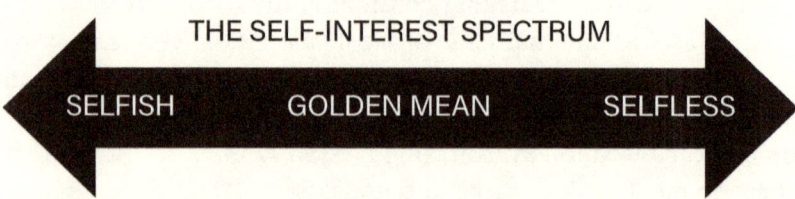

THE SELF-INTEREST SPECTRUM

SELFISH   GOLDEN MEAN   SELFLESS

So, where should we be on the self-interest spectrum to earn trust? Let's lean on Aristotle's golden mean to help us answer this tricky question. He states, "Moral behavior is the mean between two extremes."[20] In this argument, the extremes are total selfishness at one end of the spectrum and total selflessness at the other end. To be a transformational leader who earns the willing commitment of your employees, you must lean more toward the selfless end. Those you lead won't trust you if you're a selfish Ebenezer Scrooge, but they don't expect you to be a Gandhi-like, totally selfless monk either. They want you to be at that point on the spectrum where you're not eschewing your self-interests and ambitions but balancing them with the needs and best interests of the organization and those you lead—the golden mean. Truett Cathy is an excellent example of a leader who found the golden mean, balancing his company's success, the best interests of his employees, and living his personal values.

My mother, the Aldridge family philosopher, would warn me, "Everything in moderation." In this case, temper your ambition to prevent it from becoming blind or compulsive. It shouldn't be the driving force behind your leadership. The first person you lead is yourself. As long as you can look in the mirror and see a person of integrity focused on the greater good, you're leading selflessly.

Afterthought: Beware of Frauds and Hypocrites

We would be naïve to think all people live by a code of leadership conduct that I have described. There are Maintainers and Dictators who are accomplished fakers, great actors who can be very convincing. These masters of masquerade make you think they're honest, authentic, and selfless. Like chameleons, their colors are determined by who they're standing next to at any given moment. It's impossible to be perceived as authentic if a leader acts a certain way with the people they lead and another way with their peers or bosses.[21] It's also impossible to be perceived as authentic if a person acts authentically in one situation and manipulative in another.

Authenticity is consistency. Those who straddle the line between authenticity and manipulation, constantly bouncing be-

Fraud: **If you lie to others, you're deceitful.**

Hypocrite: **If you lie to yourself, you're delusional.**

tween the two, will be branded as duplicitous fakes. How many times do you have to connive or manipulate to be a manipulator? You know if you're a fake, and you can be sure that those you lead also know. They instinctively recognize fraudulent behavior. Chameleons are quickly perceived as disingenuous or lacking a moral center.[22] If a leader is playing a role that isn't a true expression of his authentic self, his followers will sooner or later feel like they've been tricked, and once that impression is out of the bottle, it's almost impossible to put it back in. These fakes come in many denominations, but the two most common are the frauds and hypocrites. Let's look at each one.

Frauds

Frauds consciously try to pawn themselves off as someone they're not. They're the people who pour hot water on ramen and try to convince you they are chefs. Even though they put their own self-interests above their organization and its employees, they work hard to deceive everyone into thinking otherwise. They act like nice people but don't follow through. They brag about taking the high road when the low road is where they regularly travel. They want their charges to believe they're leaders of strong character who are honest, authentic, and selfless when, in truth, they are not.

They are masters of deceit who can counterfeit a sense of concern for your well-being when, in fact, they could care less. Like chameleons, their behavior and personality will be whatever they think will get them ahead today. The only honest thing about frauds is that they know they are frauds; they just don't care. Many of us grew up thinking that Bill Cosby was just like his character, Dr. Huxtable, a role model of fatherhood and gentlemanly behavior. He had us all fooled. As Diane Sawyer, the former ABC news anchor, once put it, "People will forgive you for not being the leader you want to be, but they will never forgive you for not being the leader you claim to be."

Hypocrites

Hypocrites may be even more despicable than frauds because they're oblivious to the fact that they're disingenuous. They pour hot water on ramen and really believe they are chefs. Hypocrites are constantly telling and expecting people to do things that they will not do themselves. It's chronic "Do as I say, not as I do-ISM." I once observed a military commander who constantly harped on his subordinate commanders about physical fitness when he was clearly overweight and out of shape. His hypocrisy seemed invisible to him, and unfortunately, it overshadowed several of his good qualities. In many cases, leaders like this commander are delusional. The type of people who cheat at solitaire and feel good because they got one over on their opponent. They believe they're virtuous, and they want everyone else to buy into the falsehood that they are leaders of character when they are not. They rationalize their actions to justify their behavior to themselves.

Afterthought: The One-Third Rule

On the first day you step into the role of leader, supervisor, project manager, or coach, about a third of your people will automatically trust you, about a third will automatically distrust you, and the other third will be undecided. You want to keep the trusters trusting, flip the distrusters, and win over the undecided. Your goal should be to get all (100 percent) of your employees/followers/players to have complete trust in you as their leader. You do this by convincing the trusters they were right to trust you and by giving the distruster's reasons to realize they were wrong not to trust you. With the undecideds, don't worry about them initially. If you lead with integrity, they'll quickly make up their minds.

The good news is that getting all three groups on the trust train requires the same type of character- and competence-based leadership. You have to show all of them that it is in their best interests to trust you because you're a vehicle to achieving their goals, aspirations, and needs. The bad news is that no matter how much character and competence you demonstrate, there will always be employees who won't have complete trust in your leadership, no matter how much you deserve it. Your leadership should always be focused on getting to that 100 percent but realize that it's a high mountain to climb when sometimes you take three steps forward, then slide two steps back. Easy to say, hard to do.

Summary Points

Your integrity is your character in action.

- Without integrity, there is no trust.
- Can you pass the New Boss Test?
    - Do you have an ethical compass?
    - Are you the real deal?
    - Do you care about those you lead?
- Integrity is a three-legged stool:
    - *Honesty*: It's a zero-sum game; either you're honest, or you're not.
        - Your honesty is revealed by your behavior.
        - Seventy-three percent of C-level execs admit professional dishonesty.
        - As a leader, your honesty is constantly scrutinized.
    - *Authenticity*: You cannot fake it until you make it.
        - People only commit to leaders whom they see as authentic.
        - Authentic leaders inspire commitment and engagement.
    - *Selflessness:* Servant leadership is focused on the greater good.
        - Leaders have the greater good at heart over their self-interests.
        - Selflessness is not a zero-sum game.
        - Healthy ambition is healthy.

- Frauds pawn themselves off as someone they are not, and they know it.
- Hypocrites rationalize their actions to justify their behavior.
- The good guys don't always win.
- Practice the One-Third Rule: Win over the "undecideds," and convert the distrusters.
- Servant leadership is not servile leadership.

If you're comfortable with your integrity, go to the next chapter. If not, "Look in the Mirror" below.

Look in the Mirror at My Integrity

Review the following statements, then *underline* where you are and *circle* where you want to be:

- **My *honesty* is:**
    - Poor / Mediocre / OK / Good / Excellent
- **My *authenticity* is:**
    - Poor / Mediocre / OK / Good / Excellent
- **I am *selfless*:**
    - Never / Occasionally / Most of the Time / All the Time
- **I do what it takes to keep my promises and commitments:**
    - Never / Occasionally / Frequently / All the Time
- **I am loyal and supportive of my leaders:**
    - Never / Occasionally / Frequently / All the Time
- **I treat everyone on my team equally:**
    - Never / Occasionally / Frequently / All the Time
- **I do what I say I'm going to do:**
    - Never / Occasionally / Frequently / Always
- **I do what it takes to put my team's interests ahead of my own:**
    - Never / Occasionally / Frequently / All the Time
- **My trust in my team is:**
    - Nonexistent / Weak / Good / Total
- **Their trust in me is:**
    - Nonexistent / Weak / Good / Total
- **I am reliable, dependable, and consistent:**
    - Never / Occasionally /Frequently/ Always
- **My words and my deeds are aligned:**
    - Never / Sporadically / Frequently / Always

What Aspect(s) of My Integrity Could Use Improvement?

Example: Recently, during my monthly directors' meeting sales updates, I have found myself being less than truthful about my team's sales numbers. I have been totally truthful on actual to-date sales, but I have been underplaying the potential losses of current sales and inflating the number of future sales opportunities. Also, I find myself unthinkingly making derogatory remarks about senior management in the presence of my direct reports.

I Want to Improve:

My Philosophy on Integrity

Example: Be honest, authentic, and focused on the greater good of my organization and my employees. I need to face the truth and have the integrity to speak the truth to my bosses regardless of the consequences. I will give upper management and my bosses the same level of loyalty I expect from those I lead.

My Philosophy on Integrity:

My Action Plan

Example: At the next directors' sales meeting, I will be totally truthful about potential sales losses and the level of opportunity for future sales. At my next staff meeting with my employees, I will state that complaining about our upper management is unacceptable and I will set the example better than I have in the past.

My Action Plan:

9

HUMILITY

Here lies a man who attracted better people into his service than he was himself.

—Andrew Carnegie's Epitaph

WE ARE NOT born with humility. It is not innate, inherent, or inherited.[1] So, to be modest, humble, and outwardly focused, we must be in a constant internal struggle to defeat our humanness. It seems the quiet, selfless leader—the servant leader—is getting closer and closer to extinction. I once read that George Washington practiced "aggressive non-greatness." He made a conscious effort to avoid self-aggrandizement and exercise humility at all times. Can you point to any leader today who practices that level of humility? They're few and far between. Author David Brooks' contends that our society is shifting:

> ".... from a culture that encouraged people to think humbly of themselves to a culture that encourages people to see themselves as the center of the universe. Along with this rise in self-importance there is a tremendous increase in the desire for fame."[2]

When I read this passage in Brooks' book, *The Road to Character*, I immediately thought of my father, a member of the famously unpretentious Greatest Generation—one described by journalist Tom Brokaw as holding the deep-seated conviction that true character was based on the virtues of humility and modesty.[3] I knew my father had landed on Omaha Beach on D-Day, six days after he turned 20, only because my mother told me. For decades, I unsuccessfully nagged him to tell me about his D-Day experience, only to be pushed away with: "There's really not much to tell. A lot of guys had it pretty rough, but I was lucky to get through it without a scratch."

It wasn't until I was in my 40s that I heard his real D-Day story. My father was visiting us at Fort Riley, Kansas, where I was a brigade commander in the 1st Infantry Division, affectionately known as the "Big Red One." Ironically, one of the units in my brigade was the 1st Battalion of the 16th Infantry Regiment, the very unit in which my father, Private George Washington Aldridge Jr., landed on Omaha Beach on June 6, 1944. After considerable cajoling, I enticed him into visiting the 16th Infantry headquarters, which housed a collection of the unit's memorabilia, including pictures of the regiment's D-Day Omaha Beach exploits.

I warned my dad that I had allowed the battalion commander to invite some of his leaders to meet him. When we arrived at the HQ, the commander had gathered all fifty officers, the command sergeant major, and a dozen senior noncommissioned officers, all anxious to meet a WWII veteran who landed on Omaha Beach with their regiment. As my father was being shown the extensive collection of D-Day pictures, one of the young lieutenants in the group asked my dad, "Sir, would you please tell us what it was like to be a soldier on Omaha Beach that day?" With that short question, my dad did what I had begged him to do for years. Inspired by the D-Day pictures and memorabilia but mainly by the anxious young faces of the battalion's leaders in the room, he shared his D-Day story. Initially, his words flowed very slowly, only revealing broad particulars. But as he spent more time studying the pictures and responding to the officers' questions, he became more animated, detailed, and emotional. He unraveled his story in a modest, matter-of-fact language, telling of the horrors of that day and the heroism of those around him.

If you haven't seen the opening scene of the movie *Saving Private Ryan*, you should. It will give you a gut-wrenching sense of the horrific carnage the Greatest Generation endured on Omaha Beach that day. My dad talked of his experience modestly but gave enough detail that everyone in the room had a visceral feel for what a common soldier had to endure to survive on that "longest day." I had always suspected that my father's "It was not a big deal" mantra was overly modest. He was a humble man who was personified by the axiom, "Still waters run deep." But until that day, I didn't realize just how deep those waters ran.

After D-Day, my father spent the next thirty-four years in uniform, going on to serve and lead in the Korean War and two tours of duty in Vietnam. He ended his long career with a chest full of medals, including the Silver Star, the Distinguished Flying Cross, four Bronze Stars, ten Air Medals, and the Combat Infantry Badge. Not once in my life did I hear him brag or refer to any of his exploits in uniform. He was from an era where being a leader was defined by duty, not by entitlement, by responsibility, not self-interest.

That day with the 16th Infantry wasn't the first time I had witnessed my father's humility. Years earlier, when I was a young captain stationed at the Pentagon, I was having lunch in the cafeteria when a grizzled old colonel came up to me, pointed his bony finger at the name tag on my uniform, and asked, "Are you any relation to George Washington Aldridge, the Army aviator?" I replied, "Yes, sir, he's my father." The colonel sat down at my table and told me he had been a young lieutenant in the helicopter company my father commanded in Vietnam in the early '60s. He shared that when my father wasn't personally flying the lead helicopter on a mission, he would often jump on board a chopper flown by one of his junior officers. On one mission, at the last minute, one of the choppers was short a door gunner, so my dad volunteered. During the flight, they received incoming ground fire, and my father started to return fire with the H-19 helicopter's .50-caliber door-mounted machine gun. On his first burst of return fire, the eighty-five-pound gun jumped off its door rack and slammed into his face, knocking out several of my father's front teeth.

A few days after the incident, my father learned that the company executive officer (XO), his second in command, was submitting him for a Purple Heart, the medal awarded to soldiers wounded in combat. My father tore up the paperwork and told the XO, "The reason the damn gun came off the rack was that I didn't do a pre-combat check to make sure its retaining pin was locked in place like I should have. I don't deserve a Purple Heart. What I deserve is to buy everyone a round of drinks at the club for my stupidity." The old colonel told me that my dad's act of humility was typical and just one of the reasons why his soldiers had complete trust in him as their leader.

The Quiet Professionals

We need to look no further than the Greatest Generation for the perfect role models of humility. My father's humility and quiet courage wasn't an exception but the norm for the charter members of his generation. Not only did they avoid attention, it made them uncomfortable. In his memoir, *Flags of Our Fathers*, John Bradley tells the story of discovering a box of letters and photos following his father's death at 70.[4] Only then did he learn that his father was one of the six men pictured in the immortal Pulitzer Prize-winning photograph of the flag being raised on Mount Suribachi at Iwo Jima. Like my dad's reluctance to talk about his combat experiences, John's father "never spoke of the photograph or the war."

Where is that sense of humility today? We witness self-promoting leaders everywhere we look in the corporate, political, sports, and media worlds. It seems that no matter where we are, there are end-zone show-offs and self-worshiping exhibitionists constantly being thrown in our faces. I'm sure you've encountered dinner party guests or passing acquaintances who, within minutes of meeting you, gush their entire life story and spew their credentials, degrees, and accomplishments without invitation. Where are the invisible leaders who get the job done and take care of those they lead without fanfare and bravado? They're rare; therefore, they're precious. Humility is very often accompanied by anonymity. The "quiet professional" is just that—quiet. And things that are quiet usually go unnoticed. Humble leaders are, by association, selfless leaders, and like servant leaders, they often go unrewarded. It's been said that humility is a term seemingly better suited to monks and yogis than to CEOs.[5]

Humility is a byproduct of integrity. It expresses your character to the world. If you lead honestly, authentically, and especially selflessly, it's almost impossible to be anything but humble. Selflessness and humility go hand-in-hand to build follower trust. Self-made men who worship their creator are immediately seen as self-serving and narcissistic. How can you trust or respect someone who starts every sentence with "I"? You can't! A know-it-all who exudes self-importance, an oversized ego, arrogance, or unbridled ambition will quickly tip the scales of trust out of their favor. Know-it-alls rarely know it all. Many talented people have squandered their follower's trust by lacking personal or professional humility. When leaders are solely focused on themselves, how can they be focused on the organization and those they lead? They can't!

Unfortunately, it seems our leadership landscape is becoming more boisterous with pretentiousness and self-praise. Humility and modesty are becoming the exception rather than the norm. We live in a society that encourages us to think about how to have a great career but leaves many of us inarticulate about how to cultivate an inner life.[6] In today's environment, competition to succeed and win admiration is fierce. For many, it becomes all-consuming. We live in a social media culture that encourages and entices us to promote and advertise ourselves rather than live a life of modesty and humility. It seems we're in a perpetual personal and professional race to see who can get the most "likes."

Why Should I be Humble?

Being humble is what it takes to persuade your followers to trust you as their leader. It's what convinces them that you haven't placed your personal ambitions ahead of their interests. Scads of scientific research show that humble leaders create healthier and more effective organizational cultures. Those same studies conclude that a leader's demonstrated humility lowers levels of counterproductive work behaviors, unethical conduct, absenteeism, and poor performance. Being modest and humble bears little resemblance to today's cult of celebrity and distasteful self-promotion. Humility is giving credit to the team for all that is good and accepting personal responsibility for all that is bad. It's winning that "constant battle" with our selfish instincts. It's standing in the shadows and letting those you lead enjoy the attention and accolades.

I recently worked with a company going through a tough time because of COVID-19. While attending one of their monthly board of directors' meetings, I witnessed a leader who lost that battle with his selfish instincts while his counterpart won the battle. The company's two managers, who were the most severely affected by the pandemic, were called on the carpet to lay out their plan to recover from their department's considerable financial setbacks of the past year. The first department manager quickly threw his team under the bus, blaming his division's failures on poor employee performance, lack of resources, and insufficient support from the company's other teams.

The second department manager laid out the challenges he and his team faced, then presented a plan of how they were going to overcome them going forward. He ended his presentation with a short comment: "My people have done a great job. Any criticism of our performance should be directed at me, not my team. Their commitment and dedication to this company prevented what could have been a much worse situation. I am proud to have the privilege of being their leader." It's not hard to guess which manager was presiding over Organizational Mercenaries and which one was leading Organizational Patriots.

Can Professional Ambition Coexist with Personal Humility?

Many modern leadership gurus will argue that you'll be perceived as lacking drive, motivation, and self-confidence if you don't tout your talents, constantly sell yourself, and advertise your ambitions. Jim Collins, in his book *Good to Great,* strongly debunks that argument. He states that the most successful and effective leaders possess full measures of both professional will and personal humility.[7] For years, Collins studied hundreds of corporations, comparing them against rigid business benchmarks to determine what it takes to achieve long-term sustained business success. Specifically, he wanted to determine what it takes to transform a failing, mediocre, or even a good company into a great company. He found that it takes a certain kind of person, one that he calls a "Level 5 leader." His methodology ranked executive capabilities into five categories. It was the Level 5 leaders who succeeded in inspiring undistinguished companies to become "great." His research strongly debunks the idea that humble leaders lack ambition, drive, or a fierce resolve to succeed:

> "Level 5 leaders display a powerful mixture of personal humility and indomitable will. They're incredibly ambitious, but their ambition is first and foremost for the cause, for the organization and its purposes, not themselves. While Level 5 leaders can come in many personality packages, they are often self-effacing, quiet, reserved, and even shy. Every good-to-great transition in our research began with a Level 5 leader who motivates the enterprise more with inspired standards than inspiring personality.[8]"

Collins convincingly points out that we shouldn't confuse humility with timidity, subservience, passivity, weakness, or lack of ambition. Humility is based on the idea that you're no better or superior to others, but it's also about not feeling inferior to others. Just because a leader doesn't go around tooting her own horn, it shouldn't be interpreted that she doesn't have ambitious personal

A Humble Leader's Mantra

"If things went great, *they did it*!"
"If things went bad, *I did it*!"

and professional goals. Underneath that veneer of modesty can smolder an indomitable will. Humble leaders let their achievements and abilities speak for themselves through their actions, behavior, decisions, and successes. Just as ambition and selflessness are not mutually exclusive, ambition and humility are not mutually exclusive—they can easily coexist. Humility doesn't require that we not take pride in our leadership strengths and achievements. It's not thinking less of yourself; it's thinking of yourself less. It bears little resemblance to today's cult of celebrity and self-promotion.

Timeout! You Want Me to be Humble, Even If It Means Failure?

It's natural for you to ask at this point, "Wow, so you're telling me that if I do what it takes to be the humble leader you describe, there's a chance the cost may be an honorable failure and that even if I do a great job, it may go unrecognized?" I'd like to respond to your question by emphatically saying, "Absolutely not," but I can't. The uncomfortable but truthful answer is, "Hopefully not." The lightly traveled high road of humility these days is likened to the proverbial "road less traveled"; there's not a lot of traffic. As I said earlier, leaders are few and far between. If you choose to do what it takes to enter the ranks of those few, humility is one of the prices of admission.

I'm suggesting that if you lead with a lack of pretense and a modest view of your self-importance, coupled with a fierce resolve to succeed and bring all in your organization along with you, there's a high probability that you'll be recognized and rewarded for your efforts. Why not let your achievements, behavior, actions, and decisions—your leadership—speak for themselves? As Will Rogers once said, "Get someone else to blow your horn, and the sound will go twice as far." Again, I'll say, Humility is an essential ingredient to convince our followers to trust us as leaders. Let me say it more strongly: Humility is not just essential, it's necessary to win the trust of those you lead. Just as being a leader is a choice, humility is a choice. Choose wisely.

"Never let your ego get so close to your position that when your position goes, your ego goes with it."
—Colin Powell

Afterthought: Beware of Adult-Onset Arrogance

In Ancient Rome, when victorious emperors returned to the roaring crowds praising their victories, they would have a low-level servant whisper in their ear: "Remember you are mortal. Fame is fleeting." Many of today's senior leaders could use a whisperer giving them the same advice. There's an insidious tendency for many leaders in their later years to start believing that the success of their organization or endeavor is solely because of their leadership and that they're the center of their universe. As they age and experience continued success, a kind of atrophy, a withering away of their head and heart, seems to occur.[9]

The higher you go, the more you live and lead in a cocoon of privilege, and you run the risk of insularity that comes with holding senior positions. You're surrounded by people who want to please you, insulated from those who will give you honest feedback or restrain your unpleasant traits. Combined with this lack of honest feedback is the hubris that often accompanies professional success. That euphoria of success seems to infect them with a sense of conceit, leading to what I call "Adult-Onset-Arrogance (AOA)." These type of leaders start to focus on the short term over the long term, the selfish over the selfless, and their personal well-being over their responsibility to others. Success has erased their thin veneer of humility, and in the common vernacular, "They start drinking their own Kool-Aid." Their success seems to poison them with an imaginary justification for entitlement. In their minds, they don't have to play by the same rules as everyone else because they made the company successful. Like the emperor who had no clothes, they delude themselves into believing that their arrogance is invisible and they can do what they want with impunity. Psychologist

Daniel Kahneman calls this an "almost unlimited ability to ignore their arrogance."[10] Humility and arrogance are opposites. The difference between arrogance and self-confidence is self-awareness. Those stricken with AOA seem to forget the many people who made them successful: the employees who worked overtime to make their businesses profitable, the engineers who resolved issues to make the products work, and the families who supported them during the lean years.

I love the story of the Fortune 500 company CEO who, on a road trip with his wife, stopped at an old-school, full-service gas station to fill up. As he returned to his car after using the restroom, he saw his wife talking to the station attendant, pumping their gas. It turns out that she used to date the fellow back in high school before she met her husband. After she told him about the coincidence, they drove on in silence for a few minutes, and finally, he said, "I bet you're thinking you're glad you married me because I'm a Fortune 500 CEO and not a gas station manager!" She replied, "No. I was thinking if I had married him, he would be a Fortune 500 CEO, and you'd be pumping gas."[11] Don't get infected with AOA. Always remember those who got you where you are.

Afterthought: False Modesty, aka, the Humble Brag

"You know I'm authorized for six weeks of vacation each year, but for the good of the company, I forego that perk." If I heard the CEO say it once, I heard him say it a hundred times. In every conversation and meeting, he would stealthily weave in that he wasn't taking his allotted vacation time. This CEO repeatedly broadcast his "good deed," hoping to disguise it as an act of selflessness. But it came across as false humility. I call it the "Humility Bait and Switch," aka, the "Humble Brag." When you drape an act of selflessness, generosity, or kindness in a cloak of humility with the hope it will be perceived as an act of humility, you're guilty of humble bragging. The workplace is filled with self-proclaimed martyrs who constantly bring to our attention all the personal sacrifices they're making for the common good in hopes of winning our admiration and respect. They don't seem to realize that we see right through their attempt at victimhood. Rather than winning our admiration and respect, their transparent ruses earn the opposite. Genuine humility is characterized by silence. Rather than advertising your sacrifices, good deeds, and generosity, let them be discovered. Even better, let them go unnoticed. That's genuine humility, a strange concept in this Facebook age. The opposite of the humble brag is when Michelangelo, soon after he had finished painting the Sistine Chapel ceiling, was being interviewed by a wealthy patron who wanted him to do a sculpture for his palace. Michelangelo said, "I can also paint."

Summary Points

- Humility is not thinking less of yourself; it's thinking of yourself less.
- The opposite of humility is arrogance.
- Humility is an extension and demonstration of your integrity and selflessness.
- Nobody trusts a braggart or a narcissist.
- Humility is an essential ingredient to build trust in those you lead.
- A lack of humility has been the demise of many leaders.
- The quiet professional, the humble leader, is a servant leader.
- Humility frees us from having to constantly prove ourselves to others.
- Being humble and unassuming doesn't mean you're not firm in your opinions and values.
- Humility and ambition can exist simultaneously.
- Don't confuse humility with timidity, subservience, weakness, or lack of ambition.
- Humility is embracing the idea that you're no better or superior to others but that you're also not inferior to others.

- Humble leaders:
    - Consider the opinions of others.
    - Show concern for the efforts and challenges of others.
    - Pass on credit for success and accept responsibility for failures and mistakes.
    - Clean up their own messes and apologize when necessary.
    - Let someone else toot their horn.
    - Find joy in other people's success.
    - Don't always need to be right.

If you're comfortable with your humility, go to the next chapter. If not, "Look in the Mirror" below.

Look in the Mirror at My Humility

Review the following statements, then *underline* where you are and *circle* where you want to be:

- **My *humility* is:**
    - Poor / Mediocre / OK / Good / Excellent
- **I give credit for success:**
    - Never / Occasionally / Frequently / All the Time
- **I acknowledge the importance of team members:**
    - Never / Occasionally / Frequently / All the Time
- **I accept responsibility when things go wrong:**
    - Never / Occasionally / Frequently / All the Time
- **I am open to other ideas even when they conflict with mine:**
    - Never / Occasionally / Frequently / All the Time
- **I show that I'm secure in my own skin and my own abilities:**
    - Never / Occasionally / Frequently / All the Time
- **I welcome feedback:**
    - Never / Occasionally / Frequently / Always
- **I put the team's/company's interests ahead of my own:**
    - Never / Occasionally / Frequently / All the Time
- **I show those I lead respect and loyalty:**
    - Never / Occasionally / Frequently / All the Time
- **I use the terms "we," "us," and "our," more than I use "I," me," "my," and "mine":**
    - Never / Occasionally / Frequently / All the Time
- **I communicate to be understood, not to draw attention to myself:**
    - Never / Occasionally / Frequently / All the Time
- **I accept responsibility for my mistakes:**
    - Never / Occasionally / Frequently / All the Time
- **I find joy in the success in others and they know it:**
    - Never / Occasionally / Frequently / All the Time

- **I show those I lead that I appreciate their efforts and the challenges they face:**
  - Never / Occasionally / Frequently / All the Time
- **I demonstrate to those I lead that I have a healthy balance of ambition and humility:**
  - Never / Occasionally / Frequently / All the Time
- **I talk about myself too much:**
  - Never / Occasionally / Frequently / All the Time
- **I am guilty of humble bragging:**
  - Never / Occasionally / Frequently / All the Time

What Aspect(s) of My Humility Could Use Improvement?

Example: In our fast-paced industry, I often shut down my team's suggestions and innovative ideas because I want to get the job done quickly. I need to be more receptive to my team's ideas and suggestions for improvement. Too often, I say, "Just do it the way I told you." I also do not give enough credit for the good work my team does.

I Want to Improve:

My Philosophy on Humility

Example: I will credit my team and those I lead for our success and accept responsibility for those times we are not successful. I will improve my ability to be open to feedback, suggestions, and ideas. If I don't agree with them, I will respectfully let those involved know why.

My Philosophy on Humility:

My Action Plan

Example: I haven't done a good job of accepting ideas and feedback from my team; I will do better. I will seek feedback from each team member to see where I've been perceived as "blowing them off."

I often talk too much about myself. I will be more inquisitive about my employee's lives and do a better job of focused listening.

My Action Plan:

10
GRIT

**"Out of the night that covers me,
Black as the Pit from pole to pole,
I thank whatever gods may be
For my unconquerable soul."**[1]

—William Henley, author of Invictus

ON THE FIRST day of Ranger School, as over 140 of us stood in formation, our Ranger Tactical Officer, Captain Mike Lanning, told us: "Look to your left; in three weeks, that Ranger will probably be gone! Look to your right; in six weeks, that Ranger will probably be gone! In nine weeks, if you aren't mentally tough, you will be gone!" Of the seventy students in my class who didn't finish (except for those who were injured), almost all didn't graduate because they didn't have the mental toughness, the grit, to stick it out until the end.

I learned during Ranger School that some people can suffer a setback and recover; they have resilience. Others possess an indomitable spirit; they have determination. And some have indefatigable endurance and never quit; they have perseverance. Leadership wears on you without mercy. To survive as a leader, you'll need a large measure of grit, the resilience to get up when knocked down, the determination to confront problems head-on, and the perseverance to endure unrelenting hardship and endless challenges.

Do You Have an Unconquerable Soul?

Do you have grit, that indomitable spirit and strength that comes from within to help you survive and recover from personal or professional setbacks? Are you mentally tough, confronting and overcoming life's problems that are thrown in your path? Do you have psychological stamina? When the going gets tough, do you get going, or do you just give up? These are questions that all leaders should ask themselves and, more importantly, answer honestly.

Grit is the willingness and mettle to confront your problems, not avoid them. When I say "your problems," I don't mean your *personal* problems. As a leader, the difficulties, troubles, and struggles of your organization and those you lead are now your problems and your responsibility. Leaders can't afford to be fragile. So, the question is, "Do you have the emotional endurance to stay the course and not quit or burn out in an environment where problems are perpetual?" Those you lead expect and demand nothing less.

Life is hard. It's fraught with challenging situations, ethical dilemmas, mid-course career changes, burnout, seemingly intractable interpersonal challenges, family issues, failures, and health issues.[2] Dealing with your own personal and professional challenges and stresses is a feat in itself. When you shoulder the responsibility for your organization's success, then saddle upon that the problems and burdens of those you lead, it can seem daunting—because it is. As a leader, your millstone to bear is the responsibility to weather the constant barrage of problems and challenges that come your way. It comes with the territory. Each person in your charge has personal and professional challenges and problems that will eventually fall onto your doorstep. To further test your "unconquerable soul," the world in which you lead is and always will be volatile, uncertain, complex, and ambiguous (VUCA).

We have to live in the world as it is, not as we wish it to be. Bad things happen to good people and good organizations. How many companies went under because of the uncertainty caused by the complex situations brought on by the COVID-19 virus? Many of these companies were well-led, served a useful purpose, and failed because something terrible happened to good people through no fault of their own. Leading in an uncertain environment over long periods is not only physically exhausting but psychologically draining. The WWII historian Rick Atkinson describes the stresses of leadership:

> "It corrodes the soul and tarnishes the spirit, that even the excellent and the superior can be defiled, and that no heart would remain unstained. It causes mental fatigue that comes from having to make responsible, correct, impactful, life-altering choices and decisions over and over again."[3]

When bad things happen to us, it's OK to wallow in our self-pity for a few minutes, but then we have to give it a mental shrug and move on. As a leader, you can't afford the debilitating effects of prolonged self-pity. You can't become the victim. Without the mental muscle to overcome and endure the inevitable setbacks and challenges all leaders experience, your responsibilities will wear you down without mercy. You have to be active in your own recovery.

Never Let Them See You Sweat

Keeping the trust of your employees is a full-time job. In tough times, it's hard to give the appearance of supreme confidence and optimism when, in your gut, you're experiencing a tsunami of stress and anxiety. You may want to hit the panic button, but you can't. Your employees must see you as a source of inspiration and hope in times of conflict, organizational setbacks, and uncertainty. There will be occasions when you're experiencing personal difficulties, health issues, family difficulties, or other problems unrelated to your leadership role. Those personal travails must be compartmentalized and not affect your role as a leader. In these

SELF-CONFIDENCE

Reporter:
"What's the one essential talent for a quarterback?"

Tom Brady:
"Leadership. It's not a physical trait. I'm the one calling plays. If I lack any confidence, [my teammates] see right through it."

circumstances and situations, you must be seen as the rock of Gibraltar, a picture of resilience and confidence, even if that persona of self-confidence and poise is a struggle. Developing armor for the soul is easy to say but hard to do.

Life is full of surprises, and when organizations are thrust into uncertainty or crisis, two things happen immediately. First, followers look to their leaders to see how they react. If they sense doubt or fear, their confidence and trust are shaken. However, if they sense confidence, they, too, will trust that they'll come out OK. A leader who projects unwavering Olympic calm in turbulent times has a powerful positive effect on the organization. The second thing that happens is that followers wait to hear their leader's direction on what to do: Will there be analysis paralysis or a calmly directed, confident way forward? The key is to radiate absolute assurance in the outcome and never be seen as wavering from that optimism.[4] Again, indecision brings fear, whereas confidence brings calm and hope. Doing something is almost always better than doing nothing.

When You're Going Through Hell, Keep Going

Much of leadership requires performing under pressure during tough times. That's the nature of the job: making difficult decisions that impact others' lives and well-being. For leaders to be seen as a source of hope in the darkest hours, they must be visible and enthusiastically display a compelling determination to succeed. They need to focus on making the best possible decisions in high-pressure situations. Demonstrating resilience and determination in the face of hopelessness and despair is a tonic to those you lead, bolstering their confidence and hardening their resolve. It prevents the flooding of depression and fear throughout your organization. It builds or reinforces their trust in your leadership. Nobody likes a quitter, and nobody will willingly follow one. To Churchill's famous quote, "When you are going through hell, keep going." I would add, "And don't forget your team!" Your employees expect you to do just that: not quit and, when you're in hell, to get them through it. Many leaders have learned the hard way that if they're not visible, aka they're invisible, and don't outwardly display iron resolve at critical moments, then the worrywarts in the organization will prevail. It takes only a few vocal, discontented, focused naysayers to infect despair in an organization or a project with a "sky is falling" attitude. Strong and confident leadership is the antidote to those Chicken Littles.

Get Comfortable Being Uncomfortable

One of the most uncomfortable truths about being a leader is that you live in the bull's eye. Ambiguity, confusion, setbacks, unplanned change, problems big and small, and lack of order aren't events; they're business as usual for leaders. They perch on your shoulder like a gargoyle, and at times, they'll seem overwhelming. Often, it's like living a life of managed frustration. A leader must navigate between a narrow margin, suspended between the relative certainties of the past and the ambiguities of the future.[5]

We can learn from the New York Yankee Hall of Famer, closing pitcher Mariano Rivera, who perpetually lived in the bull's eye. Coming in to pitch with the game on the line, men on second and third, and the top of the lineup coming to bat, he was always one pitch away from winning or losing the game. Through self-discipline and the knowledge that being in the bull's eye was his burden to bear, he developed the psychological grit to be comfortable being uncomfortable. As a leader, you can do the same thing. Being out of your comfort zone is the norm—get used to it.

Don't pray for the day when all your problems will be gone—that day will never come. Some describe leadership responsibility as living in a perpetual state of discomfort. It would be naïve to think you can go through life as an individual, but particularly as a leader, believing you can create an environment where you can avoid, eliminate, or strategize around life's inevitable setbacks, challenges, and problems. If you haven't already, you'll eventually experience unexpected misfortunes, seemingly insurmountable problems, and challenges that will test your mental stamina. Trying to escape or avoid stress is a non-starter for a leader; there are no risk-free environments. A leader's *raison d'etre* is to confront and resolve those inevitable surprises and difficulties the world unapologetically throws your way. Your value as a leader to your organization or endeavor is based on how well you solve its problems.

For many, when they experience setbacks and see no easy fix, their inner fears and insecurities become overwhelming. These are lonely moments in which leaders are often emotionally blocked.[6] When your team has a failure or setback, how do you respond? You can't slink away and hide to focus on your own misery when the going gets tough. You must develop the capacity to respond quickly and constructively to crises.[7] You have to build the mental toughness to think clearly and make good decisions in turbulent times. As Viktor Frankl, the Nazi death camp survivor and author, teaches us, "We cannot control what happens to us, but we can choose how we respond."[8] Or as the pastor and educator Charles Swindoll states, "Life is 10 percent what happens to you and 90 percent how you react." Most leadership arenas are cutthroat. To survive, you have to deflect your personal stress with a form of psychological Kevlar.

THE GRIT TRIAD

Scholars who have studied the development of leaders have placed mental resilience at the heart of leadership success. How leaders respond to life's reversals is more important than what happens to a person. There's what happens to you, and then there's what do you do about it.[9] Rocky Marciano, the only undefeated heavyweight boxer in history, was just a mediocre boxer. So, how did he not only survive his forty-nine fights but win them all? He had the intestinal fortitude to absorb a punch, and every time he was knocked down, which was often, he got back up. He had an exceptional capacity for determination and durability.[10] Like Marciano, to survive and thrive as a leader, you have to get up when you're knocked down.

Superimpose on the need for you to be mentally tough the daunting challenge of leading in a world that's become known as the "everybody gets a trophy" or "victimhood" society. Several generations of those you're leading feel entitled. When they're confronted with any kind of personal or professional disappointment, they don't self-reflect or strive to improve. Their first response is to find someone to blame, sue, or otherwise scapegoat. They've created a hierarchy of competing victimhoods. To succeed as a leader, you must embrace psychological hardiness as something required to build trust in those you lead. Add to that burden the fact that you must build mental toughness in your followers. You must grow beyond your self-perceived limitations and develop generous amounts of the three elements of what I call the "Grit Triad":

- *Resilience* (mental toughness): the ability to recover from misfortune, failure, or catastrophe.
- *Determination* (mental hardiness): the capacity to willingly seek out problems and push through harsh and difficult situations.
- *Perseverance* (mental stamina): the fortitude to stick with a problem to its end and endure its long, hard, monotonous, and often unpopular course.

Leadership isn't for the faint of heart or the psychologically meek. It requires a level of mental toughness that forces you to punch above your weight and do more than you think you can do. You'll be challenged to merely survive, much less thrive. Let's look at the grit triad more closely.

Resilience: The Mental Muscle to Recover from Misfortune

The advice "It's not important how many times you get knocked down but how many times you get up," is just another easy-to-say but hard-to-embrace cliché. Fear, anger, grief, and confusion can paralyze us after a severe personal or professional setback. Assigning blame rather than generating solutions is an all-too-human tendency.[11] Some people, when knocked down, stay down. Those who are mentally tough, like Charles Krauthammer, get up.

While in his first year at Harvard Medical School, 22-year-old Charles Krauthammer and one of his classmates skipped morning classes to play tennis. After a couple of sets, they decided to take a dip in the pool to cool off before heading to afternoon classes. Charles dove into the pool, hit his head on the bottom, and sev-

"Resilience is the ability to recover quickly and easily, to snap back into shape again, like a rubber band stretched and released."
—George Aldridge

ered his spinal cord at the cervical spinal nerve five. He says of the accident that he immediately realized what had happened and knew that

his life would be forever changed.[12] One minute, he's a star student and athlete with the world on a string. A split second later, he's permanently paralyzed from the waist down, handed a life sentence to be confined in a wheelchair.

For many people, that would have been the end of medical school and the beginning of a life wallowing in self-pity. Instead of spending precious energy on self-pity and dwelling on the question of "Why me?" Krauthammer rose from the ashes of his tragedy and moved on. He said, "Individuals should be defined by their lives, by what they do, not by what happens to them." He chose not to be defined as a victim. He was determined to be defined as a doctor, a newspaper columnist, and an author. After fourteen months recovering in the hospital, he returned to medical school, graduating to become a psychiatrist in 1975. Following a stint in the Carter administration, then as a speechwriter for Vice President Walter Mondale, he embarked on a career as a newspaper columnist and political commentator. Working for *The Washington Post*, his column was syndicated by 400 papers across the world and he won a Pulitzer Prize for journalism. In his spare time, he published five bestselling books and was a frequent and popular commentator on network news shows.

During his last year of life, fighting a courageous battle with cancer, he continued to define himself as an author, not a victim. In his last months, he used a combination of digital and physical displays to continuously write. Krauthammer was a tough guy; he was knocked down and knocked down hard, but he got up. Not only did he demonstrate a strong will to survive, but he also revealed an unbelievable level of resilience by going on to thrive, living a life of notable consequence. He endured the unendurable. To the very end, Charles Krauthammer possessed an "unconquerable soul."

Ask yourself again, "How tough am I? Do I have the resilience to recover from a fateful tragedy as he did?" I'm not sure I do. I tell you the story of Krauthammer's life because, in my eyes, he is the epitome and role model of true grit—the resilience to recover and overcome tragedy and not only survive but thrive. As Krauthammer did, leaders must possess the resiliency to maintain stable psychological functions after highly disruptive life events. It's all about overcoming unexpected personal or professional catastrophe and not spending time lamenting it but having the grit to overcome it. Survival is about sustainability. Leaders are survivors. Leaders survive failure, disaster, tragedy, personal frailties, frustration, and bad luck while the Dictators and Maintainers scurry for the nearest bunker. The strongest leaders not only do what's required to recover from setbacks or failure but use it as an opportunity to learn and grow. People who rebound own their mistakes rather than blame others. They use failures and setbacks as classrooms and make promises and plans never to let it happen again. They take on an "I'll show you" attitude.

Determination: Failure Is Not an Option!

There's probably no better example of a leader demonstrating bulldog determination than Gene Kranz during the Apollo 13 space launch, when he yelled at his team, "Failure is not an option!" He faced a seemingly unsolvable, life-threatening problem, and he refused to accept the fact that it couldn't be solved. He mobilized and inspired his team to find a solution through strong, determined leadership. We all know the outcome. Through Kranz and his team's unrelenting efforts, the three-man crew of Apollo 13 were safely returned to Earth despite what was initially thought to be an overwhelmingly impossible task. It was called the "The Successful Failure."

His determination was manifested by his refusal to admit defeat and instead to face the problem head-on. Kranz was a master of channeling his hatred of failure in a positive direction. Through transformational leadership, his pugnacious passion for mission success was internalized by his crew. It was a powerful leadership weapon that inspired the team to find a solution to what most of them had determined was an unsolvable problem. Kranz's refusal to give up hope and his granite resolve are true testaments to the power of determined leadership.

In *Good to Great,* Jim Collins analyzes how some leaders succeed in hostile, adversarial, and ambiguous environments. He states that to be a successful leader in today's environment, like Kranz, you must maintain unwavering resolve that you can and will prevail in the end.[13] I would add that you must have the determination to confront the most brutal facts of your current reality, whatever they might be, rather than ignore or run from them. Leadership is forcing movement in a resistant world, and that takes dogged determination.

Perseverance: Enthusiasm Is Common, Endurance Is Not

Leadership success takes more than resilience to recover from misfortune or setback. It takes more than determination to seek out and confront your problems head-on. It takes mental stamina to recover from the continuous mental wear and tear that comes with being a leader. It takes incredible mental stamina to deal with 24/7/365 demands. Like Rocky Marciano, you must have the iron will to get up every time you're knocked down. Maintaining emotional stability takes deep reserves of mental toughness and psychological stamina. Leading is a day-to-day and, often, a year-to-year endeavor. The days and years bring a constant bombardment of problems, ambiguity, change, competitors, and personal demands. You've got to be unafraid if you want to persevere and endure for the long haul. Leading is easy when the times are good, and everything is going well. It's when times are tough that leading is hard. When your ability to endure and persevere is tested, how you respond is defining. Too many leaders give up just before they cross the finish line.

During WWII, the US Army learned that the most competent combat leaders were those who possessed a full measure of mental toughness. The Army also realized it didn't have the luxury of waiting for soldiers to get combat experience to hone the resilience required to survive as a leader. It needed a training vehicle to quickly find and weed out those who didn't possess the mental toughness to lead in combat. In the early 1950s, the US Army developed the Ranger School to meet that need. The purpose of the Ranger course was and still is to prepare young men and women to lead while enduring great psychological stresses and physical fatigue.[14] Ranger School is the ultimate test of leader resilience.

> "Maybe my feet hurt, and the way is hard, but I must go on. . . My soul's peace depends on it."
> —*The Pilgrim's Progress*

When I attended Ranger School, it touted itself (and still does) as the "premiere military leadership course in the world." The school takes philosopher Friedrich Nietzsche's advice to heart: "That which does not kill you makes you stronger." The nine weeks are extraordinarily taxing to both mind and body. The course is designed to physically stress students to a point short of death. In my class, it went beyond that point: Two of my fellow students died, one from hypothermia and the other from injuries sustained during a night parachute jump. Rangers typically carry between sixty-five and ninety pounds of weapons, equipment, and ammunition while patrolling (hiking, running) over 200 miles throughout the course.[15] Back-to-back training days could be twenty or more hours of arduous physical activity, with two to four hours of sleep a night. During the extended exercises, food consisted of one box of C-rations a day, about 3,000 calories. The heavy loads, physical exertion, sleep

> "What I learned in Infantry School:
>
> - No matter how cold you are, you must never look cold.
> - No matter how hungry you are, you must never appear hungry.
> - No matter how terrified you are, you must not look terrified.
>
> Because if you are cold, hungry and terrified, they will be cold, hungry and terrified."
> —*Colin Powell*

deprivation, constant hunger, and unsympathetic weather all took a harsh physical toll on our bodies and played games with our minds. The average Ranger lost between twenty-five and thirty pounds over the course.[16] I went from 178 to 160 pounds.

"So What? You Say"

One of my most surprising observations during Ranger School was that many of my fellow Rangers possessed extraordinary resilience and determination but lacked perseverance. Some quit because they didn't have the psychological stamina to endure the unrelenting misery. They didn't understand that it's not only how hard you try but also how long you keep trying that counts.

Ranger School skillfully controls the outcome of the training scenarios to give the student leader a palpable sense of failure to see how he responds. The Ranger instructors (RIs) intentionally inject stress and despair into the training scenarios to see how students react to seemingly impossible tasks. They cleverly choreographed the manipulation of cold, sleep deprivation, and hunger to push the Ranger students to the edge of their

> "You can just about stand more'n you think you can."
>
> —Texas Bix Bender, author of Don't Squat With Yer Spurs On!

limits of physical and mental exhaustion. During a patrol I led, we navigated through five hours of miserable waist- and chest-deep swamp. As the sun was setting, we finally got to our objective on dry land. The RI waded up to me and said: "Oops, headquarters just changed the mission. Turn around and head back the same way you just came and return to HQ." I assure you that despair is not too strong a description of how I and my twenty fellow Rangers felt about having to get back into the swamp in the darkness, knowing what took five hours in daylight would take much longer at night. The RIs played mind games to make you think there was no successful solution to your problem. They were masters at creating an atmosphere of hopelessness. It was all to test your grit—did you have the stuff needed to lead?

The Ranger students who survived until graduation did so because they never let their desire to get through the course be dampened by disappointment, hopelessness, or depression. Stronger than their desire to win was their refusal to lose. Their will was their prime motivation. They had steadfast resilience to recover from setbacks, disappointments, and failure. They had the iron determination to face their difficulties. They had unrelenting perseverance to stick with the mission to its end. Determination can be described by the old saying, "When the going gets tough, the tough get going." Like the Energizer Bunny, "When the going gets tough, they get going, and keep going and going and going." At graduation, every Ranger wore that toughness as a badge of honor.

> "Perseverance is resilience plus determination doused with patience and stubbornness."
> —George Aldridge

Talent Is Overrated

A high IQ and academic and professional credentials may get you in the door, but tenacity, the desire to overcome and succeed, and the refusal to give up are the traits that get you across the finish line. As weather shapes mountains, experience shapes leaders. In *Talent Is Overrated*, Geoff Colvin argues that great performance comes down to one thing more than any other: deliberate practice, which takes mental stamina.[17]

In my opinion, Tiger Woods is the world's best golfer. When practicing, he doesn't just go to the driving range and hit 200 golf balls. Vladimira Horowitz, the world's greatest pianist, didn't mindlessly play scales on the piano. These elite performers judge and evaluate every golf swing and finger stroke of the ivories, then make the adjustments needed to improve their swing and music. Developing core muscles of resilience means having a persistent and disciplined focus on weaknesses and a relentless effort to improve. To do it right is highly demanding and isn't much fun, but it's necessary. The price of top-level achievement is extraordinarily high, which is why not many people choose to pay the price. Too many people confuse activity with progress. The difference between elites and amateurs is that elites practice those things they are worst at and dislike the most, while the rest of us run around our backhand our whole lives.[18]

As Winston Churchill said about resilience, "Inch by inch is a cinch—yard by yard is hard." Effective and successful leaders bank residual psychological strength, so it's there when they need it. Don't wait to dig the well until you're dying of thirst. At some point in your leadership journey, you'll be faced with doing the hard things. Be ready!

> **"It's not the strongest of the species that survives, nor the most intelligent, but the one most responsive to change."**
> —*Charles Darwin*

Lean on the Greats

Again, let's try to heed Mark Twain's advice on how to be "wise" and learn from the experience of others. I cannot count the times that I've been mired in some professional calamity and said to myself: *This situation pales in comparison to what Washington faced at Valley Forge or what my dad endured on Omaha Beach. My problem is trivial compared to theirs; I can get through this!* On my leadership journey, I keep gravitating toward leaders who possess the characteristics we discuss in the Grit Triad. I've often leaned on my father, George Washington, Winston Churchill, Ernest Shackleton, Gertrude Bell, Lawrence of Arabia, Margaret Thatcher, Sam Damon, Ronald Reagan, Dwight Eisenhower, Elizabeth II, and others. There's a certain solace that comes from knowing that there are those who've experienced failure, disappointment, and defeat but had the resilience, determination, and perseverance to survive and ultimately triumph. I've often leaned on their stories to get me through tough times.

The ghosts of Washington, Churchill, and my father have given me the grit to persevere and persist when faced with what seemed impossible at the time. Some level of comfort can be found in knowing that if they stood tall in situations that were infinitely more dire than my situation, I can get through this. I encourage all my charges and students to study history and the lives of the greats. What better way is there to learn the level of persistence, psychological hardiness, and plain old grit to survive as a leader? Our ancestors weren't fools. The past offers truths of enormous relevance to the present.[19]

How Do We Build Grit in Others?

Much like the requirement to secure your own oxygen mask on a plane when it loses pressure before you help others, leaders must build grit in themselves before they can build it in those they lead. Resilience makes a difference because it rubs off on those you lead. As a leader, you're a role model whether you like it or not, so you're a victim of a resilience double whammy. You have to be resilient and, at the same time, inspire resilience in your followers. This is a leadership imperative. It's your responsibility to create an organizational culture of resilience, mental toughness, and psychological rigor. It's the leadership process of creating a team culture where they know they're well-prepared to do their jobs and that what they do is important and appreciated by their leaders. It's a cultural process, not a single act.

> "If I falter, push me on.
> If I stumble, pick me up.
> If I retreat, shoot me."
> —*Motto of the*
> *French Foreign Legion*

When followers see that their leaders have an attitude that they can face any adversity and succeed, then mental toughness, psychological rigor, and refusal to fail become an organizational norm. They need to see that you can treat disasters as if they were incidents and not magnify them into disasters. When they see their boss deal with painful setbacks and disappointments and not whine about it, they'll mirror that attitude.

Afterthought: "Know Thyself," A Personal After-Action Review

One of the things that Army leaders do well is a process called the AAR—After-Action Review. Following every operation, the leaders gather and quickly analyze what went well and what didn't. From the analysis comes future actions to ensure that what went well is captured for future operations and what went wrong doesn't happen again. It's experiential learning at its best. It's also a process that I've used over the years to self-evaluate my leadership. I suggest you also self-evaluate important aspects of your own leadership. Periodic personal AARs—a process of Aristotelian "know thyself"—help us evaluate how we're doing in a specific area, what's going well and what needs to improve. It's a process to make sure we learn from our own experiences. So, let's give it a try: Conduct a personal AAR. Think back and recall incidents in your life when you needed grit.

- When you were knocked down by a major unexpected personal or professional disappointment, how did you respond? Did you get up and learn from the experience, or did you give up, quit, and blame something or someone for your misfortune?
- When you were challenged with a seemingly insurmountable problem, a psychological wall, did you stop and stare at it, or did you scale it?
- When confronted by uncomfortable truths, did you accept responsibility or delusionally deny their existence?
- When you were faced with seemingly long-term unsolvable difficulties, unrelenting monotony, and unyielding irritants, did you push through by finding solutions, adapting, and overcoming them? Or did you lack the mental stamina or patience to persevere?

Regardless of how you answered these questions, resilience can be developed or improved if you have the will to do it. Developing or improving resilience in ourselves takes desire and deliberate practice over time. Granted, it's not easy, but it can be done.

Afterthought: Burnout

All leaders are human. Even the most resilient and emotionally tough person can eventually suffer mental exhaustion if they're not careful and mindful of their psychological state. If we're in leadership positions long enough, we'll get to a breaking point if we don't recognize the symptoms of that breaking point, commonly known as burnout. We all have our individual ways of dealing with stress, such as physical exercise, faith, diversions, hobbies, family, study, etc. We must have an outlet. Many potentially great leaders fizzled out early because they didn't recognize the signs. In this VUCA age, the effects of this are evident in the skyrocketing stress-related maladies suffered by followers and leaders alike. With leaders, the effects of stress are often delayed until the first breather comes around. Leaders have so much to do in stressful situations they subconsciously repress the effects of prolonged stress until they have time to reflect. Like a bow wave on a fast-moving boat, once you come to a stop, it catches up to you, and if you're mentally burned out, it can capsize you.

We all need some type of on-call psychological first aid to pull out of our hip pocket in stressful situations before we reach total despair. When he couldn't sleep, Abe Lincoln sang raunchy songs and told dirty jokes. Ike wrote notes to people he hated, then tore them up. In the Nazi death camps, Viktor Frankel dreamed about being reunited with his wife. To help me endure the stress of Ranger School, I kept a can of C-ration peaches at the bottom of my rucksack. I told myself that if I ever got to the point where I just couldn't take it anymore, before I quit, I'd break into that can of peaches. My talisman was the fact that I knew as long as I had that can of peaches, I had more to give. I still have those peaches. We all need some psychological first aid, outlet, talisman, or a mental safe place to go when things get bad. We all need our own can of peaches.

Summary Points

The Grit Triad

- Resilience (mental toughness)
    - Resilience comes in many forms: grit, mental toughness, psychological stamina, moxie, stick-to-itiveness, hutzpah, willpower, backbone, resolve, fortitude, refusal to fail, warrior ethos, guts.
    - It's the indomitable spirit and strength to recover from setbacks.
    - In tough times, leaders must demonstrate confidence and optimism.
    - Self-doubt and fear are normal leader emotions.
    - Leaders must "get comfortable being uncomfortable."
- Determination (mental hardiness)
    - It's a willingness to find, confront, and tackle problems head-on.
    - Leaders have an unwavering faith that they can and will prevail.
    - Leaders refuse to give up.
    - Leaders have a "failure is not an option" attitude.
- Perseverance (mental stamina):
    - Leaders need psychological stamina to endure and stay the course in tough times.
    - They must maintain emotional fortitude for the long haul.
    - In tough times, leaders must possess a willingness and mental strength to persist and endure.
    - Perseverance is resilience plus determination doused with patience and stubbornness.

Got grit? Go to the next chapter. If not, "Look in the Mirror" on the following page.

Look in the Mirror at My Grit

Review the following statements, then *underline* where you are and *circle* where you want to be:

- **My *resilience* is:**
    - Poor / Mediocre / OK / Good / Excellent
- **My *determination* is:**
    - Poor / Mediocre / OK / Good / Excellent
- **My *perseverance* is:**
    - Poor / Mediocre / OK / Good / Excellent
- **My ability to recover from setbacks is:**
    - Poor / Mediocre / OK / Good / Excellent
- **My ability to tolerate high levels of uncertainty and ambiguity is:**
    - Poor / Mediocre / OK / Good / Excellent
- **My leadership during times of high pressure is:**
    - Poor / Mediocre / OK / Good / Excellent
- **My willingness and determination to face problems is:**
    - Poor / Mediocre / OK / Good / Excellent
- **I give my team confidence that they'll succeed:**
    - Never / Occasionally / Frequently / All the Time
- **My ability to set a hopeful example in stressful situations is:**
    - Poor / Mediocre / OK / Good / Excellent
- **My ability to be comfortable being uncomfortable is:**
    - Poor / Mediocre / OK / Good / Excellent
- **My patience in dealing with frustration and enduring the long haul is:**
    - Poor / Mediocre / OK / Good / Excellent
- **I demonstrate that I have an unwavering faith that we will prevail in tough times:**
    - Never / Occasionally / Frequently / All the Time
- **I do what it takes to ensure I do not burnout:**
    - Never / Occasionally / Frequently / All the Time

- **I fall victim to self-doubt and fear:**
  - Never / Occasionally / Frequently / All the Time
- **I outwardly demonstrate pessimism to those I lead:**
  - Never / Occasionally / Frequently / All the Time
- **I personally exude a positive perspective:**
  - Never / Occasionally / Frequently / All the Time

What Aspect(s) of My Grit Triad Could Use Improvement?

Example: I often complain when things don't go well, especially in a crisis. I am a natural pessimist and show that attitude to my employees. I have ignored several personnel problems in my section by hoping they'd just go away.

I Want to Improve:

My Philosophy on Grit

Example: My leadership philosophy of resilience is to establish an organizational culture of resilience, determination, and persistence. I will foster that culture by leading by example. In the presence of my staff and team, I will exude a positive perspective (indomitable spirit) and sincere but realistic optimism. I will promote an environment where problems are sought, confronted, and solved, not avoided.

My Philosophy on Grit:

My Action Plan

Example: Due to the high-pressure environment of our company and the stress I feel as a leader for my team to succeed, I often outwardly demonstrated pessimism in the presence of my staff and team. I will consciously accept the concept of "getting comfortable being uncomfortable" and display a more confident attitude to those I lead.

My Action Plan:

11

COURAGE

"Fear and courage are brothers."
—*Proverb*

WE COME INTO this world as cowards. One of the major reasons physical and moral courage are so admired is because they don't come to us naturally. Self-preservation, fear, and our predisposition to avoid conflict are instinctive. It takes a strong desire to possess courage and hard work to develop it. You can grow courage. What it takes is the confidence to step into your fears, not skirt around them. Eleanor Roosevelt advised us, "You gain strength, courage, and confidence by every experience in which you really stop to look fear in the face. You must do the things you think you cannot do."

Unless you're in the military, a first responder, a rodeo clown, or in a profession where the potential of bodily danger is an integral part of your job, the probability that your physical courage will be tested is slim. In our daily lives, fight-or-flight situations are rare. However, if you're in any kind of leadership role, the probability that your moral courage will be tested is 100 percent. As David Brooks puts it, leaders "are constantly involved in moral drama."[1] That's why it's often referred to as "everyday courage." Your courage is tested every time you have to stand up for what you believe and value in the face of opposition or risk. How you react will either build, preserve, or erode your trustworthiness in the eyes of those you lead. It's not about who you claim to be—it's about who you reveal yourself to be in your actions and through your behavior. Everyday courage is doing the things you're afraid to do, but it's also doing things that you:

- Don't want to do.
- Don't like to do.
- Don't feel comfortable doing.

Courage is rightly esteemed as the first of human qualities because it's the quality that guarantees all others.[2] It takes moral courage to live your values. It's your character in action. As the writer Gus Lee describes it, "Courage is the backbone of leadership."[3] It's character with a spine. Possessing principled leadership under pressure or against opposition is a simple concept that's easy to say but hard to do. Doing hard things is hard. Moral courage gives us backbone when faced with the things we're afraid to do, don't want to do, or don't feel comfortable doing.

It's easy to say that I'll have the courage to stand up for my beliefs, tell uncomfortable truths, seek and listen to critical feedback, give credit for success, take responsibility for failure, get up every time I'm knocked down, and persevere in tough times. However, it takes moral courage to actually do those things. Every human temptation, small or large, requires some level of everyday courage to do what's right when our fear or innately selfish desires beg us to do otherwise.

It takes courage to have the:

- *Integrity* to stand up for your beliefs in the face of overwhelming opposition, disapproval, or disdain.
- *Honesty* to tell the boss uncomfortable truths and employees that they're not measuring up.
- *Authenticity* to ask for feedback when you know it may be critical of your leadership.

- **Selflessness** to do what's best for the greater good, even when it comes at a personal or professional cost.
- **Humility** to accept responsibility for failure and pass on credit for success.
- **Resilience** to get up every time you're knocked down.
- **Determination** to seek out problems and face them head-on.
- **Perseverance** to stay the course when it's long, hard, and monotonous.

The bottom line is it takes courage to lead.

What Is Leader Courage?

Anything we aspire to become is worth defining. Retired Secretary of Defense Robert Gates, in his commencement address to the 2011 graduating class of the US Naval Academy, expressed the relationship between leadership and courage this way:

> "A quality of leadership is courage: not just the physical courage of the seas, of the skies, and of the trenches, but moral courage. The courage to chart a new course, the courage to do what is right and not just what is popular, the courage to stand alone, the courage to act, the courage [as a leader] to speak truth to power.
>
> "In most academic curricula today, and in most business, government, and military training programs, there is great emphasis on team building, on working together, on building consensus, and on group dynamics. But for everyone who would become a leader, the time will inevitably come when you must stand alone.
>
> "When alone, you must say, 'This is wrong' or 'I disagree with all of you, and because I have the responsibility, this is what we will do.' Don't kid yourself. That day will come, and it takes real courage."

Gates is right: For a leader, moral courage is not a nice-to-have; it's a must-have. It doesn't come naturally or easily and isn't taught in leadership development programs. Almost all these programs focus solely on competencies and hard skills. They ignore the all-important aspects of character, the so-called soft skills. In *The Second Mountain,* David Brooks writes, "Everybody acknowledges that moral development is important, but it's something you sort of do on your own."[4] That's why it's up to you to decide how you'll tackle the subject of your everyday courage. Having moral courage is something all leaders publicly espouse and aspire to do. The rub is that most people casually assume that they'll have the courage to do the right thing when faced with a moral decision. "When I need to, I will be morally courageous" is something that's easy to commit to, but how do you preemptively steel yourself so courage is there when you need it? Said differently, how do you inoculate yourself against moral cowardice? Let's look at how we can prepare ourselves for the inevitable times when we'll need the resolve, the steel in our spine, to do the hard right and not succumb to the easier or more tempting wrong.

Dig Your Well Before You're Dying of Thirst

You've heard the advice "Live by the courage of your convictions" and "Follow your moral compass." But before you can live by your convictions, you must know what they are because that's what gives your moral compass direction. After a moral or ethical derailment, many say, "Somewhere, I got pulled off course." In most cases, they never had a course. We all need to dedicate the time to consider and codify all the aspects of our character to include how we address fear, adversity, and uncertainty. Many leaders haven't clearly defined their convictions, so when the need for everyday courage arises, they stumble and falter. We talked at length about developing a personal leadership philosophy—to decide what you stand for, then stand for it. Wisdom is the ability to recognize your flaws and weaknesses. Courage is the ability to do something about it. A pre-established leadership philosophy or code of conduct is the moral compass that points you in the right direction when your everyday moral courage is tested. Churchill learned during the darkest days of WWII that "fear is a reaction; courage is a decision."

Knowing what you stand for will make you much more likely to stand for it when you find yourself in a moral tight spot. You won't have to determine how you'll react. You'll just have to decide if you're going to keep the promise you made to yourself or break it. It's called "pre-committing" to what you stand for. If you promise yourself that you'll have the moral courage to stand up for your beliefs even if they're met with opposition or that you'll accept responsibility for your actions regardless of the outcome, and so forth, then when the time comes to live those values, you'll have the mental armor to do so. That mental armor is handy when things inevitably don't go as you'd hoped or planned.[5] I've urged you several times: "Don't wait to dig your well until you're dying of thirst." Prepare yourself now for what might come, and start working now on what has been called "that 2 a.m. courage, a serenity of soul in the midst of turmoil."[6]

Pearls of Leadership Wisdom

Gates gives us a good starting point on what it means to lead with moral courage. Let's look at each of his pearls of leadership wisdom a little deeper and see how we can use them to grow as a leader. To do this, take each of his gems and reflect on your own history. Replay in your mind those instances when your moral courage was tested. This will help you better prepare yourself for future leadership challenges. Mentally, resurrect a past episode where your courage prevailed, where you were faced with something that you were afraid to do, didn't want to do, or didn't feel comfortable doing, and you chose the morally courageous thing to do. How did it make you feel? Why are you proud of it? Then, use each of Gate's pearls to resurrect an event when your moral courage came up short, a time when you were not proud of your actions or words. What do you regret? How did and does it make you feel? What did you learn from the experience?

Aristotle said, "A man without regrets cannot be cured." We all have regrets, and regrets are not all bad. The regret of falling short when called upon to demonstrate moral courage can leave a bitter taste of guilt that remains for a long time, sometimes forever. Douglas MacArthur was right: "The courageous die but one death; the coward dies a thousand times." Said another way, "The fear of suffering is worse than the suffering itself."[7] Courage isn't the absence of fear but the ability to overcome it. The best way to overcome fear is to learn from our experiences. I certainly recall past incidents when I had a lapse of everyday courage. Most of my regrets are not of things I did but of things I should have done. My moral compass was pointing in the right direction, but for some reason, my lack of courage persuaded me to ignore it. The good that came from those incidents was that they inspired me to promise myself that I would never do those things again.

The purpose of memory isn't just to remember the past but, more importantly, to stop us from repeatedly doing stupid or wrong things. Just as physical pain alerts us that something in our body is wrong, guilt alerts us that something we've done is wrong. Regret, shame, and losing self-respect brought on by the guilt for a lapse of moral courage are powerful motivators to never to do it again. They are the mental prosecutors of your conscience. Guilt can be a powerful compass. The regret and shame may grow fainter without ever fading entirely. Often, the hardest person to forgive, even for a minor slip of moral cowardice, is yourself. That "bitter taste" usually goes away only when you've redeemed yourself.

In the following pages, let's consider Gate's pearls of wisdom and resurrect a time when you faced each of these challenges. Consider how you responded and what you learned from the experience. Here are the five pieces of advice he offered:

- Chart a new course.
- Do what's right and not just what's popular.
- Stand alone.
- Act.
- Speak truth to power.

COURAGE TO CHART A NEW COURSE

Maintainers are caretakers and conformers, while leaders are creators and transformers. Maintainers follow the script while leaders write the script.[8] As a leader, you don't have the luxury of choosing your problems or determining when they might appear. Sometimes, they'll come at you in a steady and relentless procession, other times in a cluster bomb.[9] Leaders too often face resistance to change with the retort, "It's the way we have always done it." Many problems, if not most, are only solved by changing the way they've been done in the past. It takes courage to chart a new course or to drop the old course altogether.

In 1774, George Washington was faced with a bigger danger of losing his army to the scourge of smallpox than he was of losing it to the enemy. For years, the course of action for dealing with smallpox was to quarantine those who were infected. Against monumental opposition from Congress, his generals, and his confidants, Washington charted a new course in dealing with the smallpox epidemic by adopting a new and unproven concept: inoculation. Inoculation differs from today's practice of vaccination because, with the former, they actually infected the person with smallpox. The risks were high, but he had the courage to change how things had always been done. In Washington's example, charting a new course was a matter of life and death. But in every arena and at every level, where and when necessary, today's leaders need to display the moral courage to change the way "it's always been done," even against risk and opposition.

Courage to Change Yourself

During my fifty years as a leader, in and out of uniform, I witnessed more than a few leaders get hammered by a heavy blow that knocked them off their feet. They experienced some devastating professional or personal blow: fired, laid off, downsized/rightsized, missed a promotion, lost an account, divorce, illness, or death, to mention a few. In some cases, they clearly owned the setback. They deserved what they got because of an unacceptable personal flaw or some catastrophic error of judgment. In other cases, they didn't own it because they were simply victims of unfortunate serendipity, some random bad luck utterly beyond their control. Bad things do happen to good people. I know of several rising superstars skyrocketing to professional greatness who, when blindsided by their first major derailment, deserved or undeserved, never recovered. They didn't have the courage to chart a new course, so they continued down the same old path. As a result, they seemed to fall into a malaise, blaming providence and others for their misfortune. In the worst of these cases, they fell victim to alcoholism, depression, and a life constantly focused on blaming others and hating the world for their life's situation.

Author Carlos Castaneda contrasts those who wallow in their misfortune versus those who rise above it as "the difference between an ordinary man and a warrior—a warrior takes everything as a challenge, while the ordinary man takes everything as a blessing or a curse."[10] Castaneda's warriors are those leaders who, when knocked down, regardless of whether they deserved it or not, resiliently bounce back because they have the courage to chart a new course. Warriors realize they must change to overcome some misfortune to survive and thrive. To paraphrase Winston Churchill, who experienced repeated professional failures and disappointments: Success is not final, failure is not fatal; it is the courage to continue that counts. Courage is going from failure to failure without losing enthusiasm.[11] If you haven't failed, you're probably playing it too safe; you're probably a Maintainer. Charting a new course after a personal or professional misfortune takes courage. As weather shapes mountains, problems shape leaders.[12]

COURAGE TO DO WHAT'S RIGHT, NOT JUST POPULAR

Without the courage to do what's right, regardless of the ramifications, one is not worthy to be called a leader.[13] A true test of a leader's moral courage is the willingness to stand up under pressure and make hard choices even when unpopular. Many don't, and many won't, but some do. In

> **"If you want to make everyone happy, don't be a leader, sell ice cream."**
> **—Steve Jobs**

the early years of WWII, the British Army found itself backed up against the sea and about to be soundly defeated by a far superior German Army. More than 330,000 soldiers, basically the entire British Army, were packed around the small village of Dunkirk, praying for some form of evacuation across the twenty-three-mile English Channel. Initially, it was believed that only 5,000 to 6,000 thousand men could be evacuated before Hitler attacked. Winston Churchill, then England's prime minister, made a very unpopular decision. He gave the order that only able-bodied soldiers would be evacuated. The more than 13,000 wounded soldiers would be left behind and evacuated only after the able-bodied soldiers were successfully on British soil. He knew that for any possibility of survival, Britain needed every able-bodied man who could be saved. At the time of the decision, there was no doubt that the wounded soldiers were doomed to fall into the hands of the Germans. It was something that Churchill didn't want to do. It was a decision his closest advisors vehemently argued against. But he did it anyway. He had the courage to do what was right even though it was hugely unpopular. His decision was based on the greater good for Britain at the expense of popularity and public opinion.[14] Churchill had a lifelong willingness to embrace unpopular causes and, just as bravely, to reject popular ones.[15] More on his decision later

Many of today's politicians are accused of doing what's popular rather than doing what's right. They follow the polls and desires of their "base" rather than do anything that would be deemed unpopular with that base. The problem with that strategy is if you follow the crowd, you'll never be followed by the crowd. As a leader, you need to have the courage to be unpopular when necessary. You must have the moral courage to make hard decisions. Too many people wrongly confuse leadership with popularity. As Rosalynn Carter put it, "A leader takes people where they don't necessarily want to go but ought to go." Many Maintainers have such a strong need to be liked or loved that it wreaks havoc on their resolve when called upon to do the right thing, if it's unpopular or onerous. They would rather be liked than do what's required: setting high standards, correcting people, or sacrificing personal popularity for the organization's greater good. Sure, most of us want to be liked, but sometimes, decisions that benefit the greater good are those that make us unpopular.

Courage to Accept Responsibility

Leaders must not only make unpopular decisions but also accept responsibility for them. Maintainers who rationalize or deny responsibility when an organization fails or doesn't meet expectations are moral cowards. A few days after the successful D-Day landings, General Eisenhower's aide found a crumpled note in the dustbin next to Eisenhower's desk:

Woulda, Shoulda, Coulda

A peer or boss made an off-color and inappropriate joke in front of you and your employees. Even though your gut told you to say something, you just laughed at the joke and did nothing. Your fear of the boss's retribution or your peers' disdain kept you silent and showed your employees that what the boss did was OK.

If I Could Have a "Do-Over"

When you rewind this incident in your mind, you have the courage to politely correct the offender so your employees can see you don't accept that type of behavior. You've mind-gamed the incident many times and promised yourself if it ever happens again, you'll handle it differently.

> "Our landings in the Cherbourg-Havre area have failed to gain a satisfactory foothold, and I have withdrawn the troops. My decision to attack at this time and place was based upon the best information available. The troops, the air, and the Navy did all that bravery and devotion to duty could do. If any blame or fault attaches to the attempt, it is mine alone."

Eisenhower's intelligence briefings predicted that 25 percent of the more than 155,000 men would be casualties during the first day of the largest amphibious landing in history. He was told that the success of his army in the face of a well-trained, well-equipped, and battle-hardened enemy was by no means certain. Ike was a leader of great moral courage, and if the invasion of Normandy had failed, this was the message he would have presented to the world. Of course, the allied forces prevailed on D-Day, and Eisenhower had the pleasure of passing praise for success to the troops rather than having to accept responsibility for their failure. Few leaders in history have had his moral courage and character. Leaders who stand in the spotlight and take responsibility when things go poorly earn more than respect.[16] They earn trust.

COURAGE TO STAND ALONE

Standing alone can be lonely. As the old saying goes, "It's lonely at the top." Leaders must be ready to deflect criticism by developing psychological toughness and a thick skin. The higher you go in an organization, the lonelier it will become and the thicker your mental armor will have to be. You must do the right thing—what your knowledge, experience, and gut tells you to do. Delivering bad news, giving negative feedback, or axing pet projects takes courage. Being the bad guy isn't natural or comfortable for most people. You must be tough enough to withstand excessive pressure from your superiors, peers, and subordinates who may not like your decisions or your positions.[17] It takes courage.

An extraordinary example of the courage to stand alone was demonstrated in WWII during the infamous Bataan Death March. Twelve thousand American and 63,000 Filipino soldiers were captured by the Japanese and marched sixty-five miles in the jungle to a prisoner-of-war camp. More than 10,000 of the prisoners died or were executed during the five-day march. When the survivors of the march reached the POW camp, a hasty open-air hospital was established for the wounded and sick, who were dying at a rate of 400 per day. The senior doctor at the make-shift hospital decided to hoard the few medicines they had for the prisoners who seemed likely to survive. In his judgment, giving antibiotics to the most severe cases, who were probably going to die shortly was, in effect, wasting the drugs. Many of his fellow doctors and Army senior officers were adamantly against that decision. It must have been excruciatingly painful for that doctor to stand alone with that decision; it took great moral courage. Sometimes, you must have the courage to choose the least terrible option and then stand by it alone!

Leaders have a responsibility to make decisions for the greater good of the group, which at times may anger some people, but that's inevitable. Trying to be liked by everybody is impossible. It takes courage to be callous when it's in the best interest of the organization.[18] Sometimes, the only way to go is the hard way. Whatever course you decide upon, there will always be someone to tell you that you're wrong and critics of your actions and decisions. Sometimes, it's natural to be tempted to believe that your critics are right. Ralph Waldo Emerson advises us on how to fight the paranoia all leaders will experience at one time or another: "To map out a course of action and follow it to the end requires courage." The burden of leadership is that it's the repository of problems, many of which don't have easy solutions. Leaders often find themselves in situations where they're forced to choose a course of action that's the least distasteful. In these cases, where the only bad decision is the one not made, you have to fall back on your ability to be comfortable being uncomfortable.

Courage to Face Reality When No One Else Will

We need the stand-alone courage to face life as it is, not as we hope it to be. Hope is not a method. Many Maintainers want the comfort, the perks, and the power of being a leader without the worry. So, to avoid worry, they refuse to read the writing on the wall. I'm constantly amazed at the smart people who refuse to acknowledge the elephant in the room. You'll never convince me that no one in the financial industry knew the 2008 mortgage bubble was going to burst. Or that not one of the hundreds of senior executives at Enron knew the company was just one grand Ponzi scheme. Or that the heads of many TV and movie studios had no suspicions that several of their senior executives, as well as some star employees, were abusing their female employees.

Who really believes that over the course of fourteen years and 265 accusations, not one Michigan State University administrator had any inclination that they had a doctor who was repeatedly sexually abusing young female Olympic athletes? There's no doubt that there were those who had at least some suspicions of his misdeeds and did nothing. There were many in his pecking order who refused to face reality by ignoring rumors, turning a blind eye to the pleas of the victims, or disregarding their gut feeling that something was awry. They denied the obvious because it was too difficult to accept. Not one person had the courage to do the right thing.

That degree of self-denial exists in all arenas and levels of leadership. Leaders cannot wait for problems to come to them. They must face reality by having the moral courage to look for, root out, and expose problems. Don't shirk from looking below the surface because you're afraid of what you might find. It only takes one person to have the courage to do the right thing, even if it requires standing alone. Standing alone is working without a net, and that's why it takes courage. David stood alone against Goliath, and look how that turned out.

COURAGE TO ACT

If you're brutally honest with yourself, there's probably a time in your past when your courage as a leader didn't measure up—a time when you didn't have the courage to act. These less-than-proud moments in our lives can run the spectrum, from a minor lapse of everyday courage to outright moral cowardice. Often, these "I-wish-I-could-forget" incidents are acts of omission rather than acts of commission, things we wished we'd done rather than things we regret having done. The courage to act requires overcoming fear, making a decision, and having the courage to act so your followers see you're confident in your decision. Sometimes, it just takes one person to act to start an avalanche of action.

> "All evil needs to prevail is for good men to do nothing."
> —Edmund Burke, British statesman

Courage to Overcome Fear

Courage to act defines the leader.[19] The lack of courage to act comes from our inability to overcome fear. Worry makes cowards of us all.[20] In our mental battle between having the courage to do what we know we should and our fear of doing it, we cannot let our courage be defeated by our fears. Perhaps it's fear of failure, confrontation or conflict, rejection, or reprisal that defeats our courage. For whatever reason, when we don't act when we know we should, it's usually because of some level of fear. Earlier, we discussed the concept of getting comfortable being uncomfortable. As a leader, problems, conflicts, and surprises are a given. *Expect them.*

General Jim Mattis teaches us, "You don't always control your circumstances, but you can always control your response." If you can get comfortable being uncomfortable and learn to expect the unexpected, you won't be shocked or surprised when they happen. Leaders must often appear fearless when they aren't. Ryan Pitts, a Medal of Honor recipient from the Afghan conflict, said, "Courage is not the absence of fear; it is the ability to move forward in the face of it."

Courage Is a Source of Hope in Tough Times

In his great novel, *Once an Eagle*, Anton Myrer depicts his main character, Sam Damon, as a leader who could inspire hope, confidence, and strength in the most desperate situations. On a battlefield where all hope for survival was lost, Damon arrived on the scene and calmly led the unit to victory. One of the men who had lost all hope of surviving the battle later commented of Damon, "Just to look at him was to give you courage." Damon was a fictional depiction of those leaders who can be depended on to act courageously in a disaster. He had that quiet courage that gave hope where there was none.

Not only is fear injurious to leading effectively, but it's also highly contagious. Leaders must be a source of hope, optimism, and strength during the tough times. Followers watch their leaders closely in stressful and crisis situations, struggling to determine how much confidence the leader has in surviving the situation. Leaders must become masters of demonstrating self-confidence, calm, and self-assuredness. The aura of confidence, or the lack thereof, creates either calm or panic in those being led. Followers can handle tough times if properly addressed and communicated by a courageous leader. You must have the courage to appear strong and be strong enough to lead even when the sky is falling around you.

COURAGE PERSONIFIED

Xerxes at Thermopylae:

"We will shoot so many arrows at you, it will block out the sun."

Leonidas' reply:

"This is pleasant news; we shall have our battle in the shade!"

COURAGE TO SPEAK TRUTH TO POWER

I would add to Gate's pearl of wisdom that we must have the courage to be objective and honest with our bosses *and* those we lead. Leaders must "speak truth up *and down*." We must have the courage to tell hard truths, whether to those we serve or those who serve us.

Speaking Truth Up to Those in Power

We must have the courage to deliver bad news up and challenge authority when it's necessary for the greater good. We can learn much from General Jim Mattis on the frustrations and perils of speaking truth to power. Throughout his career, from young Marine lieutenant to seasoned secretary of defense, Mattis had a reputation for giving those he served straight talk and candid opinions. His leadership philosophy of providing opposing opinions to his bosses only privately and always accompanied by recommended solutions is a successful recipe for "speaking truth to power." In his memoir, *Call Sign Chaos*, we learn of many instances where he demonstrated the moral courage to take the bad news up. On more than a few occasions, he advised senior leaders and presidents that, in his professional judgment, their strategy was misguided or, as he put it, "They were walking into minefields of their own making." At times, his recommendations were accepted, and at times, his proposals fell on deaf ears. What's so admirable about General Mattis is that whether his judgment was accepted or rejected, he obeyed without mental reservation and carried out every order to the best of his ability.[21]

There are risks to speaking truth to power. In 2012, as a four-star general and commander of central command (CENTCOM) responsible for all military forces in Iraq and Afghanistan, General Mattis argued against the White House's strategic direction in both these theaters. While he fully endorsed civilian control of the military, his sense of duty wouldn't allow him to stay silent when he disagreed with the administration's decisions about his area of responsibility. Because of that courage to speak truth to power, he paid a price. Shortly after voicing his arguments against the administration's proposed strategy, he learned via "an unauthorized phone call" that he would be fired in one hour. It takes moral courage to speak truth to power, especially when you know those in power don't want to hear the uncomfortable truth. At times, moral courage to do what you know is right will come at a personal or professional cost. General Mattis understood that sometimes you must be willing to offend entrenched interests and alienate important constituencies to do the right thing.[22] But as they say, "A clear conscience is a soft pillow."

Speaking Truth Down to Those We Lead

Research conducted by the Ken Blanchard Group found that 8 in 10 employees said their managers didn't provide them with any professional feedback. A majority, 6 in 10, said their managers didn't develop their people well enough.[23] The management literature is full of advice on how to give feedback to employees. In my consulting life, a major weakness I see in many senior managers is their inability to provide useful feedback if it borders on being negative. I would go as far as to say that most people don't receive honest and useful feedback from their bosses. Empty praise is running rampant in the workplace. Too many managers are afraid that giving negative feedback will harm the employee's self-esteem and damage their relationship with their employees. Too often, a supervisor will think, *If I tell this employee he has a behavioral problem, it will turn into a confrontation, and I don't want to have that with him.* Managers who are hesitant to provide the truth about poor performance because they fear the consequences are cowards; they lack moral courage. Placing harmony over truth has always been and still is a recipe for failure.

Being Nice May Be Nice, But Sometimes It's Poor Leadership

Sometimes, you should cut your losses quickly and not try to be too "nice." It's tough to be tough, but it's an arrow leaders must have in their quiver to draw and shoot when needed. My easygoing manner was my best and worst trait. I kept losers for too long. I held on to the belief that I could change every flawed subordinate over time with good leadership. I was more than naïve—I was wrong. It's not good enough to be right, good, nice, and easy to work with. Sometimes, you have to muster the courage to do the hard things.

The former Prime Minister of Great Britain, Tony Blair, once said, "The art of leadership is saying no, not saying yes. It is extremely easy to say yes." It's not always a Norman Rockwell scene in organizations. Sometimes, you have to be tough and use frontier justice to teach an important lesson. Your empathy for people must never cloud your judgment for doing what's best for the greater good or for excusing wrongdoing.[24] I'm not saying revert to Dictator behavior. Niceness and kindness aren't the same. Rarely, if ever, is there a need to be unkind. You can be the toughest, most demanding leader on the planet and still treat people with respect and dignity.[25]

> "I cannot give you the formula for success, but I can give you the formula for failure:
> Try to please everybody."
> —*Herbert Swope,*
> *Pulitzer Prize winner*

Some circumstances may require that you demonstrate firmness and the courage to be honest and do things that are uncomfortable. On occasion, the cannons must be fired and a little heat in your voice is necessary and appropriate. Unethical or illegal behavior, moral misconduct, and blatant disregard for organizational culture or rules are a few instances when a little heat in your voice is necessary and appropriate. When you ignore or deny the existence of an abusive or toxic subordinate on your team, those you lead will consider you complicit in their abuse and misconduct. Leadership positions are, by nature, positions of authority. When a person doesn't acknowledge, assert, and enforce their authority when it's needed to right a wrong or correct a missed standard, they have, by default, established the acceptable standard. That which is accepted or tolerated becomes the norm. Leaders must recognize the difference between being firm and enforcing standards and being mean, nasty, and cruel.

When I conduct leadership training with companies, I'm often pulled aside by a senior leader who will ask me to focus on a staff member: "Would you work with Jeff, the director of operations? He's demeaning and abrasive toward his fellow directors. He's not a team player, and no one wants to work with him." When this happens, and it does more frequently than you'd expect, I ask that senior leader if I may see Jeff's latest performance evaluation. I can't tell you how many times I see that Jeff's performance review stated, "You're doing a great job. Keep it up." When I ask why Jeff's abrasiveness wasn't addressed in his annual evaluation and why he doesn't tell Jeff now that his behavior is unacceptable, I get a list of excuses: "He's been here longer than me." "We both competed for my job, and I got it." "He'll be retiring in a year, and I'm just waiting him out."

> **"I learned that courage was not the absence of fear, but the triumph over it. The brave man is not he who does not feel afraid, but he who conquers that fear."**
> —*Nelson Mandela*

Managers who have to hire a consultant to counsel their employees about their bad behavior or poor performance lack the everyday courage to lead. Managers who ignore abusive employees or don't provide honest feedback to nonperformers may think no one notices, but everyone does. Managers who lack everyday courage erode their employees' trust in their leadership. More than a few times, I've witnessed a manager ignore, deny, or delude himself about the negative impact a single rotten apple is having on his organization. In every case, it cost him the trust of his employees. Sometimes, you just have to get your hands dirty.

Afterthought: Leadership Ventriloquism

It takes courage to do the hard things yourself, rather than handing the unpleasant tasks to one of your subordinates or someone else. There's a great TV commercial where an office manager has his assistant deliver the bad news to his employees that they'll have to work late on Friday night. The following week, he makes a big production of personally delivering good news to his employees, announcing that he's so glad to let them know that he's letting everyone off early on that Friday. It's called "leadership ventriloquism" when a manager has someone else do the dirty work of delivering the bad news because he's too cowardly to do it himself.

Managers should personally deliver any painful or unpleasant news to their employees, embracing it as their responsibility. Look them in the eye and convey the truth, no matter how uncomfortable it may be. It's moral cowardice not to do the hard things yourself. The cold hard fact is that being a leader is not for the faint of heart.

Afterthought: Fishing for Truth

The higher you go in the organization, the harder it becomes to get honest feedback from those you lead. The future of those you lead depends on your opinion of them. Most, if not all, employees will withhold any criticism of your leadership unless you make them feel safe and comfortable doing so. No one is immune from "The emperor has no clothes syndrome." Tom Brady was once asked, "What's one thing you have too much of? He replied:

"I have too many people who tell me too many nice things. I feel like I need a more critical evaluation of certain things. So many people want to try to please me. A lot of people don't want to let me down. But it's nice to get a real straight, truthful answer."

Summary Points

- Everyday courage is doing things you're afraid to do but also doing the things you:
    - Don't want to do.
    - Don't like to do.
    - Don't feel comfortable doing.
- Courage is the quality that guarantees all others.
- It takes moral courage to:
    - Chart a new course and change how things have always been done.
    - Do what's right, not what's just popular.
    - Accept responsibility for your decisions, regardless of the outcome.
    - Stand alone and do the right thing against opposition or personal risk.
    - Face reality, even when others will not.
    - Act even when afraid.
    - Be a source of hope in troubled times.
    - Do the hard and unpopular things yourself.
    - Speak the truth to your bosses, employees, and peers.

If you're comfortable with all aspects of your *courage*, go to the next chapter. If not, "Look in the Mirror" below.

Look in the Mirror at My Courage

Review the following statements, then *underline* where you are and *circle* where you want to be:

- **My *moral courage* is:**
  - Poor / Mediocre / OK / Good / Excellent
- **My courage to speak the truth to my bosses is:**
  - Poor / Mediocre / OK / Good / Excellent
- **I provide positive feedback to my employees:**
  - Never / Occasionally / Frequently / All the Time
- **I provide negative feedback to my employees:**
  - Never / Occasionally / Frequently / All the Time
- **My willingness to change doing things the old way is:**
  - Poor / Mediocre / OK / Good / Excellent
- **I am willing to do the right thing even when it's unpopular:**
  - Never / Occasionally / Frequently / All the Time
- **I accept responsibility for my decisions:**
  - Never / Occasionally / Frequently / All the Time
- **I willingly accept responsibility for team failures and setbacks:**
  - Never / Occasionally / Frequently / All the Time
- **I am a source of hope and a can-do spirit in the tough times:**
  - Never / Occasionally / Frequently / All the Time
- **I have the courage to take appropriate action with nonperformers:**
  - Never / Occasionally / Frequently / All the Time
- **I do those things I do not want to do but are necessary:**
  - Never / Occasionally / Frequently / All the Time
- **I do those things I don't feel comfortable doing but are necessary:**
  - Never / Occasionally / Frequently / All the Time

- **I win the battle with the fear of failure:**
  - Never / Occasionally / Frequently / All the Time
- **I avoid confrontation even when it is necessary:**
  - Never / Occasionally / Frequently / All the Time
- **I am comfortable being uncomfortable:**
  - Never / Occasionally / Frequently / All the Time
- **My reputation for having moral courage is:**
  - Poor / Mediocre / Good / Excellent

What Aspect(s) of My Courage Could Use Improvement?

Example: I've always hated confrontation. My biggest weakness is my reluctance to enforce standards with marginal or nonperforming employees. Because I don't like confrontation and conflict, I do all I can to avoid both. I also wait too long, only addressing it when forced to. My employees know I see the marginal employees and non-performers, and they see my lack of action. It's eroding their trust in my leadership.

I Want to Improve:

My Philosophy on Courage

Example: I will establish a team culture where everyone feels free to have the courage to live the values we espouse by setting the example. I will take responsibility for addressing those in my organization who are marginal or non-performing, a weakness I have had in the past.

My Philosophy on Courage:

My Action Plan

Example: I cannot continue to sidestep issues that have uncomfortable outcomes. As a result, I have avoided giving negative feedback to several of my employees who need to improve their work. I will personally address the nonperformance of three of my current employees immediately.

My Action Plan:

12

PASSION

"Nothing great in the world has not been without passion."
—Georg Wilhelm Fredrich Hegel, philosopher

HENRY DAVID THOREAU boldly stated that most men live lives of quiet desperation.[1] You may consider him a little melodramatic in his accusation, but I contend that from a leadership perspective, he is spot-on. Many managers and supervisors are Maintainers who unenthusiastically muddle through their supervisory roles while their employees live lives of quiet desperation. As managers and supervisors, they may have started as energetic and ambitious, but as they aged, they became passive, cynical, distilled versions of their former selves. They lack passion for anything but the status quo while waddling through their working lives banging from side to side in a rut of general disinterest. Maintainers spend their energy trying not to lose, while leaders spend their energy trying to win. The very worst Maintainers live in that rut of mediocrity, complacency, and apathy without displaying an ounce of enthusiasm for what they do or taking even a minor interest in those they lead.

There was a time when I was one of those Maintainers who unenthusiastically muddled through my supervisory role. The adage goes, "If you can find a job you love, you'll never have to work." This often-heard maxim foretells that people in jobs they love are more fulfilled than those in vocations that just pay the bills. I've experienced both sides of the coin. I spent the first two-thirds of my professional life in a job I loved—one that got me excited to go to work each morning. In that job, I passionately gave 110 percent effort for every day of those thirty years.

When I retired from the Army, I went from being a soldier to being a businessman. I'm naturally curious and thrive on learning and experiencing new worlds. My first few years in the private sector were exciting because I was absorbed in learning new and entirely different skills. However, once I was on the backside of the learning curve, my enthusiasm for what I was doing started to wane. I lost my passion; my mental batteries were slowly draining. I realized that my new life's purpose of fielding carbonated beverage dispensers wasn't something that gave me a meaningful purpose. Don't misinterpret what I'm saying as a slam against the leaders I worked for or the great people I met in the private sector. Coke and Cornelius were great companies, led and staffed by people passionate about producing the best products in the market and intensely proud of what they were doing. It wasn't them; it was me. I wasn't getting any personal satisfaction from what I was doing. More importantly, I wasn't giving my best effort to my employer or those I was leading. The man I saw in the mirror was a Maintainer. My bosses and team complemented my leadership, but they didn't know my heart wasn't in it. I hid it well.

True North author Bill George describes a leader's "sweet spot" as the intersection of your motivations and your greatest strengths. He states, "Operating in your sweet spot you are aligned with your True North and have the greatest opportunities to make a difference in the world."[2] I came to realize something I always knew: I need a leadership challenge that's focused on growing something, not maintaining it. I also need to have a purpose that serves some-

THE SWEET SPOT

"I get to do what I like to do every single day of the year. I tap dance to work, and when I get there, it's tremendous fun."
—*Warren Buffett, CEO, Berkshire Hathaway*

thing other than myself. My passion and, therefore, my sweet spot was improving organizations and teaching and coaching people in those organizations to be better leaders.

When I was asked to be the president of Via Global, a company that fit right into my sweet spot, I jumped at the opportunity. After several great years at Via Global, I decided to leave the corporate world. Ever since, I've continued to live in my sweet spot, teaching, coaching, and mentoring aspiring leaders. In that capacity, I'm fulfilled and inspired to continue in this sweet spot as long as I can. For many, finding that sweet spot never happens. So, how do you find *your* sweet spot? To answer that question, there are a few things to consider.

Passion isn't just about demonstrated enthusiasm. It's a deep-seated desire to accomplish something. The first step is wanting.[3] You have to want something bad enough to keep going when your mind and your body and everyone else is telling you to quit. Athletes, even those with raw talent and lucky DNA, must be passionate about achieving greatness in their sport. At some point, it comes down to who has the desire and drive to persevere through the boredom of repetitive training regimens, injuries, and no social life.

Like athletes, leaders must have the psychological adrenaline and passion to persevere and survive the exertion that comes with being a leader. What separates Leaders from Maintainers is that a leader has a desire to take an endeavor, an organization, an idea, or a group of people to a better place. In contrast, Maintainers just want to get by to survive. To put it bluntly, being a leader is about getting out of the safety of the foxhole, fixing bayonets, and attacking problems rather than hiding in the foxhole, avoiding conflict, and hoping problems will just disappear.

Leaders are motivated because some endeavor excites them, and they want to make a difference. They believe in what they're doing and want others to feel the same. If you don't like the word "passion," how about enthusiasm, zeal, excitement, desire, spirit, hutzpah, emotion, fervor, or even obsession? You pick it. I'm sticking with passion because it best describes what it takes to be a Leader rather than a Maintainer. If you're not passionate, excited, or enthusiastic about what you're doing, then you can't expect those you lead to be passionate, excited, or enthusiastic about what *they're* doing.

A nationwide survey conducted by the Harris Interactive, a market research firm, found that only 20 percent of employees feel passionate about their jobs.[4] If your employees aren't enthusiastic about what they're doing, they won't commit to engaging in its success. As poet Johann Fredrick Shiller warns us, "Enthusiasm [passion] is that kindling spark which marks the difference between the leaders in every activity and the laggards who just put in enough just to get by." Passion is what inspires us to do the hard things. Gates told the US Naval Academy graduating class, "Passion is a strength of purpose and belief in a cause or endeavor that reaches out to others, touches their hearts, and makes them eager to follow." It's the difference between being a Leader or a Maintainer.

Are You Passionately Leading or Disinterestedly Maintaining?

I like to paraphrase Shakespeare's quote on greatness ("Some men are born great…") to make the point that the path to leadership is different for everyone. Only a few are born to the role of leader; the Queen Elizabeth IIs are rare. Some people aspire to lead and do what they must to achieve that aspiration, while others come to leadership by chance or necessity. Most start as individual contributors or trainees and work hard to do what it takes to prove their potential before they earn the role of leader. Then there are those who have leadership thrust upon them, even though they didn't aspire to lead. As a result of some circumstance, they find themselves with leadership responsibilities. Regardless of your path, you must project to your employees that you want to be holding the reins and you want to be their leader.

Earlier, I asked you to consider the question: What are your motives for leading? Is being a leader an onerous job you must endure to, as Thoreau puts it, "fill a void in our lives with money, possessions, and accolades"? Or are you motivated by something greater than yourself? If your motivation to lead is strictly self-serving, those you lead will know. People without passion beyond their own selfish interests are seen as narcissists. Being passionate for something besides yourself provides the motivation and energy to take on the burdens of leadership. When you're passionate, you want to mobilize others to achieve your goal. Achieving sustained organizational success is only possible by inspiring followers to produce unremitting high performance. That level of effort can only be maintained for the long haul if it's motivated by an intense emotion and commitment that compels you towards *something*. The "something" I keep referring to can be your job, people, organizations, ideas, religion, causes—any endeavor that focuses on something other than yourself. When you believe in something passionately, the force of your convictions will ignite that same level of passion in those you lead.

You Can't Fake It Until You Make It

One way to quickly lose your employees' trust is to give a fake impression of enthusiasm with half-hearted acts of cheerleading, back-slapping, and good ol' boy glad-handing. If your passion isn't real, those you lead will instantly sense your insincerity and you'll be seen as a fraud.

You can demonstrate passion to those you lead in many ways. If you're a pro football fan, you know Bill Belichick, the past coach of the famously successful New England Patriots, whom I discussed in Chapter 2. Belichick is a stoic introvert who rarely exhibits any emotion, regardless of the situation. It's been said that his smile comes out "once every seventeen years, like a cicada."[5] If you compare his six Super Bowl wins with the game he lost in 2019, you'll see that the only difference in his demeanor and appearance at the end of the game is the color of his hoodie. In contrast, Kirby Smart, the current head football coach at the University of Georgia, is a physically excitable extrovert who exhibits volcanic emotions in almost every game. He gets so enthusiastic that he needs a human leash to grab his belt and keep him off the playing field. Belichick doesn't outwardly demonstrate his enthusiasm, but his players have no doubt he's passionate about winning and their well-being. They see it in his self-effacing demeanor and his forgoing of personal recognition in pursuit of higher team goals.

Even though Belichick and Smart demonstrate their enthusiasm very differently, they're both deeply passionate about football, their players, and their team, and their sincerity is palpable to those they lead. Leaders demonstrate their passion by their actions. Enthusiastic behavior won't ring true unless it's authentic and sincere. Gratuitous cheerleading is counterproductive. It's not only seen as insincere, but manipulative. Manipulators cannot inspire trust. You can't fake it. You'll be discovered. The players on both the Patriots and University of Georgia teams know that their coach's passion is deep and sincere, even if they show it in extremely different ways. One is a grumpy old man. The other is a Jumpin' Jack Flash.

Passion Is Highly Contagious—So Is Complacency

Sincere passion is infectious and highly contagious, but a lack of or watered-down passion is just as infectious and contagious. Passion is the spice of life. It's what lights the fire in your belly to keep you going when frustration, fatigue, and failures try to knock you down. Without passion for what you do, leadership responsibilities can seem like a prison.

Look at the great leaders, past and present, who've drawn millions to their flame because of their passion: Queen Elizabeth II, Jeff Bezos, Richard Branson, Mahatma Gandhi, Bill Gates, Ruth Bader Ginsburg, Steve Jobs, Martin Luther King, Abraham Lincoln, and Nelson Mandela. Their passion provided the psychological adrenalin to fuel their resilience and sustained them through their long and hard leadership journeys. Regardless of their endeavor, they were the spark that ignited the passion in others to rally around their idea, dream, or cause. Passion was the critical factor to their success and longevity. Like moths to a flame, their enthusiasm and zeal drew people to them.

One of life's unfortunate realities is that there are some jobs that don't easily lend themselves to passionate execution, which makes it difficult for you as a leader to inspire commitment and engagement from your employees. If you find yourself in a position where marshaling your passion for the job is hard enough without having to muster it in your employees, you must make a choice. You can go down the path many take and join the ranks of the life-long Maintainers and accept that "It's just the way it is here, and there's nothing I can do about it." Or you can take the path less traveled and accept the challenge that "Even in this stagnant environment with mundane tasks, I'll have to be imaginative enough to find some way to inspire my employees to move beyond mere ho-hum compliance." By the very fact you're reading this book, I'm betting you're going to take the leader's path. Injecting excitement into a group of dispassionate, glazed-eyed cubical dwellers or any group of clock-watching employees who are living for the minute they can escape their workplace is tough but not impossible.

Sometimes You Have to Make a Silk Purse Out of a Sow's Ear

What does it take to make a silk purse out of a sow's ear? What it takes is to convince your employees that you genuinely believe in what you're doing and you're personally invested and passionate about your endeavor. It's hard to find passion if your job, task, or endeavor doesn't enthuse you to some degree, but you have to. (If you can't, now's an excellent time to move on to the next chapter of this book.) I know some situations, jobs, and environments can make that very difficult—I've been there. I've been in organizations where the mission required conducting the most arduous and unpleasant tasks under extremely miserable conditions with no end to the tasks or dreary conditions in sight. But even under these undesirable conditions, the organization was extremely high performing and the morale of its Organizational Patriots was sky-high. I've also been in an organization where life was a gravy train. It was great work environment, with subsidized lunches, free gym, no professional stress, and benefits galore. But even under these conditions, productivity was marginal and the morale of its

Organizational Mercenaries was adequate at best. There was no personal sense of purpose.

What was the difference? In the first example, the leader made the best of a bad situation by assuring his employees that what they were doing had a significant impact on the organization's success. Perhaps even more importantly, he conveyed that he deeply cared for them and had their best interests at heart. As a result, they were engaged, committed, and focused on getting the job done because they were convinced that what they did was meaningful. The leader's positive attitude ignited a spark of passion, creating a workplace atmosphere of camaraderie, optimism, and enthusiasm—people woke up. In contrast, the unenthusiastic Maintainer in the second example made the worst of a good situation by making no effort to give his employees a sense that they had any connection to the success of the organization's mission. Just as damning, his employees knew he didn't care about his job or them. As a result, they felt irrelevant and distant from their company's purpose.

There's an instinctive need for humans to align with something bigger than themselves, something important beyond their own self-interests. Leaders can help employees define what that is. Merely conveying to employees that what they do is essential will take the glaze out of their eyes. A leader's enthusiasm is often the catalyst for employees to turn from being docile and cynical serfs, keeping their heads down, into enthusiastic employees bursting with excitement. Those Maintainers who go about their business without passion or enthusiasm for what they do kill the souls of their employees. Without desire and enthusiasm and a passion for engaging others in achieving your goal, your leadership journey will be long and lonely. If you have no passion for what you do, neither will those you lead.

Summary Points

- Leaders have an intense passion compelling them to take action.
- Passion is expressed by leaders as enthusiasm, zeal, drive, desire, and ardor for something bigger than themselves.
- Leaders are uncomfortable with the status quo but constantly seek improvement.
- If you're not enthusiastic or excited about what you do, don't expect your employees to be enthusiastic or excited about what they do.
- Passion and enthusiasm are infectious, but so is a lack of these qualities.
- Passion for your endeavor is mental adrenaline.
- Passion is the difference between maintaining and leading.
- Passion must be sincere, not hollow or faked.
- You do not have to be a gratuitous cheerleader to express enthusiasm.

Are you adequately *passionate* about what you do? If so, go to the next chapter. If not, "Look in the Mirror" below.

Look in the Mirror at My Passion

Review the following statements, then *underline* where you are and *circle* where you want to be:

- **My *passion* for what I do professionally is:**
    - Nonexistent / Mediocre / OK / Good / Excellent
- **I show enthusiasm for what I do:**
    - Never / Occasionally / Frequently / All the Time
- **My ability to do what it takes to stay passionate about what we do is:**
    - Poor / Mediocre / OK / Good / Excellent
- **My belief that what my company does is important is:**
    - Poor / Mediocre / OK / Good / Excellent
- **My employee's impression of my passion for what we do is:**
    - Poor / Mediocre / OK / Good / Excellent
- **My employees think my enthusiasm for what we do is:**
    - Poor / Mediocre / OK / Good / Excellent
- **My employee's passion for what they do is:**
    - Poor / Mediocre / OK / Good / Excellent
- **I do what it takes to inspire enthusiasm in my employees:**
    - Never / Occasionally / Frequently / All the Time

What Aspect(s) of My Passion Could Use Improvement?

Example: I am, by nature, an introvert. I don't visibly show that I'm enthusiastic about what we do enough. My introverted demeanor gives my employees the impression I'm a pessimist when, in fact, I'm an optimist. Unfortunately, the impression I give of lacking enthusiasm is being role-modeled by my employees.

I Want to Improve:

My Philosophy on Passion

Example: My leadership philosophy of passion is to convey the same level of enthusiasm to my employees that I feel for our common endeavor.

My Philosophy on Passion:

My Action Plan

Example: I can't change my demeanor, but I can be more conscious of my introversion and work on being more outwardly enthusiastic. I will continue to try to change my outward demeanor by being more engaged with my team and verbally advising them of my passion for what we do. I will seek feedback from my peers and employees to see if they notice a more positive demeanor going forward.

My Action Plan:

PART THREE

COMPETENCE—
WHAT LEADERS DO

13

THE POWER OF COMPETENCE

"When wealth is lost, nothing is lost; when health is lost, something is lost; when character is lost, all is lost."
—*Reverend Billy Graham*

IF CHARACTER IS the infrastructure of leadership, competence is the superstructure.[1] Character is necessary to gain trust, but competence is necessary to keep it—they go hand-in-hand. Character without competence is a recipe for failure. Your employees expect you to know your job. Before they'll fully commit to you and your endeavor, they must be confident that not only do you have character worthy of their trust but that you also possess the competence to lead them to success. Trust is the currency of leadership, and like a savings account, you want to deposit more than you withdraw. Everything you do that demonstrates your competence is a deposit leading to more trust. Everything you do that demonstrates a lack of competence is a withdrawal, eventually leading to distrust. What are the essential leadership competencies needed to build a nest egg of trust, so when you need that full commitment, it's there?

We need to ask the more profound and important question, what does it take to earn the trust of your employees and gain their confidence in your competence? To answer that question, let's do as we did with George Washington and look at Ernest Shackleton, a role model of extreme competence, to see how he led a diverse team to accomplish an arduous task while earning his men's undying trust and confidence.

The Incredible Voyage

An extraordinary story of leadership skill and professional competency took place more than one hundred years ago in one of the world's most dangerous and inhospitable places. It's a rare story of a failed mission that was brilliantly led. You may say, "That's impossible. You can't fail in your mission and still be labeled a brilliant leader!" Well, let's see.

If you were to read this job posting on LinkedIn, would you go for the interview, especially after reading "small wages and safe return doubtful"?

MEN WANTED
for hazardous journey, small wages, bitter cold, long months of complete darkness, constant danger, safe return doubtful, honor and recognition in case of success.

Ernest Shackleton, 4 Burlington St.

The authenticity of this want ad is questionable, but in 1915, any voyage to the South Pole clearly implied these dangers. What's not in doubt is that for the twenty-eight crew members needed for the voyage, more than 5,000 applicants wanted aboard.[2] The question that's been asked many times about this adventure is, Why in the world would so many people willingly volunteer to board a ship headed for certain danger and potential disaster? The answer was the name at the bottom of the ad, Ernest Shackleton.

Shackleton's well-publicized success during two earlier Southern Hemisphere expeditions gave those who signed up for the voyage confidence that he had what it takes to get them through any dangers they'd face on the voyage. Shackleton was said to have a "talent—a genius even—of genuine leadership"[3] Those who enthusiastically volunteered for the expedition were very aware of the hazardous journey's "constant danger," but they had confidence in Shackleton's competence to lead them through those dangers. Was their trust in Shackleton's competence a mistake? You be the judge.

THE PLAN

Shackleton had a vision:

- Be the first expedition to traverse the 1,800-mile uncharted continent of Antarctica from sea to sea.
- Be the first British citizen to set foot on the South Pole.
- Safely return to England with all members of his crew.

The plan for the Imperial Trans-Atlantic Expedition, as Shackleton's adventure was to be known, was to depart England on the steam-engined, three-masted, 144-foot sailing ship, the *Endurance*. With twenty-eight men and sixty-nine dogs, they would sail a three-month voyage to South Georgia, a small island off the southern coast of South America, and resupply. From there, they would sail south on the Weddell Sea to the northern coast of Antarctica, where a team of seven, led by Shackleton, would disembark and cross the Antarctic continent from west to east. The seven men would walk and dogsled to the South Pole, plant a British flag, then traverse the remaining distance to the other side of the continent, an 1,800-mile journey. On the far side of Antarctica, they would be picked up by a ship and sail to Australia. Then the entire crew would sail back to Britain to be welcomed as heroes.

Even today, an expedition across Antarctica is incredibly hazardous, but in 1914, the trip was exponentially more dangerous. There were no maps or charts of the Antarctic. The unpredictable weather was unforgiving, with temperatures often dipping to ten to twenty degrees below zero. The expedition had none of the modern comforts polar explorers enjoy today: high-tech winter clothing, composite lightweight gear, and non-perishable, calorie-dense, freeze-dried meals. They also didn't have the safety features of modern technology: satellite communication, rescue helicopters, medicines, or emergency evacuation capabilities. Not only did they have to navigate without Google Maps or GPS, they didn't even have accurate charts to map their course. All they had was a compass and an 18th-century-technology sextant. Once they sailed away from South Georgia, they had no means to contact the outside world. They'd be totally on their own.

Men Plan and Mother Nature Laughs!

Everything went according to plan until it didn't, or as boxer Mike Tyson said more recently, "Everyone has a plan until they get punched in the mouth."

Three weeks after leaving South Georgia, they entered the Waddell Sea. Mother Nature started to laugh almost immediately, and Shackleton and the crew got their first "punch in the mouth." The *Endurance* found itself at a dead stop, frozen solid in the ice pack. Stymied and stuck, the plan started to quickly unravel. As one of the crew put it, "We are stuck like an almond in the middle of a chocolate bar." After several futile attempts, Shackleton realized there was no way to free the *Endurance*. He made the decision that the crew would stay on the ship and sail back to South Georgia in the spring thaw, which he knew was eleven months away.

CHART THE COURSE, LEAD, SUCCEED

The story of Ernest Shackleton and the voyage of the *Endurance* is a master class on what it takes to turn a potential disaster into a success. It's a great tale of what leaders do and how they earn a level of trust that inspires their charges to be fully committed and engaged in their endeavor. Shackleton's success was built on a foundation of strong character but was truly defined by his many leadership competencies. His professional skills as an explorer, sailor, and navigator, developed and honed during his formative years, were extraordinary. Whether in today's world or the 18th century, all leaders must master the competencies required to succeed.

Shackleton *charted the course* by clearly defining his *vision* of what he wanted to accomplish, his *purpose* for doing it, and his *expectations* of every crew member. Once every crew member understood the course to be charted, he demonstrated his competence by *leading by example*. Finally, he achieved *success* by turning a potential disaster into a *success* story. You may be asking, What relevance does this have to me? Today's leaders have the same responsibilities as Shackleton: *Chart the course, lead by example, and succeed*. It's as simple and as complicated as that. Let's look at Shackleton's expedition and his leadership to see what and how each element contributes to building trust.

CHART THE COURSE: *Vision, Purpose, Expectations*

Shackleton's experience on two earlier voyages to the Antarctic taught him the importance of ensuring that every sailor comprehended what they were signing up for. He informed each candidate of his *vision* for the journey before they boarded a ship headed for the most inhospitable part of the world. He understood that when men sign up for "constant danger" at "small wages," they must recognize that the importance of the expedition's *purpose* warrants that danger and those wages. Perhaps the most crucial lesson Shackleton learned from his earlier expeditions was the consequence of failing to ensure that each sailor clearly understood his *expectations* for their standards of conduct, teamwork, and individual work ethic. He spent considerable effort explaining to each sailor what he was expected to contribute, both as a member of the crew and individually. He went as far as to detail each sailor's specific role and why it was important to the entire mission, making sure they understood that they would be expected to "Maintain discipline, act as a team, and do their appointed duties to the best of their ability. Each of them had been chosen because they are an expert in their field. He emphasized that their skill was essential to the expedition's success; without them doing their job to the fullest, they risked the entire endeavor and the crew."

LEAD: *Situational Awareness, Decision-Making, Lead by Example*

Shackleton's competence was demonstrated daily through his behavior, actions, and decisions. He made his presence known by keeping his finger on the pulse of their situation and staying *situationally aware* of every aspect of their lives. The crew felt the impact of his leadership in his decisions, which affected their lives. He demanded nobility from himself and expected the same from those he led. He set the example of behavior he expected of his crew. When the *Endurance* became locked in ice, he was overcome by personal depression and abject disappointment. He was careful, however, not to show his disappointment to the men, and he cheerfully supervised the routine of readying the ship for the long winter ahead.[4] He inspired optimism by being unrelentingly optimistic, hard work by working hard, and perseverance by persevering.

To prove his empathy for the crew's situation, Shackleton made sure they saw that he shared the same hardships they were experiencing. He told his crew he would never ask them to do anything he would not do himself. He insisted on having the same treatment, food, and clothing as his crew and went out of his way to demonstrate his willingness to do the same menial chores he expected them to do. He occasionally became furious when he discovered that the cook had given him preferential treatment because he was the boss.[5] He taught the golden rule by living it.

Situational Awareness

Once Shackleton realized the *Endurance* couldn't be freed until the spring, he accepted the fact that he would have to forgo his vision of a transcontinental trek. His leadership focus shifted from exploration to survival. This is an important lesson that all leaders must learn: how to let go of goals and embrace new ones.[6] He knew spending the next eleven months locked in the ice would strain the men. Keeping a close watch on the crew's temperament, he adapted his leadership actions to address the vacillating moods of the crew. During weeks without light and warmth, there were times when depression, desperation, and fear reared their ugly heads. His challenge was to keep the crew focused on their duties in these foreboding circumstances. Here is how their situation was described:

> "In all the world there is not desolation more complete than the polar night. It is a return to the Ice Age: no warmth, no life, no movement. Only those who have experienced it can fully appreciate what it means to be without the sun day after day and week after week. Few men unaccustomed to it can fight off its effects altogether, and it has driven some men to madness.[7] Day after day after day dragged by in a gray, monotonous haze."[8]

Imagine the challenge of keeping an incredibly diverse collection of individuals made up of highly educated Cambridge University dons mixed in with a rough group of working-class Yorkshire fishermen happy and hopeful for nine months in these conditions. Living and working in close quarters, under constant stress and fear, will test the strongest of us.

To keep spirits up and the crew collaboratively working together in harmony, Shackleton was required to be both a thermometer and thermostat for everyone's temperament and morale. As a thermometer, he had to measure the temperature of melancholy, boredom, and hopelessness that naturally arises in desperate situations. He had a deep sense of the moods of the crew and adapted his leadership to address those different moods. When they showed signs of hopelessness and nervousness, he acted as a thermostat by dialing down the crew's psychological temperature with humor, competition, pranks, games, and extra food. When they became lethargic, despondent, and on complacent cruise control, he turned the psychological heat up by increasing the number of working parties, keeping them busy to get their minds off their misery.

After six months of things going relatively well living on the *Endurance*, Shackleton and his crew were once again to hear Mother Nature laugh at them. On November 9, the ice pack crushed the *Endurance*, smashing its hull. They'd been living on the ship for months, but when the ice tipped it on its side, they were forced to move into tents pitched on the frozen ocean surface, affectionately called "Ocean Camp." Now, they were marooned on an ice floe, on which they would drift for another five months.

On October 23, 1915, the tectonic shifts of the ice floes started to crush the tipped ship, and shortly after that, it sank into a watery abyss. As their ship slowly vanished into a large hole in the ice, the crew knew they were watching any hope of sailing out in the spring thaw disappear. With the loss of their ship, many of the crew fell into despair and started to lose hope of survival. As Nancy Koehn points out in her book *Forged in Crisis*, after the *Endurance* sank, leaving the men stranded on the ice with three small lifeboats, several tents, and a few supplies, Shackleton realized that he had to embody the new survival mission not only in what he said and did but also in his physical bearing and the energy he exuded.[9] To inspire his men to be resilient, he was resilient.

Decision-Making

Shackleton had little choice but to do something other than sit. Again, he was forced to make a tough decision. He could choose to:

- Stay where they were and wait until spring to sail out on the lifeboats.
- Send a small party north to the sea and hope they would return with a rescue party for the others.
- Take all the men and head to the sea.

Shackleton decided the safest option was to keep all the men together. They would take the three lifeboats and all the supplies they could carry and head north to the open sea. He commanded everyone to leave all nonessential items behind in Ocean Camp. He made a dramatic gesture of leaving his treasured gold cigarette case and a bible given to him by Queen Victoria to show the crew he wasn't asking them to do something he wouldn't do. He inspired sacrifice by being the first to sacrifice.

Shackleton's plan was to head north. The crew of twenty-seven men would push and pull the three twenty-three-foot lifeboats and seven large sleds over the ice to the open sea. When they encountered open water, they would load the sleds and men into the boats, sail to the next ice flow, then go back to pulling the boats and sleds over the ice until they reached water, and so on. When the boats were loaded with supplies and gear, each weighed close to 3,000 pounds.

Lead by Example

During the trek, food became a primary source of worry for Shackleton. With strict rationing, they were able to survive on the few food stores they carried and any wildlife the hunting parties could find: seals, penguins, and birds of all sorts. Eventually, however, desperation forced them to eat the dog food and, shortly after that, sadly for the entire crew, the dogs.

During the entire ordeal, the crew's trust in Shackleton's leadership continued to grow because he set the example he demanded of them. He led from the front. He shared in their hardships. He participated in hunting parties. He chipped in with the menial tasks. He lived in the same conditions as the crew. Four months and 346 hard miles later, they arrived at the uninhabited Elephant Island, where, on April 16, 1916, they stepped on dry land for the first time in 497 days.

Finally reaching dry land after almost seventeen months of living on unstable ice floes, they collectively let out a sigh of relief. Now that they were on an uninhabited island 800 miles from the nearest civilization, Shackleton's next big decision was, What do we do now? Again, the choices were few. He could:

- Keep the crew on the coast of Elephant Island and hope that a whaling ship would pass by and be lucky enough that the ship would see them.
- Risk all the crew getting in the three lifeboats, attempt an open-sea voyage, and hope to find the coast of South Georgia over 800 miles away.

- Send one lifeboat to South Georgia, risking fewer crew members' lives if the crossing failed. That still left most of the crew stranded on Elephant Island with a significant risk of never being found if the lifeboat didn't survive.

All three options depended on hope and uncertainty. All three were bad options. Shackleton was left with the unpleasant task of picking the least bad option.

There was little hope that a twenty-three-foot lifeboat could survive an 800-mile trip in the open sea. Even if they were lucky enough to stay afloat, there was little confidence they could find the needle in the open-sea haystack, South Georgia Island. Shackleton knew they had to do something. To put the fewest men in immediate danger, he made the decision that a small crew in one of the lifeboats would attempt to reach the Grytviken whaling station on South Georgia Island. By far, the best navigator on the *Endurance* was the first mate, Frank Worsley, and it would have been an easy decision for Shackleton to put Worsley in charge of the attempt while he stayed behind with the crew.

But as he did many times, he refused to ask those he led to do something he would not do himself. He repeatedly shared the same dangers that he asked of his crew. He would captain the single lifeboat with expert navigator Worsley and four others to South Georgia. If they made it there, they would commandeer a ship and return to Elephant Island to rescue those twenty-two men left behind. This plan put the least number of men in danger. The crew left behind would be relatively safe by supplementing their supply cache over the coming months by hunting.

Departing on April 24, 1916, Shackleton and his crew of five set sail in rough seas. Constantly at risk of being crushed by icebergs or capsized by killer whales, navigating with only a compass and the stars, they sailed in what they hoped was the right direction to the whaling station. Because of Wolsey's brilliant navigation skills and a full measure of luck, on their fifteenth day at sea, they spotted the southern shore of South Georgia Island after sailing 870 nautical miles. The winds were so extreme and the seas so treacherous when they reached the coastline, they had to sit offshore for an entire day before they could attempt to land the lifeboat.

Once ashore, they realized that the Grytviken whaling station was on the opposite side of the island. Again, Shackleton was faced with few choices. They could sail the 130 miles around the coast to the whaling station or hike the twenty-nine miles over the 10,000-foot mountain range to Grytviken. Shackleton decided to traverse the mountains on foot because the seas were so rough and the coastline so unfriendly. He would leave three men and the lifeboat behind and hike to the whaling station on the north shore with two of the strongest men. The hikers would traverse the mountain range, get a boat, and return to rescue the three men left behind. Then, they would commandeer a ship to return to Elephant Island to rescue the other twenty-two men. Phew! What an endeavor!

Soon after they set out on foot, they got lost because on the chart they carried, only the coastline of South Georgia was shown—and a great deal of that was missing. The interior was blank. Thus, they could be guided only by what they could see.[10] They pressed on without stopping for fear of freezing to death. Thirty-six hours and thirty-two miles later, after several thigh-burning climbs up 10,000-foot peaks, then having to slide down ice fields on their backsides, they spotted the Grytviken whaling station. The next day, May 22, 1916, Shackleton rescued the three men left on the other side of the island.

SUCCEED

Now, Shackelton had to rescue the twenty-two crew members on Elephant Island 870 miles away through an ocean that was becoming more frozen every day. He immediately started soliciting the local whalers and the British government for a rescue ship. After three failed attempts over four months, on the fourth attempt, Shackleton finally reached Elephant Island with a ship borrowed from the Chilean government. On August 30, 1916, all twenty-two stranded men were safely rescued.

Even though the Imperial Trans-Antarctic Expedition didn't achieve its' Antarctic goals, they returned to England as heroes. While they were gone, World War I started. The heroism of Shackleton and his crew was relayed to the British soldiers fighting on the western front in hopes it would keep their morale up. Shackleton was knighted by King Edward VII and was awarded several honors by the Royal Geographic Society and other prestigious British organizations. Moreover, England branded him a hero, and his crew considered him a savior. They knew that they wouldn't have survived without his strong leadership. They knew from start to finish that he possessed a deep-seated sense of responsibility for their survival.

Shackleton publicly accepted responsibility for the expedition's failure. He had a "consuming sense of responsibility," said Alfred Lansing, author of *Endurance: Shackleton's Incredible Voyage.* "He felt that he had gotten them into this situation, and it was his responsibility to get them out."[11] He was instilled with a deep sense of loyalty and obligation to his crew. The men understood this and, in turn, offered him their commitment.[12] He assumed ultimate responsibility for the failure of the expedition. He praised and credited the courage and resilience of his crew for their survival.

Shackleton failed in his mission to be the first expedition to traverse the Antarctic continent from coast to coast. Bad outcomes and failed missions seldom make for stories of great leadership. So, why is Shackleton placed on such a high pedestal in the pantheon of great leaders? There are many reasons for the expedition's failure; some can be attributed to poor planning and perhaps a small measure of hubris. However, most were due to factors far beyond Shackleton's control, specifically, the unpredictability of Mother Nature and plain old bad luck. The Weddell Sea froze months earlier than usual, which was much more severe than in past years.

What Can We Learn from Shackleton?

The purpose of telling Shackleton's story is to impress upon you the all-important relationship between leader competence and follower trust. Just as the *Endurance* crew had absolute trust in their captain to get them through any storm, your followers must have absolute trust that you can get them through any storm. This epic adventure is a great case study of what happens when a strong character is balanced with professional competence. It was Shackleton's reputation of character that inspired 5,000 men and three women to volunteer for the perilous mission. But it was his competence that brought all twenty-eight men safely back to England. Shackleton's most significant leadership achievement wasn't just sustaining but even growing the trust each crew member had in him over the perilous two-year expedition. The question is, What aspects of his leadership built that level of trust?

I consider the most significant lesson we can learn from Shackleton to be his ability to make his leadership known and felt by his crew through his deeds as well as his words. Leadership is the ability to influence. You influence by emotionally connecting with those you lead to motivate them to willingly and fully commit to a shared endeavor. Shackleton communicated with his crew by how he treated them and talked to them, and by how his decisions affected them. They trusted his every action and decision, even if it was tough to accept and painful to execute.

Shackleton understood that communication was a human connection, not just a verbal exchange. He knew that his words were very necessary, but more importantly, he understood that the influence of his behavior was much more powerful than his words. What you do validates what you say. It's how you actually lead that wins the trust of your followers. Shackleton laid the foundation of his *vision* for the expedition, its *purpose*, and his *expectations* for the crew members with and through his words. But it was through his active leadership—his behavior, his actions, his decisions—that he won the hearts and minds and complete trust of his crew. By observing his day-to-day leadership, they knew his words could be trusted.

As we did with Washington, let's dig deeper into these imperatives and see what and how our competence contributes to building trust in our leadership. Then, let's look at how we measure each of these leadership imperatives by considering the aspects that Shackleton used to build trust in dire circumstances. As you did with character, you'll have the same opportunity to conduct a self-evaluation of each of the attributes. Again, let's follow Aristotle's sage advice to "Know thy self" and take another look in the mirror.

14

CHARTING THE COURSE

"Would you tell me, please, which way I ought to go from here?"
asked Alice.
"That depends a good deal on where you want
to get to," said the Cat.
"I don't much care where—" said Alice.
"Then it doesn't matter which way you go,"
said the Cat.
"—but I want to get somewhere," Alice replied.
"Oh, you're sure to do that," said the Cat,
"if you only walk long enough."
—Conversation between Alice and the Cheshire Cat in
Alice in Wonderland

WHAT EMPLOYEES WANT from their leaders is direction. They want to know, What's our vision? Does what we do have meaning? What's our purpose? You would hope Alice's example would only be true in fairy tales. Unfortunately, many leaders know they want to go somewhere, but like Alice, they don't have a very good idea where that somewhere is. More importantly, neither do their employees. Vision statements are common in most organizations, yet more than a few studies have shown that employees in large white-collar organizations don't even know what the vision for their company is. People crave a vision they can understand and relate to, and in which they can feel equity in its accomplishment and learn how they personally contribute to its success.

I was recently asked by the board of directors of an electric co-operative to investigate the many problems their co-op was experiencing: high turnover, on-the-job accidents, employee complaints, and a shrinking customer base. After spending time with the co-op employees, it was evident that job satisfaction was poor and morale was extremely low.

The co-op's employees were Organizational Mercenaries, doing only what they had to do to get by without commitment, enthusiasm, or engagement. When I advised the CEO of my findings, he replied: "You have to understand that life in an electrical co-op is by nature mundane, repetitive, and unchallenging. All the issues you mention directly result from the boring nature of our business." Ironically, on almost every wall of the co-op headquarters and work sites were posters advertising the importance of what they did.

Our Mission
Provide safe, affordable, and dependable power to over 10 million cooperative members

I asked him, "Why don't you use your very important mission to enthuse your employees about the importance of their jobs?" He replied, "I've tried, and they just don't care."

The Classic Maintainer

The problem wasn't that the co-op lacked an aspirational purpose or that their work was "mundane, repetitive, and unchallenging." The problem was, its CEO was lethargic, unenergetic, and unenthusiastic. He was content with maintaining the status quo by rationalizing that the co-op's issues were just "the nature of the business." He was a classic Maintainer, and his employees were classic Organizational Mercenaries.

"Nearly anyone can steer the ship, but it takes a leader to chart the course."
—*John Maxwell, author of* The 21 Irrefutable Laws of Leadership

Shackleton did a great job of charting the course for his expedition by clearly conveying to his crew where they were going (his vision), why they were going there (its purpose), and what was expected of each of them in achieving that success (his expectations). Whether it's a 19th-century ship or a 21st-century corporation, *everyone* in the endeavor must clearly know the answers to these questions:

- Where are we going?
- Why are we going there?
- What do you expect of me?

It's the leader's responsibility to provide the answers to these questions. The classic Maintainer in my example ignored my suggestions, and it ultimately cost him his job. Some leaders do a decent job of answering a few, but many neglect to answer all. Let's look at each of these questions and see how they affect the trust of those we lead.

Vision: Where Are We Going?

Charting the course is simply providing direction and clarifying where the organization is headed. If you don't provide direction, you're merely gatekeeping or caretaking, not leading. In modern terms, providing direction may be in the form of a corporate vision, a work group's mission, a company's goals and objectives, a teacher's lesson plan, or a coach's playbook. As the leadership guru Warren Bennis boldly states, "The first basic ingredient of leadership is a guiding vision."[1]

Whatever label you stamp on it, without a coherent description of where you want the organization to go, you cannot construct a well-thought-out strategy to get it there. It's the "any road will get you there" conundrum. Mountain climbers don't just start climbing—they look up and plan backward. Regardless of the size or type of organization, followers will be confused, disenchanted, and unfocused without direction. Without a sharp vision, aligning what you as the leader wants and what your followers will do is impossible. Providing a vision of where you want to go is no guarantee you'll get there, but not having a vision will guarantee you definitely won't get there.

The importance of a leader developing and communicating a vision for the organization and persuading all the stakeholders to embrace it as their own is a challenge. Vision implies the ability to see. Leaders see what others don't. As Tim Clark, author of *Leading with Character and Competence*, puts it, "A vision is a seeding of reality, a portrait of the future."[2] It's not what you see but how well you communicate what you see. Leading is about translating intention into reality, transforming your visions into verbal photographs that your employees clearly see and understand.

Leaders must keep the organization clearly focused on that picture of the future by motivating their employees to embrace the leader's vision as their own and do all they can to turn that portrait into reality. The vision is the formulation of the end-state that acts as a beacon to guide an organization through the uncertainty of change.[3] I've seen too many organizational visions that are vague mottos or lofty bromides that don't make sense. They're as dull as dishwater and seen by those who have to execute the vision as unrealistic or unattainable. Your vision must be:

- *Understandable:* rational and sound.
- *Motivational:* persuades buy-in from everyone in the organization.
- *Doable:* seen as achievable.

Let's look at each of these in detail.

UNDERSTANDABLE

Life conspires to make things complex; leaders decode that complexity. Making profound thoughts and complex ideas understandable to employees is difficult but necessary. Leaders provide focused, laser-like clarity of vision that can be easily understood by those who must execute the vision by making the unfamiliar familiar, the invisible visible, and the complicated simple. The *Human Era @ Work*, a study conducted by The Energy Project and *Harvard Business Review*, found that only 34 percent of employees said they felt a connection to their company's mission. Those who didn't feel a connection were 62 percent less likely to stay with their employers and were 45 percent less engaged.[4] Several studies show that approximately 80 percent of employees cannot accurately recite their organization's vision. A vision will not clearly be understood unless it can be explained in freshman English. It's impossible to translate it into action if it's not clearly understood. According to John P. Kotter, professor of leadership at Harvard Business School, "A useful rule of thumb is: If you can't communicate your vision to someone in five minutes or less and get a reaction that signifies both understanding and interest, your vision will not take hold."[6] If you've ever written a vision or mission statement, you realize the difficulty of making the complex simple. Simple isn't simple!

Einstein translated his fifty-blackboard equation down to one short formula: $E = mc^2$. Bill Gates gave the world personal computing capability by simplifying the technology's complexities using an old-school typewriter keyboard. Steve Jobs translated his vision of affordable portable communication into a reality for the public with the simple-to-use iPhone. These are extreme cases of making the complex understandable to the layperson, but leaders at every level must do the same thing.

I once asked a senior vice president of a midsized company, "What's your corporate vision for the future?" For more than ten minutes, in mind-numbing, jargon-filled detail, he spewed out procedures, goals, methods, budgets, and quality management practices. Nowhere was there a clear and compelling description of where the company was going. If the senior vice president of that corporation couldn't express a clear vision, how do they expect the front-line troops to understand the vision? You can only seize what you understand. For employees to translate a leader's vision into pragmatic actions, they must clearly understand it. As Colin Powell advises us, "Great leaders are great simplifiers.[7]

MOTIVATIONAL

For a vision to take hold, it must be shared by both the leader and the led. James Kouzes and Barry Posner, authors of *The Leadership Challenge*, found in their survey of one million senior executives around the world that what leaders struggle with the most is communicating an image of the future, a vision that draws others in.[8] In other words, they struggle with selling their vision.

Leaders must do what it takes to influence their employees to embrace an intense sense of commitment to their vision. To do that, their employees must not only clearly understand the vision

"Where there is no vision, the people perish"
—Proverbs 29:18

(the what), but they must also clearly understand the purpose (the why). The only way leaders can get their groups to sustain their energy over the long haul is to give them a vision that justifies a long-term commitment.[9] It's a leader's responsibility to sell the benefits of their vision to the foot soldiers who'll be accountable for achieving it.

You must translate your vision into images that excite people. When you create a clear, convincing, appealing vision, you energize people. You inspire stone chippers to be cathedral builders.[10] A compelling vision energizes people to the point that you achieve General Eisenhower's definition of leadership: "getting your people to want what you want." Many vision statements are abstract generalities that engender no passion or employee buy-in. But humans are naturally lazy unless they have a vision or goal to inspire them to act.

Here's a vision statement from a company whose products many of us use every day:

> "...we are focused on our future, strengthening our business, serving our customers, and driving long-term value for employees."

If you were an employee in this company, would you know what you have to do to turn that vision into reality? Would this vision motivate you to be more than merely compliant in your job? Would it stir your soul? Probably not. The words aren't relevant to those who have to make the vision a reality.

For years, our public education system has received scathing criticism for lacking a clear purpose and a rational program to achieve it. Comparative analysis of US students versus their international peers warrants that criticism. The Program for International Student Assessment at England's Oxford University tests fifteen-year-olds worldwide on their reading, mathematics, and science abilities. Of seventy-one countries, American students tested 38th in math and 24th in science and reading, putting them behind many other advanced industrial nations, including Russia and China.

The most critical component and the very heart and soul of our public education system are its teachers. They are underpaid, overworked, and underappreciated. They are also pulled in so many directions that it's difficult for them to concentrate on what should be their main focus—teaching children. Here's a vision statement from one of the biggest teacher organizations in the country. Is it understandable? Is it motivational? Is it doable?

> "We are professionals who champion fairness, democracy, economic opportunity, and high-quality public education, healthcare, and public services for our students, their families, and our communities. We are committed to advancing these principles through community engagement, organizing, collective bargaining, political activism, and especially through the work of our members."

If I were a teacher, this vision statement would do nothing but confuse me. It should go unsaid that I want to give every student a great education, but all the fluff in this declaration dilutes that desire. How am I, as a teacher, going to affect "democracy, economic opportunity, healthcare, collective bargaining, political activism, etc."? How does anyone build a "doable" strategy or shape pragmatic courses of action to make this vision a reality? It can't be done.

How about something like this:

Our vision as teachers is to provide quality public education to EVERY child in America that gives them the ability to meet the 12th-grade standards for:

- oral and written English,
- math, science, and computers, and
- conducting interpersonal relations in the workplace and home,

You can argue the metrics (12th grade) and disagree on the subjects (math, English, etc.). However, is this vision statement more understandable and inspirational to those dauntless and dedicated teachers who are attempting to prepare our children to survive in a fiercely competitive world? You bet it is! Getting employees to be deeply committed to achieving your vision takes something exciting and meaningful. It has to be relevant to the success or well-being of those who have to execute the vision.

Many vision statements are abstract generalities outlined in a statement that no one could object to.[11] Just because your employees don't object to your vision doesn't mean they buy into it. Your vision, your picture of the future, must connect to their hopes and aspirations. You want more than erratic, half-hearted compliance that's dependent on supervision. You want commitment, and you want that commitment to seep into every fiber of the organization. It's easy to say but hard to do. Writing a great sounding vision statement is great, but the real challenge is to motivate those who have to achieve that vision to enthusiastically embrace it as their own.

DOABLE

How often have you heard a vision statement that sounded great, even inspirational, but turned out to be impractical rhetoric and plain old hot air? A beautifully written mission statement is worthless—and perhaps even counterproductive—if it can't be executed. A leader's vision won't be compelling unless it's seen as doable. The foot soldiers that have to do the *doing* won't put their muscular commitment behind the effort unless they know it's actually possible. They have to clearly see the path from visualization to actualization. Too often, vision statements are hollow panache and are more focused on impressing the customer than inspiring employees to become committed to and engaged in the vision. Impressing the customer should be left to marketing, not your vision statement. People crave a vision that has credibility.[12]

I've witnessed many a leader's visionary ideas flounder in execution. No matter how rhetorically inspiring, it has to be doable. Transposing words into actionable deeds is the hard part. Those we lead need more than inspiring words; they need a vision of themselves moving toward it, being capable of achieving it, and believing that it's worth exerting great effort to achieve it. While the words are critically important, they're not enough. You have to act. Studies conducted by Gartner Research & Advisory paint a dismal picture of leaders' ability to present a vision to employees that's understood and motivational and seen as doable.

- *Understood:* 87 percent of employees don't understand the vision.
- *Motivational:* 69 percent don't believe in the goals set by their leaders.
- *Doable:* 90 percent don't behave in ways that align with the leader's vision.

Purpose: Why Are We Doing This?

In February 1778, General George Washington was leading what resembled a mob more than an army. That month, Baron Friedrich Wilhelm August Heinrich Ferdinand von Steuben rode into the Continental Army's winter camp outside of Philadelphia and volunteered his services to the general. Von Steuben was a Prussian officer who had served on Fredrick the Great's staff during the Seven Years' War. He was reputed to have had great success training Prussian soldiers and readying them for combat. Washington appointed von Steuben as the Army's inspector general and asked him to look at the Continental Army's collection of ragtag local militia. He asked for suggestions on bringing military order and discipline to his army and gave von Steuben free rein to start implementing them immediately.

Within a short time, things started to improve. Von Steuben introduced sanitation standards, camp layouts, administration, supply discipline, and a system of progressive training with and without weapons. Washington was amazed at how quickly the baron persuaded leaders of the Continental Army to change their old habits. He was shocked by how quickly they learned how to march, fire their weapons in unison, and maneuver on the battlefield in an orderly and regimented fashion.

Washington asked von Stueben the secret to his success in quickly bringing order and precision to his ragtag army. He advised Washington that, initially, he employed the same training methods he used when preparing the Prussian army for combat. With Prussian soldiers, he could depend on instant and unquestioned obedience. However, with American officers and soldiers, he was attacked with a barrage of "whys." Legend has it that the baron told Washington:

"I quickly realized that you Americans do best when you know the purpose of what you are to do. I told your soldiers that the reason for not relieving themselves anywhere they pleased was to prevent disease in their camps. They understood and quickly built latrines downhill from their kitchens and campsites. I told your unit commanders that the purpose of building regimented camps with tents in a row and having their men living with their operational units rather than scattered throughout the countryside was to provide a speed of maneuver when the British attacked unexpectedly. Within a week, your leaders quickly arranged the camp, as I had suggested. I advised your officers they must instruct their men in the school of the soldier, which consists of marching in formation in the same step, firing in coordination, and moving on the battlefield in a coordinated manner. When they saw the purpose of the school of the soldier was to give them the ability to quickly concentrate their firepower on the British when facing them on the battlefield, they begged for more. Once I realized I had to give a reason and the purpose for all my changes, your officers and men willingly and enthusiastically followed my instructions."

Today's Americans are no different; they want to know why they're doing something and for what purpose. As my old boss and mentor, General George Joulwan, put it in his book, *Watchman at the Gates*, "If you can instill a sense of common purpose or even just point it out, positive things happen by bringing people out of their obsessions with their own needs and emotions."[13]

Individual Purpose: Does What I do Matter?

Viktor Frankl, the Holocaust survivor and psychologist, observed that those who survived Hitler's death camps possessed a sense of meaning in their lives and an inner compass that gave them direction.[14] He went on to say that when we have no meaning and no direction, we begin to drift and become lost in despair. During his four years in Auschwitz, Frankl became curious as he witnessed a counterintuitive phenomenon: Why were so many physically robust and healthy prisoners dying shortly after captivity, whereas a great number of physically weak and severely ill prisoners were surviving, even when all reason said they should have perished? He attributed this phenomenon to these prisoners' strong sense of meaning and purpose. Frankl saw three possible sources of meaning so impactful that it carried people through unimaginable physical brutality and psychological despair. Those who survived seemed to have found an inner meaning to live in their lives: It was either through *work* (doing something meaningful), *love* (caring for another person), or raw *courage* (an intense anger to survive). Since we spend a significant part of our lives at work, it holds that we need inner meaning in our work, or we drift.

As much as you may try to motivate employees with slogans and extrinsic rewards, they will never be emotionally connected or have pride in your entity's success if they don't think what they do is appreciated. Success in any group endeavor is virtually impossible without the sustaining force of purpose.[15] Leaders must reinforce the point that their organization has a worthwhile purpose every day through their words and actions. Decades of research attest that people desperately crave a sense of meaning in their work. When people believe that what they're doing is meaningful, they'll want to do it well. For many, a sense that what they do is meaningful is missing. Of course, people want to feel they're part of an organization with a purpose, but they also want to feel they personally contribute something to that purpose. Leaders have to give followers something worth committing to.

One of people's most significant fears is that their efforts and lives are insignificant and they make no difference. A study by Shawn Achor, the author of *The Happiness Advantage*, found that "More than 9 of 10 US employees would forgo some pay in exchange for consistently meaningful work."[16] It's unarguable that employees are more committed and engaged when they believe their efforts have a purpose and their work is valued. You want them to think of their jobs as having a purpose, not just a place to draw a paycheck. But crafting a clear, motivational, and doable organizational vision that inspires employees to embrace the organization's purpose is exceedingly difficult for a leader to do. Survey after survey demonstrate that followers desperately need a feeling that they make a difference, that what they do matters.

- A *Wall Street Journal* survey found that out of nearly 2,000 respondents, 26.7 percent stated:
    - "I'm not considered essential, and my work doesn't feel important or meaningful."
- A PwC Consulting survey of 540 employees found:
    - Only 28 percent felt connected to their company's purpose.
    - More than half testified they weren't "even somewhat motivated about their jobs."
- According to OC Tanner Institute:
    - 79 percent of employees who quit their jobs did so because they weren't appreciated.

- 65 percent said they weren't recognized once in the past year.
- 82 percent said their supervisor doesn't recognize them for what they do[17]

Regardless of occupation or status, we all need a sense that what we do matters. Knowing that what we do is important, and knowing that it's appreciated, leads to commitment. Senior leaders with heavy responsibilities, like General Martin Dempsey, the former chairman of the Joint Chiefs of Staff, are no exception. With responsibility for the conduct of US military operations worldwide, General Dempsey wanted to do something enduring to make sure that the sacrifice made by every American casualty wasn't remembered one minute and forgotten the next. He placed a mahogany box on his desk engraved with the words "Make It Matter."[18] In the box were two-by-four-inch laminated cards, each prepared with a photograph and personal information of a lost soldier, Marine, sailor, or airman. Each day, he would select three cards and place them in his breast pocket to honor their sacrifice by reminding himself to ensure that his actions and decisions "Make It Matter." Marty, a leader, who I can personally attest is a leader of great character, understood that regardless of rank, age, occupation, or status, we all need to have meaning in our lives. We all need to have a sense that what we do matters.

Expectations: What Do You Expect of Me?

In four words, Dabo Swinney, Clemson University's championship-winning football coach, clearly lets his players know what he expects of them: "Best is the standard." His players clearly understand that he expects "performance that is not good, not great, BUT BEST!" Like all great leaders, Coach Swinney sets the bar high for his players and holds them accountable for achieving what he expects from them: their absolute best performance. Leadership is about holding your people to the highest possible standards while taking the best possible care of them. Organizations that set high but reasonable standards while holding people accountable to those standards clearly outperform those that do not. They have faster growth, higher profitability, and fewer failures.[19] You'd think that all leaders would set high standards for their employees, but all too many are wanting in that regard. And of those who do set high standards, many fall short in enforcing or maintaining them.

My army experience indoctrinated me with a strong belief in the value of establishing high standards and the importance of holding myself and my subordinate leaders responsible for achieving them. If the leader doesn't shape the culture of the organization, someone else will. To create a culture that brings order and predictability, leaders must draw the lines on the road they expect the members of the organization to travel between. The written and unwritten rules that guide everyone's accepted and expected conduct and reflect the organization's collective norms and values must be clearly understood by all. Too often, those expectations lack precision or detail. Not only do employees need to know specifically what is expected of them, but just as important, they need to understand, specifically, what is unacceptable. In short, they need to know what they should do *and* should not do.

Perhaps the biggest surprise I had after leaving the army and entering the corporate world was the number of organizational dysfunctions I witnessed that were due to vagueness or a lack of clear expectations between managers and employees. Time and again, I see that the root cause of an organizational problem is that the leader didn't clearly communicate or enforce the professional requirements, standards of conduct, or cultural norms he expected of his employees. Frequently, I find that the leader assumed they were understood when, in fact, they were not. The ambiguity of expectations and standards and misperceptions between leader and led is a breeding ground for employee confusion and self-interested rationalization. If you expect sustained high performance, each player on the team must not only fully understand his part and its impact on the group effort, but he must also want to carry it out.[20] Few things are more critical to an organization's success than everyone understanding what's expected of them. People who live and work in an environment of mutually understood and shared professional and cultural norms share a belief system. They're predictable to one another. They cooperate. It simplifies everything. There are many reasons for the misalignment of what leaders expect and what employees think they expect. The most common are that expectations are misunderstood, too low, or unenforced.

Misunderstood Expectations: Lost in Translation

You do not clearly define your expectations to be *understood*. You clearly define them so that you cannot be *misunderstood*. The alignment between a leader's expectations and a follower's interpretation of those expectations is often greatly misaligned because, somehow, what is said and what is heard is misconstrued or lost in translation. Very often, when leaders present their norms and standards, they lack the precision and detail needed for the employee to clearly understand what's expected. Motivating your employees to produce sustained high performance requires they know what "high performance" looks like. Feebly articulating your expected standards to your employees will result in substandard performance and poor morale. Standards must not only be clearly understood but also predictable, consistent, fair, and achievable.

In my capacity as a consultant, when I'm asked to look at an organization that's having difficulties, I interview its leaders and ask them a battery of questions to determine the professional and cultural expectations of their employees. Generally, the questions cover the topic of standards. I ask, "What are the professional, behavioral, and cultural expectations they have of their employees? And how do you convey what you expect of them?" Their responses run the gamut from vague and unspecific to minutely detailed, but almost all believe they've clearly communicated precisely what's expected to their employees.

Then I interview their employees and ask them the same battery of questions from their perspective: What are the professional, behavioral, and cultural standards you're expected to adhere to? And how does your management communicate what they expect from you? I'm constantly surprised by how wide the disconnect is between what the boss thinks he transmitted and what the employee believes he received. That misalignment of what is said and what is heard is the root cause of many, if not most, organizational problems.

At a minimum, you must sit down with your direct reports and clearly communicate to them what you expect: how we do things, our work and behavior ethic, non-negotiables, and anything you believe is important for their success. Of course, a CEO of a 2,000-person organization can't sit down with everyone in his company. An ideal organization should have workers at every level reporting to some leader whose domain is small enough to enable that leader to know everyone who reports to him on a personal basis.[21] The CEO's expectations cascade down through each layer of her subordinate leaders to their direct reports. That is how cultures are built. An organizational culture of high performance starts at the top, and it's the responsibility of the leader to initiate and cultivate. The Maintainers who defer that responsibility to others and expect their employees to magically learn the standards through implied signals and signs are doomed for failure.

**God Gave Us
The 10 Commandments
not
The 10 Suggestions.**

Low Expectations: It's Easy to be Pleased

Maintainers often draw the line on the wall far too low—many of them are too satisfied with mediocre performance. Years ago, a famous WWII soldier, General Dave Grange Sr., told me, "Your soldiers will be as lousy as you let them, and they will be as good as you make them be." The lower your expectations, the easier it is to please yourself. If you have low expectations of your team, they won't disappoint you.

Just because someone is demanding and detail-oriented doesn't make them a toxic leader. High performance comes with certain requirements. The line between failure and success is often the difference between doing something nearly right and doing it exactly right. High standards do not require that you shackle employees with onerous rules. Leaders must craft rules that encourage employees to elevate their standards, and leaders must explain why those standards and rules are necessary for success. Maintaining high standards through rigorous personal and professional discipline is essential to creating an organization that performs consistently and in the most difficult situations.[22] Standards address what's important in an organization—what makes it run well. There are things that have to be done and done well for the organization to survive and thrive.

There's a hunger for order among those we lead. From the vice president to the line worker, people want to know exactly what their boss expects of them, professionally, organizationally, culturally, and personally. People want order in their lives, and they want and expect that order to come from their leaders. They want rules, standards, guidelines, and clear expectations. The idea that we have to follow rules is ingrained in us early in life. As children, we learned manners: how to follow the golden rule, respect our elders, not to butt in line, and say please and thank you. These were rules we learned and were expected to follow. It's a leader's responsibility to clearly articulate to all employees what is expected and why it's crucial to success.

> **"We have been 'defining deviancy down'—lowering our standards of what constitutes criminal and anti-social behavior—as a coward's way of dealing with the increase in such behavior."**
> —*Daniel Patrick Moynihan, former US senator*

Unenforced Expectations: You Get What You Tolerate

Too often, standards of performance and expected cultural norms are idealized but not enforced. It's not what you preach but what you tolerate. Mediocrity begins the moment leaders fail to hold people accountable. When rules and standards aren't enforced, they begin to be flouted. Just as a football game needs referees to maintain rules and order on the field, organizations need leaders to maintain rules and order in the workplace. Without referees and leaders, anarchy would ensue. Both are needed to remind players and employees what's out of bounds and a violation of acceptable, established rules and norms. "Preventive officiating" is a term referees use to warn players that they're close to violating a rule. Leaders do the same by keeping those in the organization between the lines of acceptable behavior before they're crossed. If our established standards are empty words, there will always be some employees who will be emboldened to continually push the limits of acceptability.

Setting standards is one thing, but do you have the stomach for enforcing them? Many don't. But there's no sense in having standards unless you plan to enforce them. There will be times when your preventive officiating will be ignored, and fouls will be committed.

Discipline seems to have fallen out of favor, and many think of it as a negative concept. Quite the contrary. Discipline, currently softened to "negative feedback," is what you do *for* someone, not *to* someone. It's necessary to provide our charges with negative feedback for minor infractions, but there will be times when more severe disciplinary action is required for more grievous misconduct. It's not easy to administer discipline, but it's necessary when the conduct of an individual is clearly outside the acceptable lines of performance or behavior. The rule of thumb is to punish infrequently, but when punishment is necessary, do so in ways that establish memories.

It is weak leadership to ignore wrongdoing in an organization, whether it's a minor infraction, blatant misconduct, or an incompetent performance. It takes courage to look someone in the eye and tell them their job performance or personal behavior isn't meeting expectations. Many leaders lack the courage to enforce their own standards because they don't like conflict. When this happens, everyone loses. The organization gets poor performance, co-workers have to pick up the slack, and the poor performers continue to be oblivious to their misdeeds. More importantly, the boss loses the trust and respect of her employees by doing nothing to correct the poor performer. Leadership is about what's best for the organization. If you don't face and fix the subpar performers, the organization suffers.

The Glue That Binds

Standards and discipline are the glue that holds great teams together. If you walk by a mistake without correcting it, you should expect many and continued encores of that mistake. By ignoring a mistake, you show those you lead a lack of interest, energy, or courage to right the wrong. You have informally set a new standard. You've not only lowered the standard, but you've made it clear to everyone that you don't mean what you say.

Moreover, when you don't practice what you preach, it will cost you the trust of your team. If you don't enforce the standards you declare, they'll see you as a blowhard or, worse yet, weak-willed. Declaring and realizing are two different things. Often, managers favor the superstars on the team, ignoring their indiscretions for fear they'll antagonize the star. If you have to play favorites by selectively enforcing rules or lowering standards for a chosen few, you've institutionalized a double standard.

> **"Set the standard. Live the standard. Enforce the standard."**
> —*Mike Ettore, author of* **Trust-Based Leadership**

Coach John Wooden is considered by many to be the greatest college basketball coach in history, with a record of ten National Championships. He had a team rule against facial hair. One day, his star player, Bill Walton, entered the gym with a beard after a two-week holiday. When Coach Wooden inquired about the beard, Walton said, "Coach, I think I should be allowed to wear a beard; it's my right." Wooden paused, sighed, and then replied, "Bill, I have great respect for individuals who stand up for those things in which they believe. But the team is going to miss you."[23] Couch Wooden understood that double standards would enrage those who don't consider themselves favorites, resulting in a loss of trust and team cohesion. He understood that you must treat princes and paupers alike.

Many Maintainers fall short in motivating high performance because they have an innate need to be liked by those they supervise. They believe likeability is a critical factor in fostering collaboration and an essential ingredient for creating employee satisfaction and engagement. Do not fall into that trap! It isn't about being liked, loved, or nice—it's about tapping into the individual potential of your employees in the interest of furthering the organizational goal. I've worked for leaders I trusted and respected and was committed to, but I didn't particularly like them. I had one memorable boss who was very demanding and 100 percent business. He had no social skills or sense of humor, and his communication style was so blunt that many people took it as rudeness. However, he was true to his word and could be trusted to do what was in the best interest of the organization and his soldiers. He never asked you to do something he wouldn't do himself, and his professional competence was admired because he really knew his business. He also conveyed a strong sense that he cared for us, even though it was in subtle ways. I learned much from him. I didn't dislike him, but I didn't particularly like him, either. So, do you have to be liked to be a successful leader? Maybe not, but you do have to be trusted.

The Golden Mean

For those of you who are screaming at me that I want a draconian, micromanaged, militaristic dictatorship culture, your accusation could not be farther from the truth. I'm not advocating authoritarian or draconian regimentation. I'm advocating that leaders communicate an unambiguous description of their expectations for professional performance, personal behavior, and compliance with cultural norms.

There has to be a balance. Consider Aristotle's golden mean again. Depending on the type of organization and other impacting factors, you must find the appropriate balance between free range and draconian extremes. What is the proper balance? Too easy or too hard, micromanaging or hands off, too friendly or too distant, too stoic or too emotional, too mission-focused or too people-focused? Leadership is about balance. Granted, being disliked as a leader isn't helpful. You have to find your sweet spot somewhere between Attila the Hun and Mr. Rogers.

Afterthought: The Right Balance

Recently, I had the honor of speaking at the funeral of an exceptional leader who got it right. He had mastered Aristotle's golden mean, and his leadership was a perfect balance of demanding toughness and compassionate concern for his soldiers. He led a superbly trained unit of tough, battle-ready soldiers, extremely competent noncommissioned officers, and junior leaders. I described his leadership at his funeral as an iron fist in a velvet glove.

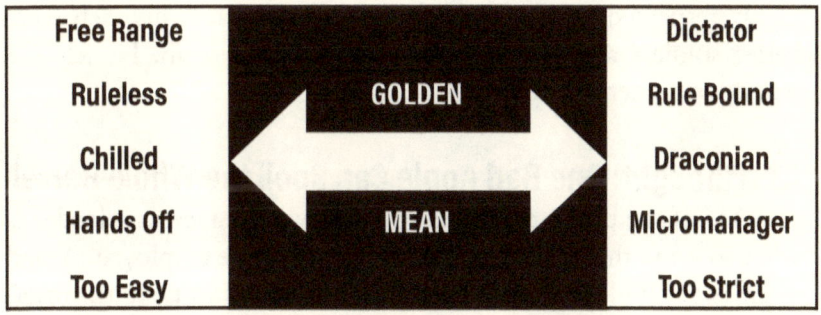

Free Range	GOLDEN	Dictator
Ruleless		Rule Bound
Chilled		Draconian
Hands Off	MEAN	Micromanager
Too Easy		Too Strict

As the commander of an infantry company of 220 soldiers, he demanded high standards from himself and those he led. He didn't suffer poor soldiering lightly and was a strict disciplinarian when needed. When you dug deeper into his likability, you found that his soldiers did more than just like him; they trusted and respected him. His troops trusted him because he pushed them to levels of performance they had no idea they could achieve. His men trusted him because they knew his demands for high performance were in their best interest, to prepare them for the rigors of combat. They respected him because he was fair and compassionate and didn't ask them to do anything he wouldn't do himself. They liked him because he led with a positive and optimistic attitude. He had a glass-half-full outlook and an almost perpetual smile sprinkled with a wry sense of humor. Every kick in the behind to do better was followed by an equal number of sincere "Well done" pats on the back. He had the ability to walk a line that was highly demanding but fair, friendly but not a friend, and serious but not without humor. He had found the leadership golden mean.

He was one of those gifted leaders of character and competence who found that perfect balance of tough love and genuine kindness. He treated people well, not as inferiors. He maintained the psychological distance required of a leader who had the daunting responsibility of preparing men for the rigors of infantry combat. His company was deployed to Desert Storm, saw considerable action, and performed magnificently. He was liked, even loved, by every soldier in his unit. His positive outlook on life, his respect for his soldiers, and his great sense of humor made him a likable and highly respected leader. When he left his company, his men were better soldiers and people because of his leadership. He left the woodpile higher.

Afterthought: One Bad Apple Can Spoil the Whole Barrel

One of the tough decisions you'll inevitably face as a leader is what to do with the high-performing, bad-apple employee. A bad apple is an employee who's productive or brings value to the organization but whose behavior negatively influences the larger group or violates the established cultural norms of your organization. You may learn that your highest-producing salesman, in his desire to close deals quickly, often skirts around information about your product that the customer may interpret as detrimental to their needs. You counsel him, reminding him that your company's sales philosophy is to be transparent about all the attributes of your product. Shortly after your counseling session with him, you learn that he has continued to withhold minor information about your product's limitations in his sales calls.

When a person is allowed to continue in his role solely because he's high-performing or perceived as invaluable to an organization, that rotten apple can quickly spoil the whole barrel. Early in my career, I learned that one bad apple in a critical position with a bit of charisma could be cancerous to the team. Several times, I waited too long to get rid of the bad apple and paid the price for it. Bottom line, act quickly. Maybe one or two strikes, and you're out. But beyond that, by keeping the bad apple, he exposes you to the risk of losing the trust of your employees and the danger that his behavior will poison your organization's culture. How you deal with bad apples is a reflection of your character.

Summary Points

- Leaders must convey to their followers where they're going (a vision), why they're going there (the purpose), and what's expected of each of their followers to achieve success (the expectations).
- *Visions* must be:
    - *Understandable:* rational and sound
    - *Motivational:* persuades buy-in
    - *Doable:* seen as achievable
- *Purpose:* Without a sense of purpose, there's no motivation.
    - Organizational purpose: Why does our organization exist?
    - Individual purpose: Why do I matter? How does what I do matter?
- *Expectations:* If a leader's expectations aren't met, it's because they were:
    - *Misunderstood:* What is said is not what is heard.
    - *Too low:* The lower your expectations, the easier you are to please.
    - *Unenforced:* It's not what you preach but what you tolerate.
- Leaders must balance disciplined execution and behavior with consideration and caring for employees.
- Tolerating bad apple regardless of their professional successes threatens a leader's respect and trust.

If you're comfortable with your ability to *chart the course*, go to the next chapter. If not, take a "Look in the Mirror" below.

Look in the Mirror at My Ability to Chart the Course

Review the following statements, then *underline* where you are and *circle* where you want to be:

- **My ability to provide a clear vision to my team is:**
  - Poor / Mediocre / OK / Good / Excellent
- **My employees understanding of my company's *vision* is:**
  - Poor / Mediocre / OK / Good / Excellent
- **My employee's motivation to embrace our vision as their own is:**
  - Poor / Mediocre / OK / Good / Excellent
- **My employee's belief that our vision is doable is:**
  - Poor / Mediocre / OK / Good / Excellent
- **My employees believe what our company does is important:**
  - Never / Occasionally / Frequently / All the Time
- **My employees believe that what they do as individuals is important:**
  - Never / Occasionally / Frequently / All the Time
- **My employees know exactly what's expected of them:**
  - Never / Occasionally /Frequently / All the Time
- **My ability to discipline poor performers, the "bad apples," is:**
  - Poor / Mediocre / OK / Good / Excellent
- **My ability to balance disciplined execution and employee consideration is:**
  - Poor / Mediocre / OK / Good / Excellent

What Aspect(s) of Charting the Course Could Use Improvement?

Example: I need to be more prudent in enforcing professional standards and expectations. I'm good at correcting poor performance, but I don't correct employees who deliver a mediocre performance, knowing full well they're doing the minimum to get by.

I Want to Improve:

My Philosophy on Charting the Course

Example: I want to ensure that all my employees clearly understand my company's vision, embrace our company's purpose, and realize they're important to its success. I also want to ensure that all my employees are clear about what is professionally and culturally expected of them and that I treat all employees equally in enforcing those standards and expectations.

My Philosophy on Charting the Course:

My Action Plan

Example: I will sit down with each of my employees over the next thirty days and determine if they clearly understand our vision and embrace our company's purpose. I will also ask if they feel that what they do has meaning in accomplishing that purpose. In addition, I will ask each employee if I am seen as fair and sensible in upholding our standards. I will ask my deputy the same thing about my perceived double standards. Based on what I find in the discussions, I will adjust my leadership and behavior to overcome any negative aspects of my leadership.

My Action Plan:

15

ACTIVELY LEADING

"Deeds Not Words"

—36th Infantry Regiment Motto

IN MY CONSULTING life, I was once asked by a company's board of directors to work with its CEO, who was having issues with high-employee turnover, poor morale, and union complaints. After interviewing several employees at various levels, I met with the CEO. I advised him that his employees had lost trust in the company's HR department because of its blatant favoritism and discrimination in hiring and promotion processes. He responded, "I delegate all those issues to my very capable HR vice president. I handle the strategy-level issues; I don't have time to get into the weeds of personnel issues! I consider my job as more of a Winston Churchill, not a Jerry Springer!" The HR vice president was causing a significant adverse effect on the company's performance. The CEO knew it, but he chose not to get involved. As a consequence, his employees had lost trust in his leadership, resulting in the critical issues noted above.

I advised the CEO that competent leaders participate in their business at the appropriate level. Here comes that golden mean concept again: It's leadership with a strong bias toward action that keeps a business between the lines. Leaders must show up, be visible, and check, recheck, and challenge those executing the vision with positive and provocative questioning. They must passionately influence execution with hard-nosed standard setting, relentlessly seek new or better ways to achieve success, and constantly guide employees in the right direction. This CEO was a classic Chateau Manager.

Chateau Managers

"Chateau Managers" is a term I coined from the description given to those WWI generals who would issue battlefield orders to the troops, then scurry back to their chateaus. They would leave their orders to be carried out by the soldiers on the front lines. From the safety of the chateau, they had no idea how the battles were going, and more importantly, they had little or no influence on the battle's outcome. They made their presence known by periodically making a brief appearance on the battlefield, but they did nothing to make their presence *felt* by those carrying out their orders.

Like those Chateau Generals, some managers today will present an inspirational PowerPoint that lays out their vision, goals, and objectives for the company, but then they immediately hurry back to their corner office, leaving their guidance to be carried out by their employees on the front lines. From the comfort and security of their offices,

"A desk is a dangerous place to watch the world."
—John le Carre, author

they have little to no awareness of what's happening in their organization; therefore, they have little to no influence on the outcome of their directives. Their presence may be momentarily *known,* but they do little to make their leadership *felt* by those carrying out their orders. These Chateau Managers don't understand that until their words result in action, they're merely hot-winded platitudes and impotent PowerPoint presentations. As one of my favorite TV characters, Frank Reagan of "Blue Bloods," says, "Lead by example instead of by antidote."

While lofty visions of the future can be inspirational, they must be accompanied by the hard work of translating them into down-to-earth specificity. A leader's ability to turn words into deeds separates the successful from the also-rans, the winners from the losers. Leadership is measured not by the beauty of your aspirations but by the actual accomplishment of your goals. It's not enough to aspire, wish, and hope—you must act. Your words are merely the scorecard by which your deeds are graded. Building trust takes an unrelenting demonstration that both your character and competence are worthy of trust.

Making your presence known to your employees and getting buy-in to the course you've charted for them is necessary but not sufficient by itself for leadership success. You have to make them feel that you have their best interests at heart and are interested in what they're doing. They have to feel that you care for and about them.

> **The best fertilizer for the soil is the shadow of the boss.**
> —*Mexican proverb*

You can't just show up when you want something. Only by actively participating in the execution of the business can you make your leadership felt. Let's look at what being *known and felt* looks like.

80 Percent of Success Is Just Showing Up

A leader's words may be interesting, but it's how they act that's critical. Leaders are doers, not observers. They get involved. They're on the playing field, not watching from the sidelines, giving Monday morning critiques. What it takes to achieve organizational success is a leader's competence to effectively navigate the rough waters of change, conflict, and ambiguity. To do that, leaders must be intimately and intently involved with the people and operations of their organization.[1] Success is measured by how well leaders find and solve problems and lead their organization to success. It is their *raison d'etre*.

Earlier, I mentioned the fictional character from the book *Once an Eagle*, Sam Damon, who showed up during a critically desperate situation on a battlefield where his men were dejected, despondent, and ready to quit. By merely showing up, his presence brought hope where there was despair, ultimately changing the course of the battle. It doesn't matter that this incident is fictional. It demonstrates a profound truth: The leader's presence makes a difference. A leader who actively participates has a positive and uplifting effect, whether on the battlefield, the shop floor, or the carpeted halls of corporate towers.

One leader who understood that the impact of his presence was exponentially more powerful than the effect of his words was Winston Churchill. His radio speeches during World War II were inspirational and moving. They made him known to every British subject. But it was his regular presence on the bomb-damaged streets of London's neighborhoods where he made his presence felt. On those rubbled alleys and avenues, he showed England and the world what courage and leadership looked like. It's one thing to say "Carry on." It's quite another thing to do it. It was his active leadership, his presence after the nightly raids, that motivated Englishmen to "Keep calm and carry on."

By showing up where hours earlier the bombs had fallen, assessing the damage, giving orders, and showing sincere concern, Churchill made it felt by all in England that he was leading them to victory. It demonstrated to them that he had their best interests at heart and was aware of and deeply cared about their pain and suffering. As his country's governmental leader, he understood his presence was important for the people. By being present, he gave them comfort that there was hope. He was exactly where he needed to be, doing exactly what he needed to do, at precisely the right time.

The powerful impact of a leader's physical presence is undeniable. In small teams, a leader's presence is a normal occurrence. In large and geographically dispersed organizations, it's easy to fall back on the excuse that regular personal contact with everyone in the organization isn't possible or practical. However, just because the situation doesn't make it easy or convenient for a leader to physically touch everyone regularly isn't an excuse to be a Chateau Manager. Churchill didn't physically see every Englishman, but his presence was known and felt by

> **"A body can pretend to care, but they can't pretend to be there."**
>
> —*Texas Bix Bender, author of* **Don't Squat With Yer Spurs On!**

every citizen of the British Empire. Jack Welch, the legendary CEO of GE, couldn't meet face-to-face with each of his employees who were spread out across the world, but his tough-and-blunt presence was known and felt by every one of GE's 300,000 employees. There are many leaders in this same category: Mary Barra, Steve Jobs, Jeff Bezos, Meg Whitman, Howard Schultz, and more. They all had their stamp impressed on the people in their organization. You have to show up to prove to your employees that you care about them. You have to show them that you have their best interests at heart and are interested in what they're doing. When the top dog makes a strong point of being known and felt, that leadership ethos cascades down into the organization.

When commanding a brigade of 3,700 soldiers, I found it to be a challenge to follow my own advice. So, I developed a management matrix to discipline myself and make my presence felt by every soldier in my brigade. I wanted to visit every direct report weekly and every unit monthly. Once a quarter, I scheduled a gathering of all my soldiers to give them a state-of-the-brigade overview. During my two years as commander, I rarely deviated from my planned visits. The warning is that the larger the organization, the greater the challenge is to make your leadership known and felt, but it has to be done.

Only by Making Your Presence Felt Are You Leading

Not only do you have to show up, but through your behavior, actions, and decisions, you must show that you're competent. Leaders make their presence felt by being where the action is so they can scan, focus, and act. You make your leadership felt by your participation in translating your ideas, vision, and strategy into concrete and pragmatic action steps. It's through your behavior and decisions that you ensure disciplined execution at all

> **"Vision without execution is hallucination."**
>
> —*Walter Isaacson, from* **The Wall Street Journal** *article, "The Lessons of Leonard"*

levels and in all areas of the organization. If you're an absent leader and out of the loop, how can you be aware of what's going on?

How can you coach your team, provide direction, show support to those in the trenches, monitor and measure performance and deadlines, spot and solve problems, and, when necessary, offer a pat on the back or a kick in the rear? You can't—you have to show up! You have to be present!

Leaders must close the often-confusing gap between their vision and the successful execution of the goals and objectives of that vision. There are business leaders who like to think that the top dog is exempt from the details of running the company. I can't tell you how many times I've heard statements like this in my consulting life:

- I leave the people issues to HR, the technical issues to the engineers, the IT stuff to the geeks, the legal issues to the lawyers, and the marketing and sales issues to the sales team.
- I don't get into the details of running the organization; it's below my pay grade.
- I give the company my marching orders; now it's up to my employees to execute them.

This attitude is a recipe for organizational failure, but it happens all the time. It's why 23.2 percent of new businesses fail in the first year, 48 percent have failed by the fifth year, and only 34.7 percent of them are still around in the tenth year.[2] I call it an epidemic of "underleading." Lou Gerstner, the former CEO of IBM and RJR Nabisco, warns us, "What is critical to understand is that people do not do what you expect but what you inspect."[3] Most often today, the difference between a company and its competitor is the ability to execute.[4] As Larry Bossidy, the former CEO of Honeywell, opines:

> "People think of execution as the tactical side of business, something leaders delegate while they focus on the perceived "bigger" issues. This idea is completely wrong. Execution is a discipline and a system, and the leader of the organization must be deeply engaged in it. He cannot delegate substance."[5]

Bossidy is right. Leadership isn't handing your vision or a strategy to employees at the annual off-site or presenting a list of individual goals and objectives to an employee at their annual review and then leaving them to their own devices. Leading requires active participation. Leadership is the alchemy of turning words into deeds, visions into achievements, dreams into reality, and plans into accomplishments. The most powerful way to communicate and positively influence organizational success is through your engagement, by ensuring that things that are supposed to happen do happen. Strategies most often fail because they aren't well executed. Only the leader can ensure collaboration, accountability, and synchronization between and across competing fiefdoms. Leaders cannot influence unless they are present, accessible, and approachable to those they lead. There's no way a leader can know what's going on in the trenches if they're spending all their time behind a computer or at endless staff meetings.

So, You Want Me to Micromanage?

Absolutely not! Micromanaging Maintainers are as dangerous to organizational success as Dictators. They meddle, criticize, second-guess, and change things because it's different from how they would do it, even if the other way is better. Micromanagement is a recipe for an instant loss of trust and a breeding ground for resentment. Micromanagers strangle initiative, creativity, and commitment. But when I hear, "I don't micromanage. I delegate. I empower. I trust my people to do what I tell them to do. It's not my style. I'm a hands-off leader," my response is, "You're abrogating your responsibility as a leader. Sometimes, you have to get your hands dirty."

Salesforce, a company of 49,000 employees with a revenue of more than $55 billion, is an excellent example of a business where the CEO has made his presence known and felt by every employee without giving them a sense that he's micromanaging. Every week, Marc Benioff conducts a teleconference that's open to all 49,000 employees. In those sessions, he makes his presence felt by discussing and reinforcing things that are important to him. He's not micromanaging; he's leading.

Leadership Equation:

Competence → Trust → Influence → Leadership

Remember, I stated that leadership is the influence that's powerful enough to motivate our followers to commit fully and be totally engaged in our common endeavor. I went on to say that a level of influence powerful enough to inspire that intensity of commitment comes when our employees know we possess a level of competence they deem trustworthy. So, what competencies must a person master to be successful? To the right is a list of some of the skills that management gurus and MBA programs state a leader must master to succeed.

This book is long enough as it is, so instead of digging into each one, let's take the advice of the management guru Peter Drucker, who warned us, "There is nothing quite as useless as doing with great efficiency what should not be done at all."[6] Said another way, "Do the right things well." Depending on your leadership landscape and aspirations, not all of these will apply to your situation. You have to identify the skills that are important to succeeding in your profession. Many competencies important to a tech company CEO are different from those required of a high school principal, which are different from a project manager, which are different from a Marine major.

However, there are several competencies that should be on every leader's playlist, regardless of the type of organization they lead. Let's focus on those competencies that are instrumental in making your leadership known and felt to build a level of trust powerful enough to inspire your Mercenaries to become your Patriots. As we did with George Washington, let's review the competencies that made Earnest Shackleton a great role model for successful leadership: situational awareness, leading by example, teaching/coaching/mentoring, and decision-making. Not only do these skills inspire trust in those you lead, but the absence of any of them will also inspire distrust. Successfully demonstrating these leadership competencies is what it takes to make your presence known and felt in your organization.

Leader Competencies

- Situational awareness
- Leading by example
- Coach/teach/mentor
- Decision-making
- Strategic thinking
- Professional knowledge
- Vision setting
- Execution focused
- Empowering
- Communication
- Judgment
- Tact
- Customer service
- Accountability
- HR management
- Financial management
- Creativity
- Flexibility
- Strategy development
- Prudence
- Emotional intelligence
- Political skills
- Social intelligence
- Conflict management
- Change management
- Risk-taking
- Negotiating
- Work-flow management
- Adaptability
- Diversity
- Developing others
- Relationship-building
- Team-building
- Networking
- Problem-solving
- Innovation
- Empathy
- Add Your Own

Unless you're situationally aware of what's happening in your organization, how will you know what decisions to make? Unless you're leading the example you want your employees to embrace, how will they know what's expected of them? Unless you're actively teaching, coaching, and mentoring your followers, they'll do things however they want. Unless you make timely and correct decisions, regardless of your strength of character and competence, your trust as a leader will wane and your tenure will be short. These competencies are the ingredients that inspire those you lead to be committed and engaged and are relevant in every leadership situation, profession, and arena. Let's look at each in more detail in the following chapters.

Summary Points

- Actions speak louder than words. While words are necessary, they're not sufficient; deeds must accompany them.
- Until a leader's words result in action, they're just hot wind.
- A leader's ability to turn words into action separates the successful from the also-rans.
- Leadership success isn't measured by aspirations but by accomplishments.
- It's not enough to aspire, you have to act. Your words are merely a scorecard by which your deeds are graded.
- Leaders must make their presence both *known* and *felt*.
- Leaders must make it known to their employees that they have their best interests at heart, are interested in what they do, and care for and about them.
- Only by being seen as actively participating, through your actions, behavior, and decisions, can you make your leadership felt.
- You have to "show up" to prove to your followers that you care about them.
- You have to "show up" to make sure what's supposed to be happening is actually happening.
- Lack of leadership presence "is the overwhelming common denominator in most cases of sub-optimal workplace performance in all types of organizations and at all levels, which has adverse effects on productivity and quality."[7]

If you're comfortable that you're *actively leading*, go to the next chapter. If not, "Look in the Mirror" below.

Look in the Mirror at My Ability to Actively Lead

Review the following statements, then *underline* where you are and *circle* where you want to be:

- **My ability to do what it takes to inspire action around my words is:**
    - Poor / Mediocre / OK / Good / Excellent
- **My ability to make my presence *known* to my team is:**
  Poor / Mediocre / OK / Good / Excellent
- **I do what it takes, through my actions, behavior, and decisions, to make my leadership *felt* by my employees:**
    - Never / Occasionally / Frequently / All the Time
- **My ability to make my leadership known and felt by all my employees is**
    - Poor / Mediocre / OK / Good / Excellent
- **I make contact either face-to-face or otherwise with every employee:**
    - Never / Occasionally / Frequently / All the Time
- **My followers would say they see me:**
    - Never / Occasionally / Frequently / All the Time
- **My followers would say they have contact with me:**
    - Never / Not Enough / Often Enough / Too Often
- **My employees would say I micromanage them:**
    - Never / Occasionally / Frequently / All the Time

What Aspect(s) of My Ability to Actively Lead Could Use Improvement?

Example: A recent climate survey reflected a feeling by employees that my front office was too distant from what's happening in the organization. Two key survey questions were "Do you feel your managers know what's happening in your area?" and "Do your managers appreciate the work you do?" Over half of my employees responded negatively to both questions.

I Want to Improve:

My Philosophy on Actively Leading

Example: I want to grow an organizational culture of symbiotic trust between the leaders and the led. I want the managers to know what's going on in the trenches and the workers in the trenches to know that the managers know what they do and appreciate what they do. I want all my subordinate leaders to get out of their offices and visit the field and workplaces often. I want them to be active leaders.

My Philosophy on Actively Leading:

My Action Plan

Example: I'm going to share my leadership philosophy of active leadership with my subordinate leaders and have each present to me how they plan to incorporate that philosophy into their work life. I will also start hosting a monthly lunch for employees who have birthdays that month. Most importantly, I want to create an opportunity for me to hear their ideas on how we can do better.

My Action Plan:

16

SITUATIONALLY AWARE

"You can observe a lot by watching."

—Yogi Berra, former New York Yankees player and manager

ON JANUARY 15, 2009, Captain Chesley Sullenberger filed his flight plan with the Federal Aviation Administration for his trip from New York City's LaGuardia Airport to Charlotte Douglass International Airport. Shortly after, at 3:25 pm, US Airways Flight 1549, with 155 passengers and crew aboard, took off and headed south toward North Carolina. During takeoff, the plane struck a flock of Canada geese at an altitude of 2,818 feet, 4.5 miles from the LaGuardia airport, causing both engines to shut down. Captain Sullenberger radioed a mayday call to the air traffic controllers, advising them, "This is Cactus 1549, hit birds. We've lost thrust on both engines. We're turning back toward LaGuardia." The tower advised Captain Sullenberger that all flights were on hold and he was cleared to land on runway 31.

Captain Sullenberger quickly assessed his situation and realized he couldn't make it back to the airport. His only option was to set the airplane down on the Hudson River. He transmitted to the tower, "We can't do it. We're gonna be in the Hudson." In the span of three minutes and twenty-one seconds, he commanded the passengers and crew to "brace for impact," as he maneuvered the plane directly over the river. From an altitude of 3,060 feet and an airspeed of 213 mph, he began his glide descent onto the Hudson, passing just 900 feet over the George Washington Bridge and smoothly ditching the aircraft in the middle of the river.[1] Sullenberger's quick thinking, extraordinary concentration, and flying skills averted what could have been a catastrophe. As a result of his total situational awareness, all 155 passengers and crew were safely evacuated from the floating aircraft.

Ten months later, on October 21, 2009, Captain Timothy Cheney filed a flight plan for his trip from San Diego to Minneapolis-St Paul International Airport (MSP). Shortly afterward, at 5:01 pm, Northwest Airlines Flight 188, with 148 passengers and crew aboard, headed to Minnesota. The plane was scheduled to land at MSP three hours later. Two hours into the flight, Denver air traffic control lost radio contact with Flight 188. Controllers from both Denver and Minneapolis frantically attempted to re-establish contact with the aircraft nine times without success. Other pilots in the area tried to contact the flight without a reply. Northwest Airlines company dispatchers sent text messages to the pilots that went unanswered. The flight was without radio contact for over an hour and a half. The situation became so tense that the Air Force readied fighter jets to check on the welfare of the plane, and officials at the White House Situation Room were alerted.[2]

Just as the fighter jets were about to scramble, Minneapolis-St Paul air traffic control re-established radio contact with Flight 188, which had overflown its airport by over 100 miles. The aircraft's captain said he was unaware of their location until a flight attendant asked when they were due to land. The investigation into the incident revealed that Captain Cheney was "going over schedules on his laptop" and had lost awareness of the time and situation. As a result, he was officially reprimanded for being "disengaged and impervious" to the danger his actions posed to the passengers and crew.[3]

What was the difference between Flight 1549 and Flight 188? The answer is obvious: One of the pilots was paying attention while the other pilot was not! Captain Sullenberger (Sully) was situationally aware while Captain Cheney was, to use aviation terms, "asleep at the stick." Being a leader is much like being a pilot. A pilot files a flight plan to advise the FAA where he's going, then flies the plane with the intent to successfully and safely land at the destination in his flight plan. A leader presents his vision to his employees (charts the course), then actively leads them on that course with the intent of successfully fulfilling the goals outlined in his vision. Like Captain Cheney, who filed his flight plan, then put the plane on autopilot, assuming the controls would steer the aircraft in the right direction, some managers present their vision, then set its execution on autopilot, assuming their employees will steer the organization in the right direction. Leaders, like pilots, must pay attention. They must stay "situationally aware."

What Is Situational Awareness?

Situational awareness is a concept that's been a regular part of life in aviation, health care, and the military for many years. Unfortunately, outside of these arenas, it hasn't been recognized as a specific leadership imperative. In its simplest form, it's defined as "knowing what's going on around you." It describes a person's focus and comprehension of the situation encountered in a mission, job, or environment. For a leader, the "environment" encompasses all those things that are important to the success of their undertaking or have the potential to derail it. While "knowing what's going on around you" may sound simplistic, it can be a real challenge for a manager in a fast-paced, complex, and stressful environment.

Leaders need to be situationally aware of things that affect the commitment and engagement of their employees. Your vision, decisions, cultural intentions, and organizational objectives are nothing until they're put into action. As one of my favorite quarterbacks, Tony Romo, once said, "None of it matters until you do it." A true test of your leadership is how well you recognize problems before they become catastrophes. Too many managers are surprised when improperly executed decisions or misinterpreted intentions become major problems or emergencies. Many, if not most, could have been easily addressed and fixed in their early stages if the manager had effectively made himself situationally aware. Sully and Captain Cheney's environment was their flight plan, weather, and air traffic.

Leading is an active and participative endeavor. Unfortunately, some delude themselves into believing they can lead from their bunker, office, or computer, or through their management processes and direct reports. Just as the Chateau Generals shouldn't have depended on their lieutenants to learn how the battle was going, you shouldn't depend on others to learn about the health of your organization's operations. Situational awareness gives you the ability to see and analyze with confidence those actions, processes, and events that positively and negatively affect your organization's goals and objectives. Whether you're in a combat zone, on the shop floor, or in the C-suite, firsthand situational awareness is critical to your organization's success. It may not be the only way to stay informed, but it *is* the most effective way. It's a skill that can be developed and continually improved if you make the effort.

The Germans have a term—*fingerspitzengefuhl*—that means "having your fingers on the pulse." It describes people with acute situational awareness that gives them the ability to respond appropriately to a situation before it becomes a crisis. Leaders who have their fingers on the pulse of their organization can proactively react to potential problems before they become catastrophes. Shackleton had *fingerspitzen*, an ability to sense his crew's ups and downs. He used it as a thermostat to adjust his leadership to meet changing situations. Churchill had *fingerspitzen*. His walkabouts through the rubbled streets of London gave him a visceral sense of British citizens' pain, morale, and mood. It gave him an extreme close-up of the situation rather than a panoramic view from 10 Downing Street. Churchill once said, "I want to take the face off the clock and look at the gears."

Who Is Curt Shilling?

An example of a person who didn't have their finger on the pulse of what was important—and paid the price for it—played out in the 2010 special election to fill the US senate seat long held by Ted Kennedy, who had passed away the previous year. The

Massachusetts state attorney general, Martha Coakley, threw her hat in the ring. As a long-time Democrat, Coakley should have easily defeated her Republican opponent, Scott Brown, for a seat that had been held by Democrats for decades. Throughout the campaign, however, it was evident that she didn't have her finger on the pulse of what was important to Massachusetts voters. The straw that broke the camel's back came during a radio interview. When Coakley was asked what she thought of Curt Shilling, the legendary Boston Red Sox pitcher loved and revered by every Sox fan, she stumbled and didn't seem to know who he was.[4]

Her gaffe had nothing to do with her character, integrity, or honesty—it just showed she had no awareness of who the Massachusetts voters were. To this day, Shilling is idolized by Sox fans because of the famous 2004 "Bloody Sock Game," where he pitched through extreme pain and a blood-soaked, severely injured ankle to win the sixth game of the American League Championship Series. With his help, Boston came back from a 3-0 hole in the series to beat their hated archrivals, the New York Yankees, and went on to sweep the Saint Louis Cardinals for their first World Series in eighty-six years. The rabid Sox fans who lived and died by the Boston baseball season couldn't fathom voting for someone who had no idea what Shilling meant to them. Many believe her fundamental lack of situational awareness cost her the election. It would be like running for office in Charlie Brown's neighborhood and not knowing who Snoopy was.

Once you've clearly charted the course for those you lead, you have to do what it takes to actively lead them on that course. Active leadership requires that you're aware of what's happening in the trenches, and that can't be done from afar. For doctors to check a patient's heartbeat, they have to put their fingers on the patient's pulse. For leaders to check the heartbeat of their organization, they have to put their fingers on all aspects of their organization that are important to its success. Regardless of venue or scope of responsibility, all leaders must do what it takes to "take the face off the clock and look at the gears."

Keeping a Finger on the Pulse

Shackleton and Churchill had an acute awareness of what was going on in their worlds and an exceptional sense of the moods of the people they were leading. That situational awareness was much more than intuition and instinct. It was a product of their relentless reconnaissance and efforts to stay informed and aware of everything that was important in their world. They were able to read between the lines and see into the shadows because they got out of their comfort zones and walked between those lines and into those shadows. Their reputation for what psychologist and author Daniel Goleman has termed "emotional intelligence,"[5] the ability to read people's thoughts and moods, wasn't some magical, innate skill but rather a product of the many hours they spent with their people, communicating with them face to face. They understood that leaders needed to be at the critical point in the arena to feel and see what was going on so they could determine what they had to do to lead to success.

Like military leaders who position themselves on the battlefield where the fighting is the worst, managers need to have their finger on the pulse of the most tenuous and vulnerable part of their business. When you get into the inner workings of your organization, you can spot problems and stop the bleeding before you have to apply a tourniquet. When you're forewarned of impending problems, you're forearmed to do what's necessary to fix them in their infant stages or, better yet, prevent them altogether. Let's look at the most common situational awareness potholes so you can steer around them.

Ignorance Is Bliss

Many top dogs think they're exempt from the details. On the contrary, employees want their managers to be situationally aware so they can effectively provide direction, set the example, coach, teach, mentor, and make timely decisions. A business leader's major job is to ensure success through disciplined execution, which requires being aware of what's going on where the rubber meets the road—the plant floor, the project site, and the point of sale.

Being a leader demands that you notice. You can't sit back and just hope things are going well. Hope is not a method. Leaders build trust by showing their employees that they are hyper-aware of those things that impact their environment and lives. You have to know your organization. Can you be as detailed a subject matter expert as those who work for you? Many times, no. However, it's necessary to have a level of situational awareness about what they do to know if things are going as they should. An orchestra's conductor may not play the flute, but he knows when the flutist hits a sour note.

In Ken Lay's case, things were going great at Enron. They were making money hand over fist. The company was growing and becoming more profitable at such an astonishing pace it seemed too good to be true. That's because managers in the bowels of Enron were generating bogus profit numbers using Ponzi scheme strategies to keep people, including their leaders, confused. It worked—until it didn't. Like all Ponzi schemes, eventually, someone has to pay the bill. The eventual bill payers were the Enron employees who lost decades of retirement savings and the company's stockholders who lost their entire investment. When Enron crashed around him, Lay, who was the CEO at the time, claimed he didn't possess the subject matter expertise to understand what his subordinates were doing.

Some managers, like Ken Lay, live in a comfortable cocoon, surrounded by their protective direct reports. They depend on their staff or self-ordained experts—consultants—to keep them abreast of what's happening in their business. Like the Nobel Laurette Bob Dylan opines, "You don't need a weatherman to know which way the wind blows." If those cocoon-protected executives would wet their finger, step outside of their comfort zone, and stick their finger in the air, they could personally determine the direction of the wind. When you have to depend on someone else to tell you what your employees are doing or thinking, you're not leading, you're presiding.

If You're Out of Their Sight, You're Out of Their Mind

The higher you go in an organization, the easier it is to invent excuses to be less accessible to your employees. With a broader scope of responsibility and a larger number of people to lead, it becomes much harder to stay situationally aware of what's happening in the depths of your business. Granted, time is a zero-sum game, but regardless of your enterprise's size or circumstances, you should plan to get your finger on the pulse of your employees regularly, because they need you. In my consulting life, I frequently hear leaders say, "I plan to," "I want to," or "I hope to get out and see my people as soon as I can find the time to do it."

A line manager with six employees, whom he works with daily, can easily stay abreast of what's going on in his team and be readily accessible to them. A project manager with fifty people working at several locations has a bigger challenge: keeping his fingers on the pulse of what's important and making himself accessible to all those he leads. A company CEO with 1,250 employees scattered across the globe must work very hard to stay adequately informed of all that's important to her endeavor's success. She must be extremely diligent about making herself accessible to those she leads on a regular basis. Yes, it's difficult, but it's necessary! Said another way, leaders must develop the self-discipline to do *what it takes to* make themselves accessible to those they lead. A leader is not a figurehead but someone who gets to know their employees and is available to help overcome unexpected obstacles, acknowledge employee efforts, provide guidance when needed, and answer questions and concerns. Doing that can be approached in two ways: passively and actively.

What It Takes to Make Yourself Accessible

Passive leadership accessibility is the easier of the two approaches. All good managers use a menu of passive systems to monitor the critical aspects of their business. Carefully crafted and focused passive tools, such as dashboards, daily/weekly/monthly/annual updates, scorecards, and HR climate surveys can provide decision-makers with useful information and a critical heads-up about problems before they happen. One of the most frequently touted passive accessibility programs is the "open door policy," which is intended to provide a safe opportunity for followers to meet with their leaders to voice their concerns, questions, or ideas. I've always had a well-advertised open-door policy, but my experience has been that people are very reluctant to be seen waltzing into the boss's office.

Although passive accessibility methods free up time, there are significant tradeoffs that make it the least effective way to make yourself accessible. Even though passive accessibility is better than no accessibility, at its very best, it can only provide filtered second- and third-hand information. Nothing is as effective for knowing what's going on as direct contact with the guts of your organization. Like a battlefield commander, there's no substitute for going up to the front lines and making a personal reconnaissance to determine the ground truth. To paraphrase Rich Lesser, the longtime CEO of the 22,000-employee Boston Consulting Group:

LEADERS OUT OF TOUCH

In a Microsoft global survey of 160,000 respondents:

A majority of workers stated: "We are struggling or just surviving in these pandemic work conditions."

Whereas their leaders said: "We are thriving."

—Microsoft Survey, "The Next Great Disruption Is Hybrid Work—Are We Ready?" March 22, 2021

> "When you become a leader and you have enormous influence over people's careers, people start screening what they say to you. They put a bubble around you, and you have to work hard to pop that bubble."[6]

The Only Place to Get Ground Truth is On the Ground

What separates the Leader from the Maintainer is the former's ability to get truthful and accurate assessments of how their leadership is doing, specifically how their intentions are being met. "Management by walking around" is a term that seems to be out of fashion, but there's nothing more powerful and potent than the shadow of the boss where the employees are doing the work. When you purposely seek out your employees and engage with them to learn what's going on in their slice of the world, you demonstrate that you're interested in them as employees and people. Actively getting firsthand information either verifies or refutes the second- and third-hand filtered reports you get from intermediaries. The only way you can learn the ground truth is by being on the ground.

The idea that a leader has to get out into the world is nothing new. The wise Russian tsar-reformer, Peter the Great, had it right in the 17th century. He recognized that he'd have to see it for himself to determine if his radical reforms to improve the lives and the plight of his people were being implemented as he intended. To get his fingers on his people's pulse, he donned the common folk's garb and combed the countryside, mingling with the people incognito to get complete awareness of the situation. He's the first example of being an "undercover boss" that I know of.

Whether you lead one person or a thousand, you must find a way to make yourself accessible to everyone in your organization. Getting out and about to make yourself accessible will provide informal opportunities to listen, learn, and penetrate deeper into your flock than your dashboards and formal metrics ever can. You become finely attuned to the rhythms, tempo, and issues that your charges are living with daily. By actively being accessible, your employees will become more comfortable with approaching you. Just as important, it will exponentially increase your level of real knowledge of how your goals and objectives are being executed. It will give you an honest picture of whether you're merely presiding over Mercenaries or actually leading Patriots. It will inform you whether your endeavor's operations and processes support the culture you want to inoculate within your team. It will show you where your leadership is needed. Active accessibility creates informal opportunities and candor, whereas passive modes and hierarchical settings kill openness.

As a battalion and brigade commander, I made myself accessible by walking around the motor pool and the barracks, eating with soldiers in the mess hall, and attending sporting and social events. Eisenhower said all leaders must personally see how the troops "are holding up." I learned more about the mood, combat readiness, morale, and general goings-on from those wanderings than any other method. It also showed my troops that I cared for them. When approached by soldiers with problems and issues, I took their concerns seriously and either fixed the issues or told them why I couldn't. This type of leadership provides a significant boost to morale and cohesion. Management (leadership) by walking around sounds simple, but it's a travesty how many leaders don't do it.

Kill a Few Messengers, and the Bad News Goes Away!

Have you ever hesitated outside your boss's office door with some unpleasant news or problem, dreading that step across its threshold? I once worked for a gifted Army commander who came to our unit with a reputation for being a soldier of solid character and exceptional competence. However, we quickly learned that his one flaw overshadowed his many qualities: He was a slayer of messengers. When things were going well, he was an amicable and pleasant boss. But when a staff officer or one of his subordinate commanders presented him with a problem or bad news, he would pitch a temper tantrum that was a tsunami of profanity mixed with demeaning comments and threats. Most importantly, he did nothing to contribute to solving the problem.

As one of his most senior staff officers, I worked with him more closely than anyone else. For some reason, I had the special dispensation of not being a victim of his outbursts. When I approached him about his temper, he said, "I don't suffer fools gladly. By putting pressure on these young staffers and commanders, they'll learn how to solve problems at their level and quit bringing them to me to solve!" And, of course, he was right. After about the fourth or fifth profane public humiliation of a messenger bearing bad tidings, problems ceased to make their way to our headquarters.

His strategy of making himself unapproachable so that problems would be solved at the lowest level worked...until it didn't! While some issues started to get solved at a lower level, many of the problems required his participation and would get swept under the rug because his subordinate leaders were afraid of how he would react to them.

His unapproachability eventually caught up with us. One of his subordinate commanders was so squeamish about the browbeating he knew he'd get that he decided to hide the issue from the boss. He hoped he could resolve the problem or that it would just disappear. A problem that could have been easily resolved in its early stages with the boss's intervention was left unchecked and festered until it became a catastrophe. Unfortunately, as a result, the subordinate commander was relieved of his command. Even worse, the boss didn't learn from the experience. In fact, his unapproachability became even more severe.

This is an extreme case of a boss who has intentionally made himself unapproachable. If we go back to our discussion of Dictators, you'll find that many of them are cut from the same cloth as this commander. But most leaders who aren't approachable are that way for reasons much more subtle and, in many cases, unintentional. Just because you've embraced passive and active measures to be accessible doesn't guarantee that you'll be approached by those you lead. Here are some common misconceptions about approachability:

- Telling everyone you're approachable will make you approachable.
- Being accessible will make you approachable.
- Being pleasant, smiling, and acting amicably will make you approachable.
- Publishing an open-door policy will have people lined up to approach you.

What It Really Takes to Make Yourself Approachable

When our charges feel comfortable enough to start bringing us their opinions, ideas, concerns, and especially their complaints to us, it's a sign that we've finally won their trust. They're confident they can approach us without fear of repercussion, recrimination, criticism, or professional risk. Regardless of how many modes of passive and active accessibility you've developed, unless you have a level of trust with your charges that makes them comfortable that they can approach you, it won't happen. You'll never get the truth. Being approachable is about being trusted. While being *accessible* is about breaking down physical barriers between leader and led, being *approachable* is about breaking down barriers of mistrust and building bridges of trust. First and foremost, don't kill the messenger!

Best Practices: Breaking Down Barriers to Approachability

Even if you're competent in all that I've suggested above, sometimes it can still be tough to break down those barriers of mistrust, reluctance, or discomfort that are carried by many of those you lead. Most people are reluctant to be candid with the boss. They're afraid of repercussions if they voice negative comments. If they voice positive comments, they're worried they'll be perceived as "brown-nosing" by their peers. I'm often asked for specific techniques on how to break down barriers. Look at your organizational structure and culture, and see how you can set the conditions where followers feel comfortable and safe to be open and candid. John Chambers, the former CEO of Cisco Systems, held a monthly birthday celebration. He explains why: "Anybody with a birthday that month gets to come to breakfast and quiz me. No directors or VPs in the room. It's brutal, but it's how I keep my finger on the pulse of what's working and what's not."

I used a variation of that technique as a battalion commander in Germany. I hosted a monthly breakfast for the twenty to thirty of my troops heading back to the States after serving two to three years in our unit. I wanted to accomplish two things at the breakfast. Most of all, I wanted to convey my sincere appreciation to each soldier for their years of faithful service. Additionally, it was an opportunity to get their candid feedback on how things were going in my battalion. I didn't want them to fear any retribution for their openness, so we had breakfast a day or so before they flew back to the States and after they had officially departed the battalion and had their completed evaluation reports in hand.

As we ate, I asked each soldier to tell us about their next assignment or what they would be doing after getting out of the Army. Once the breakfast cutlery had been removed, I used the opportunity to ask them for their assessment of how we were doing as a Germany-based infantry battalion. As a gesture, I passed my hat with the silver oak leaf of a lieutenant colonel on its brim to the soldier sitting next to me and said:

> "I'm going to give you an opportunity to turn the tables on the boss. You've just been promoted, and now you're the battalion commander of the 1st Battalion, 36th Infantry Regiment. Tell me three things that you wouldn't change in the battalion and three things you would immediately change. In other words, what are three good things and what are three bad things?"

The hat circled the table until every soldier had the opportunity to provide their input. It was gratifying to hear the good things the battalion was doing, but the most useful information came from "the three things I would change immediately are _____" question. Frequently, the frank honesty forced me to pause and consider my own leadership. Of course, I checked out every negative comment to ensure it wasn't just a personal gripe. Many were. However, many were legitimate problems that needed to be addressed. When I heard about a problem from several soldiers over several months, it usually proved true. "Staff sergeant xxx, in D Company, is abusive." "Several latrines in the motor pool have been broken for weeks." "The Charlie Company mess hall runs out of food at breakfast several times a week." I also learned what was working well and should stay on course. "The monthly PT contest between companies you recently started has really improved everyone's focus on PT." "First Sergeant Galloway is a tough hombre, but he really takes care of his men." "The mail service has gotten much better with the new mail clerk."

Whether it's a birthday celebration or a monthly breakfast, sometimes you just have to be innovative to penetrate the reluctance of many of your followers to be open with the boss. Every leader's environment is different, but with imagination and a sincere desire to make yourself accessible and approachable, you'll reap huge benefits from the situational awareness discovered from the effort.

Afterthought: Accessibility and Approachability— the Fine Line

You want those you lead to be comfortable being open with you. Finding the right mix of distance and closeness between leader and led is an important leadership skill. Managing the tension between authority and approachability can be tricky. You want to be friendly but not a friend. A leader must be accessible and approachable but shouldn't allow too much familiarity. You can be dedicated to the well-being of your subordinates without trying to be their "pal" or "one of the guys." A leader must remember that he'll likely have to make decisions that won't be popular, and getting close to people makes those decisions harder.[7]

Also, don't misinterpret being accessible and approachable as providing an open mic for the malcontents and disgruntled in your organization. Of course, you want to hear about things that aren't going well—criticisms, problem areas, and complaints—but just as importantly, you want to know what's going well and what can be leveraged to do better. You also want productive ideas, opinions, and thoughts. Unfortunately, there will always be a small contingent of employees who'll take advantage of your accessibility and use it as a soapbox to waste your time. In many cases, they just want to be heard. Don't fall into the trap that many do of spending 90 percent of your time listening to the 5 percent or fewer who'll never be content regardless of the situation. Your time is an asset and shouldn't be wasted.

Summary Points

- Situational awareness is having your finger on the pulse of your organization and knowing what's going on around you.
- Situational awareness is a leader's comprehension of the situation that affects the mission, job, task, or environment.
- A leader's environment encompasses everything that's important to the success of their undertaking or has the potential to derail it.
- Leaders need to be situationally aware of all the things that affect their employees' commitment and engagement.
- Leading is an active and participative endeavor. You cannot lead from the corner office or from your laptop.
- Leaders with their finger on the pulse of their organization can proactively respond to potential problems before they become catastrophic.
- Employees want their leaders to know what's going on in their world.
- Being a leader demands you notice; you can't sit back and just hope things go well.
- Nothing is as effective for learning the truth than making a personal reconnaissance.
- The only way to learn ground truth is to be on the ground.
- Whether you lead a thousand people or just one person, you must make yourself accessible to everyone in your organization.
- Just because you're accessible doesn't mean you're approachable.
- Being accessible is about breaking down physical barriers between you and those you lead.
- Being approachable is about breaking down barriers of mistrust and building bridges of trust.
- Finding the right mix of distance and closeness between leader and led is a vital leadership imperative.

If you have a *good finger on the pulse of your organization*, go to the next chapter. If not, "Look in the Mirror" below.

Look in the Mirror at My Situational Awareness

Review the following statements, then *underline* where you are and *circle* where you want to be:

- My *situational awareness* of all things important to our success is:
  - Poor / Mediocre / OK / Good / Excellent
- I spend the right amount of time out of my office visiting employees:
  - Never / Occasionally / Frequently / All the Time
- I look for problems in my organization before they become catastrophic:
  - Never / Occasionally / Frequently / All the Time
- I do what it takes to make myself accessible to every employee:
  - Never / Occasionally / Frequently / All the Time
- My ability to calmly take bad news without killing the messenger is:
  - Poor / Mediocre / OK / Good / Excellent
- My ability to break down barriers of mistrust in my company is:
  - Poor / Mediocre / OK / Good / Excellent
- My reputation as a listener is:
  - Poor / Mediocre / OK / Good / Excellent
- My ability to get employees to open up to me is:
  - Poor / Mediocre / OK / Good / Excellent
- When I talk to employees, my ability to give them total focus is:
  - Poor / Mediocre / OK / Good / Excellent

What Aspect(s) of My Situational Awareness Could Use Improvement?

Example: My deputy advises me that I come across as stern and severe. Even though I have an open-door policy, employees are apprehensive about approaching me. When I engage with my employees, I sense they're telling me what I want to hear rather than what they want to say. As a result, I'm not sure I have a good finger on the pulse of my organization.

I Want to Improve:

My Philosophy on Situational Awareness

Example: I want to have situational awareness of all aspects of my organization that contribute to its success or could potentially cause its failure. I also want to be accessible to all my employees beyond the formal methods, like my open-door policy, and create an environment where they feel I'm approachable.

My Philosophy on Situational Awareness:

My Action Plan

Example: I'm a prisoner of my calendar. I will start scheduling a recurring walking tour of my employees' offices and workspaces at least once a week on specific days and times. I will design a matrix to see all my employees in the building and grade myself on making contact with each one.

I will work on overcoming my outwardly introverted personality and engage more with my employees to convey my appreciation for what they do.

My Action Plan:

17

TEACHING—COACHING— MENTORING

"The relationship between a boss and a subordinate is the same relationship as a teacher and a student."

—Dr. W. Edwards Deming, business theorist

TEACHING WITHOUT PURPOSE is a crime. It's like teaching a child how to pronounce words but not telling them what they mean.[1] Good teachers, coaches, and mentors are masters of conveying purpose to all they impart. Let me offer a real-life example of a great coaching moment to illustrate what I mean.

We were on the last day of an exhausting thirty-five days of training at Grafenwoehr, Germany, climaxing with an infantry battalion live-fire assault on a fortified enemy position. The live-fire exercise was a complex operation requiring the synchronized fires of fourteen Bradley Fighting Vehicles, fourteen Abrams tanks, six howitzers, six mortars, four Apache attack helicopters, and a company of more than one hundred dismounted infantry soldiers. As I looked through binoculars from the turret of my command vehicle, I could see that the tank company and the Bradley company were in their assigned attack positions. The artillery battery commander radioed that he was set and ready to fire while the engineer company and chemical smoke platoon reported they were good to go. The mission called for the attack to be kicked off with a preparatory barrage of coordinated fires of the Apache gunships, Abrams tanks, and artillery. Once the prep fires on the objective were complete, they would be lifted, and the follow-on assault of a dismounted infantry company would sweep across the enemy positions supported by cannon fire from the Bradley's to finish the job.

Everything was set to go as I anxiously awaited the arrival of the Apaches to start the attack. As much like a sledgehammer as the assembled firepower seemed, the execution of the operation had to be orchestrated as delicately as if it were a performance of the "Swan Lake" ballet. This was training, not actual combat, but as with all battalion live-fire exercises, hundreds of soldiers were in harm's way. Synchronizing the fires of the Bradleys, tanks, artillery, mortars, and the Apaches was a formidable challenge, requiring meticulous precision. If we lifted the preparatory fires too early, the enemy would have time to reinforce themselves in preparation for our infantry assault. If we lifted them too late, our dismounted infantry would be victims of friendly fire.

As a new battalion commander, this was my first time leading such a large live-fire exercise. The successful synchronization of the operation and, more importantly, the safety of my soldiers weighed heavily on my shoulders. In the back of my mind lingered the fact that shortly before I took command, just a mile from where we stood, a training accident during a similar live-fire exercise took the lives of two of the battalion's soldiers.

While I waited in the turret for the helicopters to arrive, I was mentally rehearsing the trigger points to start and stop each operational phase at precisely the right time. My pucker factor was already maxing out when my driver announced over the intercom that there was a "big general" pounding on the back ramp of my Bradley. I jumped down from the turret and was surprised to see my division commander, Major General George Joulwan. After I gave the general a quick salute, he asked, "I understand the Apaches are a few minutes out. Have you got time to tell me what you have going on?" Of course I did. I gave him a quick overview of my concept of operations. He asked, "What worries you the most about your plan of attack?" I told him that my biggest concern was getting the synchronization of lifting fires between each phase precisely right. General Joulwan went into full coach mode at that point: "Walk me through your plan and trigger points," he said. As he listened to my concept of operations, he would stop me with a "Yes, that's great, go on!" When I got to the trickiest part of the operation, shifting the Apache rocket fires to start the infantry assault, he stopped me, pointed to a tree-covered ridgeline to our left, and asked, "Have you considered bringing the Apaches in on the left on the other side of that hill? That would put a physical barrier between the gunships and the infantry." I hadn't, but I instantly saw the benefit of doing what he suggested. A few minutes later, the Apaches arrived. I had them move to the new position on the left. The operation kicked off and was successful without incident.

What General Joulwan did that day was classic coaching. Coaching takes place where the action is happening. At the live-fire exercise, he stood by and observed how I was navigating a challenging situation and interjected positive feedback at critical points where I was on the correct course. Where he observed a better way to "synchronize" based on his many years of experience, he suggested a better or more efficient way to do it: "Why not move the gunships to the other side of the hill during the assault?"

The Leader as Teacher, Coach, and Mentor

I had the good fortune to work for some great leaders in and out of uniform. General Joulwan was the leader who stands out as the best coach, teacher, and mentor. As a cadet at West Point, he was on the football team and frequently used the game's analogies to make a point, earning him the nickname "Coach." He seemed to be clairvoyant. Coach would show up at every critical training event or operation, like that rainy day at Graf. With more than 17,000 soldiers and thirty-five other battalions in his 3rd Armored Division, I never understood how he had time to visit my battalion at almost every critical training event. He treated every one of these encounters as an opportunity to teach or coach, and I always learned from his visits. Leaders in every type of organization should do the same: consider every encounter a teaching or coaching opportunity. The highest form of demonstrating your competence is to impart that knowledge to those with less experience by teaching and coaching.

General Joulwan had a powerful personality and an imposing presence that, on first meeting, was intimidating. However, it didn't take long for me to realize he was genuinely interested in making me the best leader I could be. He was a teacher, not a preacher. Like all good coaches, he pulled things from me I hadn't considered by asking the right questions to hammer his teaching points home. Unlike many senior leaders, I felt secure with him because he wasn't judging but coaching. He didn't reveal my shortcomings, of which there were many, in a demeaning way. You knew he wasn't testing you to reveal your weaknesses but coaching you because he wanted you to excel. He made you better than you were. Not only was General Joulwan an enthusiastic coach, but he was also a great teacher and mentor. Many people consider coaching, teaching, and mentoring the same thing. I agree that coaching and mentoring are forms of teaching. However, I contend that in the context of leadership, they differ. Each deserves to be considered as a specific skill that leaders need to understand and use appropriately. Let's examine how the three are applied differently and why each is important:

- **Teaching:** Teaching is when an experienced practitioner imparts knowledge to a student in the form of basic skills, concepts, and techniques. It takes place anywhere the teacher can convey that knowledge to a student in an environment conducive to focused learning. It can occur in a classroom, in a small team, on the shop floor, in a cubicle, or any place where the teacher can focus the student's attention on the subject to be learned. Teaching focuses on specific lessons, why they're essential to the student, and a process to ensure the lessons have been learned. Teaching is imprinting in the student's brain what to do, how to do it, and why they're doing it. Teaching is *not* lecturing.

- **_Coaching:_** In coaching, as with teaching, an experienced practitioner also imparts knowledge to the student. The difference is that the coach doesn't convey that knowledge in a classroom environment but in the real world. They coach where things happen and where the lessons taught earlier can be observed and judged. Coaching happens during the action on the playing field. A good coach spots the nonobvious but impactful events unseen by the player or employee at the moment of action and uses it as a coaching opportunity. The coach sees clarity in what others do not see, cannot see, or have overlooked. Coach John Wooden once said, "A coach is anyone who can give corrective advice without causing resentment."

- **_Mentoring_**: Rather than teaching concepts and skills or coaching to improve those skills, mentoring focuses on broader issues, such as values, organizational best practices, career advice, or general professional knowledge. Mentoring can be as formal as company-sponsored programs or as informal as an old friend or boss helping a young colleague. Mentors are talent growers, and their purpose is to guide the less-experienced person over time to achieve their maximum potential. The mentor/mentee relationship must be based on symbiotic trust. The mentee must trust the mentor's counsel, regardless of how painful the advice may be. As the saying goes, "Some of the best mentors are also tormentors." Many mentor/mentee relationships can last a lifetime. General Joulwan mentored me for years after I left his command. If you're still confused between each type, let me give you two examples that highlight the differences between teaching, coaching, and mentoring.

COACH AND PLAYERS: How to Play Offense

- *Teach:* The college basketball coach has his five freshman recruits in the locker room, and on a whiteboard, he teaches them the first offensive play he wants them to memorize. On the board, he draws what each of the five players is supposed to do, where to go, and why they must go there. Then he takes them to the court, where all five players slowly walk through each step of their assignments while he demonstrates how he wants them to pick and roll against the other team. The team practices the play slowly in a "by the numbers" drill several times. The coach has them walk through the drill several times until he's satisfied they have learned their lessons and understand their individual routes and assignments.

- *Coach:* The coach then brings in the upperclassmen and sets them up in defensive positions. He has the five freshmen run the new play against the defending upperclassmen. The coach does his magic from the sidelines during the full-court, full-speed practice session. He coaches by encouraging, admonishing, and advising during the action. "Dribble closer to that pick." "Great shooting off the screen, but don't take that shot so far from the net." When things get to the point where he sees a valuable lesson can be learned, he stops the play, pulls in the players, and coaches them on what they're doing wrong or how to do it better. Then he starts the play again, lets the players make the adjustments, and continues his coaching from the sidelines.

- *Mentor:* At the end of his junior year, a star player tells the coach he's being courted by professional scouts who want him to skip his senior year and enter the NBA draft. The coach sits the player down and gives him the pros and cons of skipping his senior year. He relates stories of previous players who left early, did well, and had great professional success. He also shares accounts of other players who regretted their decisions. The coach mentors the player on what he thinks is best for him based on his current ability and maturity, giving him the plusses and minuses of leaving school a year early. He also offers to connect him with past players who successfully transitioned early to the professional ranks and those who later regretted their decision to leave school a year early.

VP AND MANAGER: Briefing the Board

- **Teach:** The executive vice president of a publicly held company meets with the newly hired finance manager to prepare him for the upcoming quarterly board of directors meeting. The new manager will be responsible for briefing the company on its current financials at these sessions. The VP tells the manager exactly how the CEO wants it done, slowly walking him through the data, the process, and the steps dictated by the CEO. He advises the manager that the CEO is very particular about what and how the data is presented in the PowerPoint slides and warns him that there is no license to do it differently. Then, using last quarter's data, the VP demonstrates how the briefing should be conducted. He then directs the new manager to prepare the financial data as he was just taught and be ready to brief it at a dress rehearsal board meeting next week.

- **Coach:** A week later, the VP arranges a mock board of directors meeting using company staff members. The new manager starts the mock session, and about five minutes into the meeting, the VP coaches him: "You did a good job setting a clear sense of purpose for your briefing." A few minutes later, the VP stops the manager again and coaches him: "You noticed Mike has just taken over your briefing and has gotten you off-topic by asking you questions you'll address later in the briefing. One of the members of the board is famous for doing just that. You have to stay on topic by politely telling him his concerns will be addressed shortly." When the practice session is over, the VP gives the manager a critique of what he did well and where he needs to improve, then answers any questions the manager may have.

- *Mentor:* A couple of years later, the now-seasoned finance manager realizes he has ambitions to move up in the company. The manager sees from the bios of the company's senior executives that the VP who helped onboard him a few years ago started his career in the same finance section as the manager is in now. The manager asks the VP if he would be amenable to sitting down for a few minutes to advise him on moving up in the organization. As with most senior leaders, the VP consents, and they schedule a meeting that begins a long mentor-mentee relationship.

"Shaping Souls": Your Legacy Are Those Leaders You Leave Behind

If you haven't already had an opportunity to teach, coach, or mentor someone, I promise you that the psychological reward of seeing your charges become better versions of themselves because of your efforts is powerful stuff. When you see that you've made a positive difference in the character or competence of those you're leading, the feeling is almost electric. Remember the question I asked people: Who was the most influential person in your life who made you the leader and person you are today? The answers overwhelmingly pointed to people who imparted knowledge to them during their lives: parents, teachers, coaches, and bosses. I once heard someone say that "Leadership goes beyond the transmission of skills—it entails the shaping of souls." The most powerful way to "shape souls" is by showing your employees that you care enough about them to spend your time and energy to make them better and more successful by teaching and coaching them to become the best possible version of themselves.

A true test of your leadership is what happens not when you're there but after you leave. It goes back to our "woodpile" example. What is your leadership legacy? Is your organization better off for your leadership? Will you leave the woodpile higher than you found it? If you left today, would anyone care? Perhaps most important is, what do you want to be remembered for? The culture of your organization or team and the leaders you leave behind are your legacy—good or bad. Leaders are responsible for vigorously teaching and coaching the next generation of their leaders. One of the most powerful ways to teach is through your example, behavior, actions, and decisions.

> **LEGACY**
> **You are not dead as long as you are remembered.**
> —*Russian proverb*

It's a fact: Good parents grow good kids, good coaches develop good coaches, and good leaders build good leaders. It's their legacy.

Do you consider yourself a good coach and teacher? You may not be as good as you think you are. Many studies show that managers who think they're good at coaching and teaching are not. In one study, 3,761 executives assessed their coaching skills, then their assessments were compared with those of people who worked with them. The results didn't align well. Twenty-four percent of the executives significantly overestimated their abilities, rating themselves above average, while their colleagues ranked them in the bottom third of the group.[2]

So many supervisors aren't effective at teaching and coaching because they don't consider it a primary leadership function. It's something they believe just naturally happens during their workday. I've often heard, "No, I don't consciously think about teaching and coaching, but I do it all the time." My advice is to look at how you lead through the lens of teaching, coaching, and mentoring. Ask yourself, Am I taking every opportunity to use my experience and expertise to make those on my team better?

Afterthought: Growing Your Own Is Cost-Effective

The military doesn't have the luxury of hiring outside help for their middle or senior leadership positions—they have to grow their own. The military's survivability is based on its leaders' ability to produce more leaders, not more followers. The Army doesn't have an HR department that can go on LinkedIn and place a want ad for candidates with *"20 years' of proven performance in infantry combat operations, training, and leadership to be commander of a mechanized infantry battalion."* The Army has created a succession management process to grow men and women with the requisite character and competence to fill its senior leadership positions. It's an efficient process that ensures that when they need that battalion commander, there's a stable of qualified candidates to fill the role. The process is based on continuous teaching, coaching, and mentoring of young potential leaders throughout their entire career.

The private sector could do well by doing the same. Not growing their own leaders costs companies millions every year. The survivability and prosperity of an organization depends on its willingness and success in nurturing and growing its future generation of leaders. Many companies pay lip service to the idea of leader development and succession management. Very few have detailed and focused succession management plans that prepare their junior managers to fill future leadership positions. How often do we hear of a new CEO being hired from outside a company and fired shortly thereafter because he wasn't a good fit? It's because the company didn't do a good job of growing its own future leaders. A well-executed leadership development and succession management program is an investment in your people. A senior executive recently told me, "If I put too much effort and resources into developing my employees, they'll get overqualified and leave the company." When I heard that, I asked him, "What if you don't invest in them and they stay?"

Summary Points

Don't be a Maintainer who:
- Sees yourself as the boss, not a teacher or coach.
- Gives your employees too much "what to do" and not enough "how to do it."
- Doesn't let those you lead fail.
- Doesn't delegate because "It's just easier to do it yourself and not have to explain how to do it!"

- Doesn't take the time to teach the right way when something is done wrong.
- Lets teaching moments pass because you don't have the time or energy to teach.
- Gives orders rather than lessons.

Be a teacher who:

- Imparts knowledge to those you lead in the form of your industry's basic skills, concepts, and techniques.
- Uses every opportunity to impart knowledge to your employees.
- Coaches where things happen—on the court, in the office, on the shop floor.
- Spots nonobvious but impactful lessons.
- Gives corrective advice without causing resentment.

Be a mentor who:

- Teaches values, best practices, and career advice to junior leaders.
- Guides junior talent to their fullest potential.
- Not only teaches skills but shapes souls.
- Leaves the woodpile higher.

If you're comfortable with your *teaching/coaching/mentoring*, move on. If not, "Look in the Mirror" below.

Look in the Mirror at How I Teach/Coach/Mentor

Review the following statements, then *underline* where you are and *circle* where you want to be:

- **My ability to teach my employees important professional skills is:**
  - Poor / Mediocre / OK / Good / Excellent
- **My ability to teach *how to do it* rather than dictating *what to do* is:**
  - Poor / Mediocre / OK / Good / Excellent
- **I use on-the-spot opportunities to impart knowledge to my team:**
  - Never / Occasionally / Frequently / All the Time
- **I ensure that what I teach is learned to a high standard:**
  - Never / Occasionally / Frequently / All the Time
- **I take every opportunity to coach where things are happening:**
  - Never / Occasionally / Frequently / All the Time
- **I give on-the-spot corrections and praise to my employees:**
  - Never / Occasionally / Frequently / All the Time
- **I stop and coach when I see nonobvious but important points to be learned:**
  - Never / Occasionally / Frequently / All the Time
- **My ability to give corrective advice without causing resentment is:**
  - Poor / Mediocre / OK / Good / Excellent
- **My ability to mentor and impart values, career advice, and knowledge is:**
  - Poor / Mediocre / OK / Good / Excellent

What Aspect(s) of My Teaching Could Use Improvement?

Example: In our frenetic work environment, I too often tell my employees what to do without using the opportunity to teach them how to do it. However, when I do make corrections, I come across as giving negative feedback rather than coaching them on how to do it better. This causes resentment and gives the impression that I don't appreciate the employee's situation, which is not true.

I Want to Improve:

My Philosophy on Teaching/Coaching/Mentoring

Example: I want to be a good teacher and coach to my employees. Also, I will mentor those junior leaders who I see as having potential for future leadership in the company.

My Philosophy on Teaching/Coaching/Mentoring:

My Action Plan

Example: I will take my four junior leaders, whom I see as having potential for future senior leadership, and start mentoring them. I will schedule walking tours throughout our company and look for opportunities to coach. I will start weekly brown bag lunches with employees who report directly to me in order to teach skills necessary for success in our industry and urge my junior leaders to do the same with their direct reports.

My Action Plan:

18

LEADING BY EXAMPLE

"In crisis, leaders get bigger or smaller."

—Nancy Koehn, author of Forged in Crisis

LEADERS ARE OFTEN judged not by what they say but by what they do. Setting the example is fundamental to getting people to believe in who you are and what you stand for.[1] Nobody understood this better than Colonel Lewis Burwell "Chesty" Puller. The situation in November 1950 for the American forces defending the Chosin Reservoir in Korea can only be described as desperate. Fighting on rugged, hardscrabble terrain in subzero temperatures, the 30,000 US soldiers and Marines were outnumbered by 120,000 enemy troops. Colonel Puller's Marine regiment found itself cut off from the main US fighting force, surrounded, and vastly outnumbered by the attacking Chinese troops. One of Puller's battalions reported that they had just repulsed a strong enemy attack and had taken heavy casualties. The battalion commander requested to pull back before the next Chinese assault because they were low on ammunition. Colonel Puller radioed the commander: "I promise you I will get ammo to you. But until then, fix your bayonets and hold your position at all costs!"

As the legend goes, shortly after the battalion commander issued the order to his men to "fix bayonets and stand your ground," a jeep pulled up next to his command post and outjumped the regimental commander with a bayonet-tipped rifle. The Chinese repeatedly attacked. The Marines successfully defended against each assault as Puller moved through the positions, exposing himself to enemy machine guns and artillery fire, ensuring correct tactical employment, reinforcing the lines as needed, and personally overseeing the treatment and evacuation of the wounded. Puller left the battalion only after the ammo resupply he had promised them finally showed up. The Navy Cross's citation for his actions in the Chosin campaign reads, "By his unflagging determination, he served to inspire his men to heroic efforts in defense of their positions."[2]

I use this battlefield illustration because Chesty Puller was a leader who clearly understood how to use the power of personal example to influence those he led. Marines on the ground reported that the minute he stepped out of his jeep, he remarked with a smile, "We're surrounded; now we have the bastards right where we want them!" It was at this point that a sigh of relief rolled across the battalion like a tidal wave. The arrival of one more bayonet didn't make the difference. It was Puller's aura of optimism that brought hope to a seemingly hopeless situation. It was his palpable self-confidence that put steel in the spine of the surrounded Marines. It was his bravery that gave his Marines courage. Puller set the example that he demanded of his Marines. He proved true to his word by getting the ammunition to the battalion as he said he would. He won their loyalty and respect because they saw him sharing in their hardships and fighting by their side.

Leadership Is Influence

The most powerful way to convince your followers you're worthy of their trust is through your good example during the bad times as well as the good. The quickest way to lose that trust is through your bad example. Your example puts your character and competence on parade for all to see. Setting the example gives legitimacy to your words. It's the way you demonstrate and, therefore,

"I need to be seen to be believed."
—Queen Elizabeth II

prove who you are. Character matters, but it's not known until it's shown. Your character must be demonstrated and publicly validated by your actions, behavior, and deeds. To be believed, it has to be seen. You have to show direct behavioral evidence that you are who you say you are. You have to role-model the behavior you expect from others. You have to practice what you preach. Your followers have to see you in the midst of their hardships and struggles before they'll believe you have their best interests at heart and really care about them. The jury is out on who you are and what you stand for until it's conspicuous. "To lead" is an action verb; you have to *do it*. Ultimately, it doesn't matter who you are, what you say, or how you say it, leadership is about what you *do*.[3]

Knowing how to do something and doing what it takes by leading by example are two different things, however. Puller lived the example he required of his officers and men. His word was his bond. He didn't demand of his Marines anything he didn't demand of himself. Puller led by example, but many leaders do not. They may understand that "example is fundamental" to getting people to trust you, but they don't possess the will to do "what it takes."

Though most of us will never be asked to lead in such dire or difficult circumstances as Puller and his men, the basic principles for inspiring trust in our leadership and commitment to our common endeavor are fundamental principles for any organization. Whether you're the CEO of a global enterprise with thousands of employees or a community leader supervising three volunteers, the principles of leading by example are the same. Like Puller, you must:

- *Set the example:* Role-model the behavior you expect of others.
- *Be true to your word:* Practice what you preach.
- *Share in the hardships:* Be there during the bad as well as the good.

The first principle isn't optional. You're always setting an example. You're a role model whether you want to be one or not. The second two principles are optional. Let's examine these three principles and why each is so important to building trust.

SET THE EXAMPLE

Puller's motto, "lead by example," wasn't an empty slogan. In every command position he held, from second lieutenant to lieutenant general, he never failed to personally set the example he demanded of his officers and men. In combat, he rigidly refused comforts he couldn't give his Marines. He lived with his men, carrying his own pack, eating the same food, and sleeping in the same miserable conditions. He required the same of his subordinate leaders, refusing to allow them to enjoy any comforts not available to their men. The legendary stories of Puller's lead-from-the-front example inspire Marines to this day. There is no argument that Puller led by example, as evidenced by his massive list of combat decorations for extraordinary valor.[4]

History gives us many leaders, like Puller, who, through their example, influenced people to buy into who they were and what they stood for: Martin Luther King's nonviolence when he was the recipient of repeated violence, Washington sharing the same misery as his men for the eight winters of the Revolutionary War, Nelson Mandela forgiving his jailers after eighteen years of imprisonment, Winston Churchill's empathy as he walked through the bombed London streets hours after the air raids, Shackleton's optimism during the most dire times.

> **"Preach the gospel at all times— when necessary, use words."**
> *—Saint Francis of Assisi*

Many leaders rationalize that their followers don't notice or don't care about the slight inconsistencies between what they say and what they do. They think they're immune to the blatant inconsistency between their deeds and words. Take the example of Al Gore, the self-styled "Mr. Environment."[5] Did he really think people wouldn't notice or care that as he passionately espoused the dangers of climate change, he lived by a different standard in his own life? As he toured the country in his private jet and basked in the spotlight of climate change fame, he lived in a house four times the size of the average American's that consumed twelve times as much energy, with energy bills averaging $12,000 a month.[6]

Setting the example means that when you draw the line on the wall of what you expect from your employees, you must live up to that same line. The example you set, whether positive or negative, will be the standards of your organization. It's like the old saying, "The first person we lead is ourselves." Following the same rules you set for others is vital to earning the trust of those you lead. When leaders behave in ways that violate the standards they expect of others, employee cynicism goes up, and job performance and morale go down. Gore deluded himself into believing that the imbalance between his deeds and his words was invisible to the public. He did everything possible to portray himself as a leader—except set the example!

BE TRUE TO YOUR WORD

The first time you're tagged as a "Do as I say, not as I do leader," any trust you've banked up to that point will be cashed in. What does practicing what you preach really mean? It means that you do what you say you're going to do and follow through on your promises. It means you understand that you must demand of yourself what you demand of others.

> "Corrupt politicians make the other 10 percent look bad."
> —Henry Kissinger, former US secretary of state

Nothing corrodes followers' trust faster than when a leader says one thing, then does something entirely different. The recent COVID-19 pandemic provides a perfect example of leaders who demand we follow their rules while they flagrantly ignore them. Shortly after dictating to his citizens, "I am locking down California. STAY HOME!," California Governor Gavin Newsom was caught having dinner at an exclusive restaurant with a large group of friends. Speaker of the House Nancy Pelosi, who strongly advocated closing businesses and called those who refused to wear masks "cowards," was photographed getting her hair done without wearing a mask in a salon that was supposed to be closed. The "Do as I say, not as I do leaders" are on both sides of the aisle. In a radio interview, Texas Senator Ted Cruz, during the 2021 winter disaster that left sixteen dead, told millions of fellow Texans, "Stay at home!" The next day, he boarded a plane to Cancun to join his family on vacation.

These are just a few of the many examples of political leaders who have implied "do as I say, not as I do" by their actions. It's no wonder that trust in politicians has been declining and is at an all-time low. Leaders communicate by example. The Pew Research Center, a nonpartisan think tank in Washington, DC, started asking Americans in 1958, "Do you trust the government to do the right thing most of the time?" In 1958, 77 percent of Americans responded yes. That percentage has steadily declined to 24 percent in 2023.[7] This drastic loss of trust is because we expect leaders to practice what they preach, and most Americans believe too few leaders in politics do. Our followers judge every word we say and every action we take to see if we're practicing what we're preaching. I can't say it too often: "Our words are merely the scorecard by which our deeds are graded." Every time a leader deviates from the accepted official or unofficial norms, he loses some level of follower trust.

Trust In Government

Percentage of US adults who have trust in the government to act in the best interests of the public:

All the time: 2%
Most of the time: 22%

—*Source: Pew Research Center, May, 2023*

Too many politicians today violate their own mandates within a few days of foisting them on their citizens. When caught, their solution is to spin a paint-by-the-numbers apology, hoping to minimize their blatant double standards, refuse blame, or deny the truth. There seems to be no accountability beyond the gratuitous *mea culpa*. No wonder we're cynical. The brazenness of their acts flaunts an attitude that they feel entitled to live by different rules than they expect of us. They act as if the sin is not in the doing but in the getting caught.

Like our examples, leaders who don't practice the behavior they preach to others create resentment, discontent, and a sense of separateness in the people they supposedly lead. It's not just the big things that erode followers' trust but also the little things. Sneaking out to have dinner with friends when you're trying to influence your constituents and voters to stay at home may not seem like a big deal. But it is. These politicians all seem to have caught a bad case of Adult-Onset Arrogance.

Politicians don't have a monopoly on saying one thing and doing something else. Americans' confidence in most US institutions has been steadily declining for the past several years.[8] It seems like we're in an era of constant apologies and confessional statements from leaders who were caught violating their professed standards of behavior. When caught for not living up to their dictates or attempting to covertly skirt the system, they give a hollow and seemingly insincere apology. They assume it will atone for their misdeeds and that no trust will be lost because of their "heartfelt" confession. There's no remorse or sincere contrition; it's just an "I'm sorry I got caught" attitude.

AMERICANS' CONFIDENCE IN MAJOR US INSTITUTIONS DIPS

Share of Americans who have a "great deal" or "quite a lot" of confidence in the following institutions:

1.	Military	64%
2.	Police	45%
3.	Presidency	23%
4.	Church	31%
5.	Public schools	28%
6.	Justice system	14%
7.	Big Business	14%
8.	Newspapers	21%
9.	TV news	11%
10.	Congress	7%

—*Source: Gallup Confidence in Institutions Poll, June 2022*

Unfortunately, those leaders who flaunt a sense of entitlement and privilege lead by example, but it's a bad example. You must be true to your word if you want to be trusted by those you lead.

SHARE THE HARDSHIPS

To earn trust and commitment, leaders must also be seen as sharing in the hardships and struggles of their followers. What does sharing hardships really mean? It means you share in the bad times as well as the good. It means you hold yourself accountable to the same standards you set for your followers. It means you experience the same stresses your employees are experiencing. It means you endure the same unpleasantness and job insecurities your employees are enduring. Why is sharing hardships necessary? It shows that you don't hold yourself above them. It demonstrates you care about what they're going through and don't consider yourself privileged or entitled.

Puller's motto, "Lead by example," was not an empty slogan; he lived with his men and shared their hardships. There were no officers' messes in his outfit. He fell in line with the privates, carrying his own mess gear, and in true Marine tradition, Puller would be the last man in the chow line.[9] In his book *Leaders Eat Last*, Simon Sinek tells of his surprise when he visited a US Marine unit and witnessed its leaders standing at the end of the chow line, eating only after all their troops had been served. There are several reasons Marine (and Army) leaders eat last. First, it ensures the mess sergeants have planned well enough to feed everyone. If they run out of food or the qual-

> **"It is painful, continual, and difficult work to be done by kindness, by watching, by warning and by praise, but above all by example."**
> —*John Ruskin, Victorian philosopher*

ity of the chow isn't as good at the end of the line as it is at the front, it'll be the leaders who suffer—not a good thing for that mess sergeant's future. But also, in high-tempo combat operations or field exercises, circumstances may make it impossible for even the best mess sergeants to prepare a great meal. Said more crudely, the chow stinks through no fault of the cooks but what's served is better than MREs, a cold, dehydrated, tasteless field ration. In this case, it shows the troops that their leaders are sharing the same lousy food as they are. In either situation, it's a conspicuous demonstration that their leaders aren't exempt from the hardships they expect their troops to endure. Eating last is repaid with loyalty and hard work from the troops.[10]

Also, when you know you're asking people to do tough things, and you share and are seen sharing in those tough things, it makes asking your followers to do tough things easier. General Harold Alexander's conscience was clear in June 1940. As the officer responsible for evacuating the defeated British Army off Dunkirk beach, he was the last man on the last boat, making sure all 338,225 men went before him. It provides a little comfort knowing you're proving that you wouldn't ask of them that which you wouldn't ask of yourself. It also produces a special camaraderie of shared suffering between you and those you lead.

Tough Times Bring Out the Best in Leadership

Circumstances don't make a man; they reveal him. Tough times and crises bring out both the best and worst in leaders. Leading in the good times is easy. Inspiring others to be committed to a common goal gets much tougher in the hard times, and that's exactly when a leader's trust is needed the most. Sharing the hardships of those you lead is a powerful principle leaders ignore at their own expense.

The recession of the early 1970s brought out the best in one leader who clearly understood the importance of sharing the struggles of his employees. After years of great prosperity, Bill Hewlett, CEO of the company that carried his name (Hewlett-Packard), found that his company of 16,000 employees was suddenly treading water, trying to stay afloat in a deep recession. The easiest way for a company to cut costs in an economic downturn is to lay off employees. In fact, during the 1970s' recession, that's exactly what many CEOs did: They laid off millions of the rank-and-file to please Wall Street. Meanwhile, these same CEOs and their top executives held tightly to their own positions and privileges.[11]

Hewlett's staff advised him that if he laid off a tenth of his 1,600 employees, HP could ride out and survive the recession. He decided to ignore that advice at a time when he knew it would be very tough for

- **Dictators are at their worst when things are at their worst.**
- **Maintainers are absent when things are at their worst.**
- **Leaders are at their best when things are at their worst.**

his employees to find another job. In a memo to his employees, Hewlett explained:

"Usually in business, it is the little guy on the line who takes it on the chin, while management and higher-ups stay at work. It is only right that everyone share the pain, up and down the line."[12]

He developed a plan where everyone in the company, including senior executives and himself, would incur a 10 percent pay cut and take an unpaid day off every two weeks. Everyone was in the same floundering boat; the leaders suffered the same hardships as the rank-and-file and would do so until HP came out of the recession. As you can imagine, Hewlett's act of sharing the hardship, when other CEOs acted so selfishly, earned him the undying loyalty and gratitude of HP's employees for decades to come. Hewlett's efforts to keep everyone employed during incredibly tough times is a classic example of a leader sharing the same hardships and struggles as his employees. His example personified "Tough times never last, tough people do."

Tough Times Bring Out the Worst in Leadership

During the recent pandemic crisis, many rank-and-file employees were handed a pink slip while their bosses handed themselves a big payday. It's understandable that the pandemic's business losses would cause companies, large and small, to suffer and, in the worst cases, force some to file for bankruptcy. However, the self-serving behavior of many senior executives during the pandemic reveals the worst type of leadership.

Early in the pandemic, a *Washington Post* article called out eighteen companies in which the executives rewarded themselves with hefty bonuses just days before declaring bankruptcy.[13] The spin given by company boards and senior execs to rationalize these generous paydays just before filing for Chapter 11 (bankruptcy) went something like this: "To retain and continue to motivate [these senior executives] through the volatile and uncertain environment affecting the retail industry, they must be compensated appropriately." The response to this rationalization by those who were laid off without any severance during the worst unemployment crisis since the Great Depression was "these bonuses unfairly enrich the very same corporate managers that led the company into bankruptcy."[14]

If you're like me, when you first read the headlines that executives had given themselves big financial rewards just days before they announced the failure of their company, you said to yourself, "That's got to be illegal!" As it turns out, it's not! Executives can give themselves big paydays as long as they do it before they "officially" file for Chapter 11 bankruptcy. It may be legal, but it doesn't make it right. Many would consider it unethical and immoral. It's

Payday Before Mayday

The Washington Post

Bonuses before bankruptcy: Companies doled out millions to executives before filing Chapter 11.
—*October 26, 2020*

Forbes

Hertz Files for Bankruptcy After 16,000 Employees Were Let Go and CEO Made Over $9 Million
—*May 23, 2020*

OBSERVER

JC Penney Paid Top Execs Huge Bonuses Before Firing Workers, Edging Toward Bankruptcy.
—*May 15, 2020*

Patch

Toys 'R' Us CEO and at Least 4 other Company Execs Shared $8.7M Bonus Despite 31,000 employees who they put out of work get nothing.
—*May 12, 2018*

selfish and should place a heavy burden of guilt on the conscience of those who do it. It quickly adds to the growing mistrust of business leaders in general.

What Does This Have to Do With Me?

At this point, you might be thinking, *"So what? I'm not a CEO. I'm in no position to give myself a bonus or lay off employ-*

ees. What's this got to do with me?" Granted, these are extreme cases, but the choice between selfishness and selflessness exists to a degree in every leader's life. Several years ago, I was consulting with a large power cooperative where there was a distinct resentment between what they called the "inside employees versus the outside employees." The co-op's CEO had created a culture where it seemed he was leading two separate teams. The "inside" people—the senior staff, the clerks, the accountants, HR, the call center, and other assorted desk jockeys—were perceived as seeing themselves as better than the "outside" people—the drivers, the linemen, and the service agents. When the CEO retired, the board hired someone with a reputation for being a team-builder—and a strong track record to support that reputation. Shortly after he took the helm, a major winter storm hit the co-op's electrical grid, bringing down miles of power lines and putting them in emergency operations. Under the previous leadership, during these emergencies, the inside team, unlike the outside team, was allowed to work from home. The new CEO changed that. He required the inside people to come in and work from their offices. He had them reorganize into the same 24-hour shifts that the outside people had to do—12 hours on and 12 hours off.

He understood the importance of being seen as sharing in his crews' hardships, but he also understood the importance of ensuring that his subordinate leaders were seen as doing the same. He asked his senior co-op leaders to get out in the harsh elements with his crews. They took sandwiches, hot soup, and coffee, and visited the linemen where they were doing their work. He set up a duty roster that posted at least one of the co-op's senior leaders in the field 24/7 for the duration of the crisis. For the first time in decades, the linemen saw their leaders and the inside team involved in what they did. The inside team got a better appreciation of the hardships the people out in the field had to endure, and the linemen now felt like the co-op was one team.

This resentment between different factions in an organization is a common phenomenon. It most often occurs when there's a relationship gap between different fiefdoms or tribes in an organization. Gaps between management and line, blue collar and white collar, and hourly workers and salaried workers are common. It's exactly what I found in this co-op. There was great camaraderie between the members of the inside employees and great kinship between the members of the outside teams but deep resentment between the two groups. As senior managers get further away from the bottom-tier

British General William Slim to his Officers, Burma 1942
"As officers, we must be willing to lead during hardship and danger. You are there to lead. As leaders, you will neither eat, nor drink, nor sleep, nor smoke, nor even sit down until you have personally seen that your men have done those things. If you do this for them, they will follow you to the end of the world. And, if you do not, I will break you."
—*Source: Frank Owen, Burma Star Association*

workers, they pay less attention to their wants and needs. Like the new CEO in my example, it takes a concerted effort to close that gap between the different tribes in your organization. Many lower-tier employees feel marginalized and unimportant. Every employee must sense they're part of the team regardless of where they are in the organization's pecking order. General Martin Dempsey spent an entire book, *Radical Inclusion*, on the importance of breaking down barriers between fiefdoms. As he puts it, "Leaders [must] develop an instinct for inclusion, an uncommon commitment to reach beyond collaboration all the way to trust."[15]

Afterthought: The Buck Stops Here

Leading by example means taking responsibility for your team's results. A leader boldly stating "I am responsible for everything that happens in this organization" means nothing until those you lead see through your daily behavior that those words are backed by your deeds. As leaders, we must accept responsibility for our organization's shortcomings and failures, and pass on the responsibility for success to the men and women in our organization. Responsibility cannot be delegated or contracted out. Being responsible for failure as well as success isn't for the faint of heart, and it's why not everyone is cut out to be a leader. It was said of

Shackleton, "In success, he shared credit; in failure, he shouldered the blame." We often hear the axiom:

> "The responsibility for the success or failure of an organization falls on the shoulders of the leader. The leader should pass the credit for the success to the team, but if the organization fails, the leader should take the responsibility for that failure and accept the consequences."

Responsibility is the price of leadership.[16] Unfortunately, the concept of a leader "taking responsibility for failure" often falls on deaf ears. Many organizations are run by Maintainers who blame other people or circumstances for their failures. Leaders must consistently pass on credit for success to their followers and take responsibility for organizational failures. It's hard to do but necessary. Being seen as holding yourself accountable is what it takes to create a culture of accountability in your organization.

Summary Points

Leaders should set the example, be true to their word, and share in the hardships of those they lead.

Set the Example: Role-Model the Behavior You Expect of Others

- The most powerful way to convince your followers you're worthy of their trust is through your good example in both the good and bad times.
- Your example puts your character and competence on parade for all to see.
- All leaders are role models, whether they want to be or not. They're always setting an example through their actions, behavior, and decisions.
- Setting the example gives legitimacy to your words.
- Character matters, but it's not known until it's seen.
- Your character must be demonstrated and publicly validated by your actions, behavior, and decisions.

- The jury will be out on who you are and what you stand for until it's conspicuous.

Be True to Your Word: Practice What You Preach

- Everything you say and do is constantly judged by your followers to see if you're practicing what you preach.
- Don't be a "Do as I say, not as I do" leader!
- Connect your words with your deeds.
- Be dependable; do what you say you're going to do.
- Keep your word.
- Demand of yourself what you demand of others.

Share in the Hardships: Be There for the Bad and the Good

- Hold yourself accountable to the same standards you set for others.
- Experience the same hardships and stresses as those you lead.
- Do not ask those you lead to do something you wouldn't do yourself.
- Leadership, or the lack of it, is greatly revealed in the tough times.

If you're comfortable that you are *leading by example*, go to the next chapter. If not, "Look in the Mirror" below.

Look in the Mirror at How I Lead by Example

Review the following statements, then *underline* where you are and *circle* where you want to be:

- **My ability to *lead by example* is:**
    - Poor / Mediocre / OK / Good / Excellent
- **I role-model the behavior and professional demeanor I expect of others:**
    - Never / Occasionally / Frequently / All the Time
- **I criticize my bosses and other offices in our organization:**
    - Never / Occasionally / Frequently / All the Time
- **What I say is backed up by what I do; my deeds and words are aligned:**
    - Never / Occasionally / Frequently / All the Time
- **I exhibit "Do as I say, not as I do leadership."**
    - Never / Occasionally / Frequently / All the Time
- **My dependability—doing what I say I'm going to do—is:**
    - Poor / Mediocre / OK / Good / Excellent
- **I demand of my employees nothing more than I demand of myself:**
    - Never / Occasionally / Frequently / All the Time
- **I share the same stresses and hardships as those I lead:**
    - Never / Occasionally / Frequently / All the Time
- **My leadership stays constant in bad times as well as good:**
    - Never / Occasionally / Frequently / All the Time

What Aspect(s) of My Leading by Example Could Use Improvement?

Example: I want to change my employees' perceptions that I don't suffer the same hardships as they do. In a recent company climate survey, I learned that many of my employees state that I'm not visible, and I haven't shown them that I have their best interests at heart.

I Want to Improve:

My Philosophy on Leading by Example

Example: I will be a leader who sets the example of the personal and professional behavior I expect of those I lead. I will make sure those I lead see me sharing in their hardships and know that I understand the difficulties associated with their jobs. During crisis periods, I will be a role model for all employees.

My Philosophy on Leading by Example:

My Action Plan

Example: I will be much more visible, accessible, and approachable during the tough times. I will make my presence seen, known, and felt at crisis events by going to my employees' work sites and offices. I will make sure my subordinate leaders do the same. We will fight the urge to stay close to the communications center in crisis and depend on our deputies while we get out with the field teams.

My Action Plan:

19

DECISION-MAKING

I'll never forget that rainy pre-dawn morning decades ago when I had to make a decision that would significantly impact the lives of my soldiers. With knots in my stomach while pondering what to do next, I looked up and saw my troops uneasily staring at me in anticipation. Finally, my platoon sergeant asked, "What do we do now, lieutenant?"

EVERY NEW LEADER experiences some version of "What do we do now, lieutenant?" at some point in their leadership journey. We'll make thousands of judgment calls throughout our professional lives. Leadership is about choices, since we're constantly being required to decide which direction to lead our followers. As we rise from our first leadership role to positions of increased responsibility, the importance of our decisions is magnified by the increasing impact they have on the lives of those we lead.[1] Leaders are primarily problem-solvers. It takes sound judgment to determine how to turn difficult problems into actionable and pragmatic solutions. One of the most important things leaders do is make judgment calls that produce successful outcomes. Judgment is too complex a subject, too dependent on expertise, experience, intuition, and countless other uncontrollable variables to pin it down to a single simple definition. Rather than dig into the complexities of what makes good judgment, I want to focus on the outcomes of judgment calls, i.e. decisions.

Leaders have to make decisions all day, every day, week after week, decision after decision. The value you bring to an organization is your ability to solve problems and how well you manage confusion and ambiguity by making quality decisions. With decision-making, even if you stay strictly between the lines of your core values, you may still make a wrong decision. Anytime you choose between competing options with vastly different outcomes, you run the risk of choosing the wrong one. With every decision, serendipity, the unknown, and plain old luck have a vote in its outcome. The trouble with luck, both good and bad, is its randomness.[2] You may make a decision that reflects your stellar integrity by doing the right thing rather than the expedient thing. You may make a courageous decision that's unpopular but benefits the greater good. You may make a selfless decision that comes at a great personal cost. You may make a gritty decision whose consequences are fraught with potentially weighty professional risks. Even though you've stayed true to your personal and professional code of conduct, the decision still has the potential to be a bad one. The old Hebrew proverb says, "Men plan, and God laughs." Just because circumstances beyond your control have the potential to foil your decision, that shouldn't be used as an excuse for not making decisions. Without the courage to make decisions, more often than not, you won't remain in the leadership saddle for very long. The measure of your success as a leader is the sum of all your judgment calls and decisions.

It's impossible to make the right call every time. However, to survive as a leader, a high percentage of your calls must be strikes, not balls or wild pitches. It's really pretty simple: Managers who make decisions that produce good outcomes quickly build reputations as good leaders. Managers who make decisions that produce poor outcomes build reputations as poor leaders. Of course, there's the third category: those who can't seem to make any decision. These people earn a reputation as ineffective leaders. As Noel Tichy and Warren Bennis point out in their book, *Judgment: How*

Winning Leaders Make Great Calls, "The cumulative effect of a leader's judgment calls determines the success or failure of their organization."[3]

There are things you can do to prepare yourself to make quality decisions. First, you must make sure that everyone in the organization clearly understands one basic decision-making rule: who is authorized to make which decisions. This critical rule helps the leader make better and fewer decisions. Second, don't be surprised and get ambushed by the inevitable decision-making landmines you'll most certainly encounter. Be prepared to make decisions with incomplete information and not enough time. Also, be ready for challenges that will test your core values. Lastly, have a "go-to" decision-making process or model in your leadership decision-making toolkit. You don't want to waste time getting stuck in the loop of having to decide how you're going to solve a problem when it's laid in your lap. Scores of decision-making models are available in academic sources and business literature.

> "In any moment of decision, the best thing you can do is the right thing, the next best thing you can do is the wrong thing, and the worst thing you can do is nothing."
> —*Teddy Roosevelt*

Rule No. 1: Where Does the Buck Stop?

I was taught in the Army that I was responsible for everything my unit did or failed to do. What that translates into is that I was responsible for all decisions made in my organization, whether they were mine or one of my subordinate leader's. Of course, you can't make every decision. Some will be your responsibility; others will have to be delegated. Your number-one rule as a decision-maker should be to make sure everyone in your organization clearly understands which decisions you reserve for yourself and which you feel comfortable delegating.

There's a tendency among many Dictators and Maintainers to hold all decision-making authority for themselves. These micromanagers smother their employees, stifle commitment and engagement, and drive their creative employees out. As a general rule, all decisions should be made at the lowest level possible, where the person making the decision has the knowledge, resources, and authority to create a successful outcome. To do that, it should be clearly understood by everyone in the organization who can decide on what issues.

All decisions that put the endeavor, the company, or the team at risk of irrevocable damage or catastrophic failure should solely be in the leader's domain. As Jack Welch, the former CEO of General Electric advised, leaders should only make decisions that only they can make. That sounds intuitively obvious, but I've seen a troubling trend where leaders relinquish their decision-making authority to experts, consultants, and their staff. Deciding is not about consensus. Input from purveyors of advice—consultants, HR, legal, and any number of "experts"—is valuable and can be instrumental and integrated into the leader's final decision. However, that input isn't a substitute for the leader's judgment. When the company's life and future depend on the decision, leaders cannot subcontract or delegate the decision to others. Ultimately, the debate and discussion can be fierce and passionate, but the leader makes the final call and takes the responsibility for the outcome.

I'm not suggesting that you shouldn't consider the advice of consultants and your in-house counselors, but remember, you are ultimately accountable for the outcomes. Consultants are betting without having skin in the game; they're gambling with your money, your reputation, and, in extreme cases, your job. As Warren Buffett advises us, "Beware of geeks bearing for-

> **TYRANNY OF EXPERTS**
> **"They tell me Wagner's music is much better than it sounds."**
> —*Mark Twain*

mulas."[4] The leader is the one taking the risks without a net. If things go to pot, the worst that can happen to the experts and consultants is, you don't ask them back. They just walk away with your money. The ultimate responsibility for the failure of an organization lies in the lap of the leader. Therefore, any decision that risks a business's overall health and well-being rests on the shoulders of the leader. Clearly establishing decision-making authority is vital to organizational success.

Landmines

Decision-making can be stressful because our choices have an afterlife that can be minor or catastrophic, temporary or perpetual. The environment in which you'll experience the most stress is when you're pressured to make decisions quickly, with incomplete information, and you have no choice but to decide between competing solutions that have vastly different outcomes. That stress exponentially increases when your decision has a potentially severe or catastrophic impact on your organization. Let's look at some historical examples where a decision had to be made quickly, with incomplete information and choices that offered vastly different outcomes. In every situation, the leader was confronted by challenges to his character. As you read the examples, ask yourself which course of action you would have chosen.

RISKY DECISIONS TAKE COURAGE
1777—George Washington,
New Jersey Headquarters

Advisor #1: "General Washington, your men are grievously suffering from smallpox. The infection rate and the number of bedridden soldiers is rising every day. I recommend you allow me to infect them with a small dose of the smallpox virus to inoculate them. If we don't do something about the epidemic now, most of your 40,000 soldiers will succumb to the disease and you will be leading an Army that cannot fight!"

Advisor # 2: "General, you cannot even consider this absurd idea! It's just too risky! First of all, mass inoculation has never been done and many learned physicians predict it will not prevent the disease but rather make the soldiers critically ill. Also, as you know, the Continental Congress has outlawed immunization. If they hear that you are openly flouting their law, they will most certainly relieve you of command of the Continental Army. Worst of all, I warn you that immunizing your soldiers will result in infecting your entire Army with smallpox, and you will be leading an Army that cannot fight!!"

"What do we do now, General Washington?

All decisions come with risk. Those with the potential for big payoffs or significant setbacks always present the most difficult choices. But leaders have to make the call. They have to weigh what is a foolish gamble versus what is a considered, yet necessary, risk.

You'll most likely never be faced with life-or-death decisions like George Washington. But if you're leading a group of any size, at some point, you'll be called upon to make decisions that affect the success or failure of your endeavor. You must consider the risk, weigh the options, and make the choice that gives your organization the best chance of success.

Perhaps you led an entrepreneurial project that started a year before the 2020 pandemic hit. Your fifteen-person company was doing so well that you had to hire another ten employees to keep up with demand. Then the pandemic struck. Bam! You just lost 60 percent of your business. You're getting conflicting advice and pressure from company stakeholders. Your team says they're willing to take a pay cut to keep all fifteen staff members. But your bank wants you to downsize by fifteen employees immediately or says you won't survive. What do you do?

Decisions imply choices, often with huge differences in outcome. Choices imply risk, and risk implies the opportunity to be wrong. Do not ignore your instincts! Leaders are expected to make sensible exceptions to general rules. Often, they must take calculated risks and make decisions in conditions of great uncertainty and confusing half-truths, knowing that once the decision is made, it cannot be unmade. That's why being a leader isn't for the faint of heart. Leaders must have the courage to willingly take measured risks when necessary and listen to their gut. In Washington's case, he risked inoculating his soldiers. Fortunately, his instincts were right, and it worked. His army recovered quickly enough to return to the battlefield shortly after the mass inoculations.

UNPOPULAR DECISIONS TAKE HUMILITY
1940—Winston Churchill,
War Room, London

Advisor #1: "Prime Minister, we have more than 300,000 soldiers stranded on the Dunkirk beaches waiting to be evacuated. With our current maritime capability, we'll only be able to evacuate between five to ten thousand men across the channel before the German's attack and capture the rest. Your current orders state that we'll evacuate the walking and ambulatory wounded first, ahead of able-bodied soldiers. I recommend we rescind that order and leave the wounded behind. England must have every able-bodied soldier we can evacuate if we want to have any hope defeating Hitler's forthcoming invasion of our island!"

Advisor #2: "Sir, that is an absurd idea. If you make this decision, you will be remembered as the most unpopular PM in the history of England. I'm sure Parliament will never agree to such a heartless move. More importantly, the British people and public opinion in general will cast you as a heartless coward for leaving our wounded boys at the mercy of the Hun savages. I highly recommend, for your reputation, your conscience, and your political future, that you do not consider this unthinkable move!"

"What do we do now, Prime Minister?"

The more responsibility you have and the greater the number of people you lead, the higher the probability that some in your organization will deem your decision wrong, even though it is the best decision for the group. It still takes a full measure of humility to follow your judgment or gut when you know it will be intensely

Monday-Morning-Quarterbacked. It goes back to Old Abe, who said, "You can't please all of the people all of the time." When decisions have to be made for the greater good, it's often at the expense of the few, and those few will become the most vocal.

Harmony is nice but not always possible. As parents, we're as happy as our most unhappy child. As a leader, you can't be as unhappy as your most unhappy employee because no matter what your decision, there will always be somebody disgruntled with it. Churchill knew that if he chose not to put the wounded at the head of the line for evacuation, he would be furiously criticized. He understood that leadership was about leading his base, not being led by his base's opinions.

In today's world, there are political decision-makers who, if faced with a dilemma like this, would have their staff check the polls to determine which decision would be most popular with the voters and how to best spin it. It takes great humility to do what's right at the expense of your popularity. Leaders must choose what's best for the greater good, and that often comes at the cost of being popular. You cannot bend in the winds of public opinion and do what brings you short-term popularity at the expense of the long-term welfare of your organization.

Churchill's decision not to evacuate the wounded did not become public until years later. His call to the British people for help resulted in a flotilla of more than 800 vessels. He evacuated 338,226 soldiers from the Dunkirk beaches to England. Every wounded and able-bodied soldier was evacuated.

LOSE/LOSE DECISIONS TAKE SELFLESSNESS
1941—Chief Surgeon,
Prisoner Hospital,
Camp O'Donnell, Bataan

Advisor #1: "Doc, we have more than 800 patients lying on the floor of this makeshift hospital suffering from infected wounds, malaria, and malnutrition. We just received a smuggled cache of medicine and drugs, but we're still urgently short of what we need. I recommend we determine which patients have the greatest probability of survival and hoard the medicines to use only on those patients we feel certain will live. Giving drugs and medicines to relieve the misery of those we know are going to die is just wasting the medicines."

Advisor #2: "Doc, we cannot play God. Hoarding the medicines will violate everything we stand for. I highly recommend we distribute the medications equally and use the medicine on the most severely ill and try to make their last days as painless as possible!"

"What do you want us to do, Doc?"

Wouldn't it be great if all decisions were win/win? Everybody would get what they want and walk away feeling like they won. But many times, life and business aren't fair, and the final decision has to be one classified as the "least bad choice." Look at the decisions Shackleton had to make; in most cases, he was forced to select the best, bad choice.

Leaders are regularly faced with decisions that are difficult to make and execute. Decision-makers have to try to get to the point where they're "comfortable being uncomfortable." The burden of being the leader is that you're the repository of your organization's problems, many of which have no adequate, easy, or popular solutions. You may find yourself in a position where you're forced to decide and all your options are undesirable. In some cases, no one wins, and everyone loses to some extent. No one enjoys being backed into a corner where you have to pick between the lesser of two or more evils and live with the consequences of the unpleasant choice. You have to combine hard-nosed decisiveness with passion. Your empathy for people cannot cloud your judgment for doing what's best for the greater good.[5] When you make a decision that has negative consequences, you have to do your best to compartmentalize your emotions and stay focused on the task at hand. No one likes letting people go, downsizing, cutting budgets, or forcing people to get shots or wear masks. As the doctors had to do at Bataan, only administering medicines to the patients they determined had the best chance of surviving, leaders must balance empathy and compassion with a high degree of detachment and focus on the greater good.

TIMING YOUR DECISIONS
1) Imperfect Information: Ready - Fire - Aim

2002—George W. Bush,
Situation Room, White House

Advisor #1: "Mr. President, our intelligence community has determined that Iraq and Saddam Hussain are amassing material to build a weapon of mass destruction. I recommend we invade Iraq and destroy that capability."

Advisor # 2: "Sir, currently we do not have definitive proof that Hussain does, in fact, have any WMD capability. If we invade Iraq, we will further destroy any semblance of government they have now, and we will be opening a can of worms that may have a long-term negative impact on the balance of stability and problems in the Middle East for years to come."

"What should we do, Mr. President?"

Timing is a decision-making skill that improves with experience, study, and observation. You have to operate at the speed of the problem. Sometimes, a thirty-second decision may have to rest upon thirty years of experience and study.[6] There are many urban legends about timing. One is to wait until the last minute to make critical decisions so that you have all the information. In other words, let the situation play out to its fullest. But who among us can correctly pick the exact correct "last minute"? When exactly do you have to translate your decision into reality or action? That's the question. Many times, decisions are made too quickly. The reasons for firing before taking a good aim are many: individual or group bias, fear, conflicting points of view, wrong information, and wanting a specific outcome so badly that it blinds and prejudices the available information.

Two types of landmines have been the demise of many leaders. On the one hand, you must beware of surrounding yourself with people and subordinates who simply echo and validate your opinions. I always wanted people who would give me diverse opinions and perspectives. I made it a point to select advisors who weren't shy or afraid to challenge my assumptions and decisions. I didn't want sycophants who smiled and validated the outcome they think I wanted to hear. Perhaps President Bush needed a stronger voice when he was trying to decide whether to re-enter the Middle East.

On the other hand, you can't let the most dominant advisor in the room sway the choices in his direction just because he has the most powerful personality. When your decisions have a significant impact on the lives of others, they deserve a serious investment of your time and reflection. Having to make a decision quickly with incomplete information is every leader's nightmare. Too many leaders fall victim to wanting a quick fix to a deep problem. President Bush's decision to re-enter the Middle East was made based on wrong information; there were no weapons of mass destruction. As General Colin Powell and others later admitted, it was the wrong decision.[7]

2) Analysis Paralysis: Ready Aim, Aim, Aim, Aim, Never Fire

2000-2010— CEOs, Blockbuster, Blackberry, Kodak, Radio Shack, Circuit City, Polaroid, Sears, and K-Mart

Advisor #1: "Boss, our current business model is on the verge of becoming obsolete. We need to pump more money into R&D and market research to develop new services, products, and a business model to get a step ahead of our competitors, or we'll soon be extinct."

Advisor #2: "Sir, we don't have to worry—our products and services are timeless. We need to continue to focus on sales and marketing. Let's put off market research and R&D expenditures until the next budget cycle. I'll conduct a study to determine what our competitors are doing, then we can adjust. We have plenty of time.

"What do you want us to do, Boss?"

Here's one of the contradictions I mentioned earlier: After advising you not to make a decision too hastily, now I'm telling you not to wait too long to make a decision. It's all about timing. An essential quality of leadership is the courage to decide. Deciding not to decide is stalling, which is a decision in itself. In most cases, waiting to make the perfect decision leads to making no decision. Leaders must recognize when the moment to act demands action. Many of today's leaders have faltered because they hesitated, taking too long to select a course of action.[8]

Indecision often leads to missed opportunities. There's no point in defining or determining a problem if you don't intend to do something about it. The lack of moral courage to make a tough decision, when that decision is important and necessary, has been the demise of many leaders. The past decade has given us many examples of senior decision-makers sinking into the quagmire of analysis paralysis, which led to missed opportunities. They waited too long to decide. Foolishly, they chose not to decide until they had 100 percent of the information thoroughly vetted by their lawyers and public relations spin masters. In today's world, where trust travels at the speed of social media, managers can't wallow in analysis paralysis or hide in their PR safe zones, waiting for 100 percent of the information before they act. Don't let uncertainty be an excuse for prolonged inaction: Leaders have to make judgments based on intuition and hypotheses that cannot be proven at the time of the decision.[9] Acting imperfectly is always better than doing nothing.[10]

As you can see from the CEOs in "Analysis Paralysis," their advisors warned them, but they didn't want to or didn't have the stomach to decide. It cost them their company. When a decision has to be made, make it. There will rarely be a perfect time to decide. Leaders who are *undecid-ERs* make everyone else suffer. You have to boldly fight the urge to kick that can down the road.

Decide, act, and move on. Indecision and procrastination are the parents of failure. Napoleon is attributed with this admonition to his generals: "You can ask me for more horses, more canon, more soldiers; you can ask me for anything you like, except more time!"

ETHICAL DECISIONS WILL TEST YOUR INTEGRITY
2000–2019 CEOs
Enron, Wells Fargo, WorldCom, Bear Stearns, Tyco, Lehman Brothers, AIG

Advisor #1: "Sir, the issues of integrity and illegality we just found going on in our organization must be publicly addressed. We need to own up to what we've found and take whatever means we can to address it. We must admit fault, demonstrate contrition, and show a plan to make those right whom we have wronged. We must convince our customers that it will never happen again!"

Advisor #2: "Boss, look, with the right spin, we can gloss this over to not look as bad as it really is. We have compiled a list of actions that deflect the impact of what's happened, and with some good public relations spin, we can make it seem like a minor mistake by just a few of our employees. If we label them "rouge agents" and publicly fire them, this will blow over by the next news cycle."

"What do we do, Boss?"

Your decisions must be built on a foundation of character and integrity guided by your moral compass. If not, there's no directional basis for decision-making. When a leader is faced with a clear ethical or moral right or wrong decision, the doors are one way. The choices become binary—yes or no. We have to ask ourselves, "Do I follow my conscience, my moral compass, or ignore it?"

Several of the leaders listed in "Ethical Decisions" supposedly didn't know of the situation's illegality until it was brought to their attention. At that point, several decided to either hide it or wait it out, hoping to recover from the situation without notice. In several of the examples, it was a conscious decision to commit the crime, hoping they'd get away with it. Regardless of whether the deception was an act of omission or commission, it was still unethical.

As in life decisions, leadership decisions have consequences. Decision-making is about choices, and the choices you make reflect your character. When you have a preconceived personal code of conduct based on a set of core values, your decisions are more likely to follow that code or reflect those values.

Toolkit

Not all decisions require a comprehensive decision-making tool. Using intuition, experience, and judgment, most can be made quickly without going through a complex process. Sully Sullenberger didn't use a formal decision-making model when he successfully landed his plane on the Hudson River. He depended on years of experience and on-the-spot quick thinking when he decided to land on the river rather than return to the airport. However, when faced with complex problems requiring more than a quick decision, too many leaders flounder in analysis paralysis, spending precious time deciding *how* to decide,

DECISION-MAKING MODELS

Ethical D-M Model
Rational D-M Model
Shared D-M Model
Multi-Criteria D-M Model
Adaptive Reuse D-M Model
Intuitive D-M Model
Military D-M Process
All can be found on Google.

robbing them of the time that should be spent actually solving the problem. All leaders should have a comprehensive systematic process in their toolkit to conduct the analysis required to make the best decisions in complex situations.

The academic and business worlds offer many decision-making models, processes, and matrices. The environment in which you lead will dictate what's best for your situation.

You may have developed your own decision-making process or model. I became comfortable using the Military Decision-Making Process (MDMP) during my years in the Army. It's designed to assist the decision-maker in selecting the best course of action in complex, time-constrained environments. However, the process is generic enough to be used in almost any situation, and I continued to use it in my civilian roles after leaving the Army. Eisenhower used the Military Decision-Making Model (MDMP) to decide which beaches to assault on D-Day. However, it's so simple and flexible that you could use it to decide what car you should buy to replace the clunker you're driving now. Regardless of what you choose, I strongly suggest you have a familiar go-to process already in your toolkit before you're forced to solve a complex problem. As I've repeated again and again, "Don't wait until you're dying of thirst to dig a well!"

Afterthought: Time Leeches and Monday Morning Quarterbacks

Here's a scenario that played out for me all too often. I'm in the middle of a high-stress situation, forced to make a quick decision in a short period that has a significant impact on my organization. I'm at a critical point where I need to focus on the situation with just the counsel of my most trusted advisors. Outsiders, usually people who have no equity in the decision, even though uninvited and knowing I'm swamped, will approach me and ask, "How are you doing? Have you got a minute? Have you thought about this?" I want to scream, "Not well. No, and yes, we threw that idea out hours ago." The point is, when you're in a crisis, be ready to get bombarded with a cacophony of suggestions on which the bombardiers hold no responsibility for failure. Don't let these leeches suck you dry of the time and the laser focus you need to make a good decision. There's a reason that racehorses wear blinders—so they won't get distracted by the chaos around them. It keeps them focused.

Also, while there's a chronic shortage of leaders willing to make the tough decisions, there's never a shortage of people who are quick to critique and criticize your decision. I don't remember where I heard this; it may have been a quote of a quote of a quote, but it holds true: "Criticism is a tax for being a leader; the best way to cope with it is to budget for it." Be ready for the chorus of Monday Morning Quarterbacks who will come out of the woodwork to second-guess your decision. These are the same guys who insist they have the gift of hindsight, always claiming to have seen it coming *after it came*. Take Aristotle's advice: "There is only one way to avoid criticism: Do nothing, say nothing, and be nothing."

Summary Points

- Leadership is about choices; you're constantly being required to decide which direction to lead.
- With increased responsibility comes the increased impact of your decisions on all concerned.
- A leader's success is measured by the sum of his or her decisions.
- Only make the decisions that only you can make.
- All decisions should be made at the lowest level possible.
- All decisions that put the endeavor, the company, or the team at risk of irreversible damage or catastrophic failure should solely be the domain of the leader.
- Leaders cannot subcontract or delegate responsibility for the outcome of their decisions.
- Whatever decision you make, there will always be someone to tell you you're wrong.
- Risky decisions take courage and confidence.
- Unpopular decisions take humility and selflessness.
- Be ready to make decisions that benefit the organization's general welfare, even if they're unpopular.
- Not all decisions are win-win.
- Stay true to your moral compass and core values for all decisions that approach an ethical fault line.

If you're comfortable with your *decision-making skills*, go to the next chapter. If not, "Look in the Mirror" below.

A Look in the Mirror at My Decision-Making

Review the following statements, then *underline* where you are and *circle* where you want to be:

- **My *decision-making ability* is:**
  - Poor / Mediocre / OK / Good / Excellent
- **I only make decisions that only I can make:**
  - Never / Occasionally / Frequently / All the Time
- **I make all decisions that risk putting the organization in jeopardy:**
  - Never / Occasionally / Frequently / All the Time
- **My ability to avoid analysis paralysis by making timely decisions is:**
  - Poor / Mediocre / OK / Good / Excellent
- **I demonstrate the courage to make decisions without 100 percent information:**
  - Never / Occasionally / Frequently / All the Time
- **I make decisions based on the greater good, not what's just popular:**
  - Never / Occasionally / Frequently / All the Time
- **My ability to be comfortable with being uncomfortable is:**
  - Poor / Mediocre / OK / Good / Excellent
- **I wait too long to make difficult decisions**
  - Never / Occasionally / Frequently / All the Time
- **I make decisions too quickly:**
  - Never / Occasionally / Frequently / All the Time
- **My reputation as a decision maker is:**
  - Poor / Mediocre / OK / Good / Excellent
- **My history of making correct and timely decisions is:**
  - Poor / Mediocre / OK / Good / Excellent
- **My ability to consider and predict second and third order effects of decisions is:**
  - Poor / Mediocre / OK / Good / Excellent

- **My ability to delegate decisions to others is:**
    - Poor / Mediocre / OK / Good / Excellent
- **I take responsibility for my decisions even if they turnout to be wrong:**
    - Never / Occasionally / Frequently / All the Time
- **I clearly establish who can make what decisions in my organization:**
    - Never / Occasionally / Frequently / All the Time

What Aspect(s) of My Decision-Making Could Use Improvement?

Example: I know I'm a fence sitter. I delay making a decision until I'm comfortable that I'm making the absolutely right decision. Sometimes, it's too late. And I want to do a better job of delegating decisions to my junior leaders and shop foremen. I'm so overwhelmed with my workload that decisions that should be made quicker are delayed until I can focus on them. I'm making too many decisions that could and should be made at a lower level.

I Want to Improve:

My Philosophy on Decision-Making

Example: I will make decisions that only I can make. I will delegate all decisions that can be made at a lower level to a leader with the judgment and appropriate information to make a sound decision. I will hold authority to make all decisions that have the potential to put the company at risk of not meeting goals or could cause damage or catastrophic failure.

My Philosophy on Decision-making:

My Action Plan

Example: I'm going to conduct a complete analysis of the recurring decisions that my team makes. I will authorize my subordinate leaders and their foremen to make those decisions if I determine they have the judgment and information necessary to do so. I'm going to review all the tasks associated with our decision-making requirements and delegate those that can be made by subordinate leaders.

My Action Plan:

20

SUCCEEDING

"The overall goal of leadership is to increase effectiveness and build a history of success within the organization."

—General Martin Dempsey, author of Radical Inclusion

SOME HAVE SAID, "There is likely a place in paradise for people who try hard, but what really matters is succeeding!"[1] You've charted the course, clearly communicating a doable and inspirational vision to those you lead, and they're committed to your vision. You are actively leading, you're keeping your finger on the pulse of the organization, you're setting the example, you're teaching and coaching, and you're making sound decisions along the way. All that's left to do is succeed. But what is success? Let's go back to Stephen Covey's "Keep the end in mind." Before we can determine if we are successful as leaders, we need to decide what leadership success looks like. We need to ask ourselves, "What is my definition of leadership success?"

Remember my dad's advice for leadership success: "Accomplish your mission and take care of those you're leading." You must define what leadership success looks like to you so you can do what it takes to achieve it. However you define leadership success, it must at least have some version of the two components of my dad's definition: Get the job done, *and* take care of those you lead. In both cases, the litmus test is this: Is your organization and the people in it better because of your leadership? Are you leaving the woodpile higher? Are you a Maintainer who'll be quickly forgotten when you leave, or are you a leader who'll be long remembered for the success you brought to the organization and the people in it? Let's look at both these gauges of leadership success individually.

Get the Job Done

The only true measure of leadership is whether the team succeeds or fails. Trying doesn't count—you have to deliver.[2] Leadership is one of the last places where pure meritocracy is alive. No matter how much character and competence you possess, you won't last long as a leader if your endeavor doesn't succeed. Failing honorably is still failing. The task of leadership has always been, and always will be, to inspire the best in others so they can and will contribute meaningfully to the success of your organization or endeavor. Leaders are judged by results. If your win-loss record isn't heavily weighed on the win side, you probably better update your LinkedIn resume. You must succeed to succeed. All organizations want leaders, but most get Maintainers. Research from Gartner Research estimates that between 50 percent and 70 percent of executives fail within eighteen months of taking the role.[3] This high percentage of failures is because most come into their leadership roles as Maintainers. They don't possess the character and/or the competence to succeed.

So, how do you judge your success in getting the job done? The real test of your leadership is whether your company, organization, or team is better off because of your leadership. From an organizational perspective, determining if you're leaving the woodpile higher is relatively straightforward and objective. Don't make it too complicated. You either meet or exceed your organization's metrics of success, or you don't. You either achieve your goals and objectives, or you don't. You either make the numbers, or you don't. Your

> **"Whoever said, it's not whether you win or lose that counts probably never lost."**
> —*Martina Navratilova*

team either wins the account, or they don't. You're either profitable, or you're not. When you're tested, you rise to the challenge, or you don't. The bottom line: Is my organization succeeding because of my leadership? Have I made a difference? Have I left the woodpile higher?

Take Care of Your People—It's How You Get the Job Done

An important leadership truth is to get the job done, you must earn the trust of your followers or employees. Your success as a leader depends on your ability to inspire whole-hearted commitment and enthusiastic engagement from those you lead. If your employees don't view your character as uncompromising and your competence up to the task, you have little or no chance of earning their trust. When you've done what it takes to inspire your Mercenaries to become Patriots, success will quickly follow. Your value as a leader isn't what you personally accomplish but how you motivate others to accomplish much more than any individual can do on their own. It's about translating individual success into group success.

Judging your success in "taking care of your people" is much more subjective than judging your success in "getting the job done." How do you decide if you've earned the trust and loyalty of those you lead? How do you ascertain if you are a Leader or a Maintainer? In the military, it's determined by how those you lead answer the following questions about you: Would you willingly follow this leader in combat? Or would you trust this leader to be your son or daughter's commander in combat? In the private sector, it's determined by how they answer the question, Would you follow this leader to another company if you could?

You know you've made a difference in people's lives when they're more devastated if you say, "I am disappointed in you. I know you can do better." than if you gave them a verbal or written reprimand. When followers don't want to let you down, when they want to make you proud, when they want to emulate you, then you have the license to look in the mirror and call yourself a leader. When that happens, you feel those you lead aren't following you but accompanying you. When you know your leadership has influenced people to reach their fullest potential, there's no more fulfilling satisfaction. To be described or recalled as a good leader who made a difference in people's lives is the ultimate success. When that happens, you know you've done what it takes to be a leader of character and competence, and no matter what your future fate, no one can ever take that away from you.

21

THE FINAL AFTERTHOUGHT

A life is not important, except for the impact it has on others.

—Jackie Robinson's epitaph

I STARTED THIS book by declaring that we're in a leadership crisis. A leader's role is to do what it takes to successfully accomplish a task, improve a situation, overcome a difficulty, solve a problem, and generally make things better. Said another way: Leaders make the woodpile higher. We're in this crisis because in so many public and private sectors, tasks aren't being accomplished, situations aren't being improved, difficulties aren't being overcome, and things, in general, aren't getting better. The reason is lack of leadership!

"Do not walk through time without leaving worthy evidence of your passage."

—Pope John XXIII

We have too many Dictators blaming everyone but themselves for their failures and too many Maintainers who claim the task, situation, difficulty, and problem "ain't my job." Both are quick to tell us what the problems are without offering solutions. What we don't have are enough Leaders who are willing to do what it takes to own the responsibility for doing the business of accomplishing, improving, overcoming, and generally making things better.

You don't have to look far to see that things aren't getting better but worse. Those in charge are not succeeding. Their organizations and the lives they impact are not better for them being there. Shortly after Colin Powell passed away, Peggy Noonan, *The Wall Street Journal* columnist, asked a question about his passing:

> "Are we still making their kind? Or have we got so many things wrong we aren't quite producing them anymore? Are we still making these astonishing individuals built along classic American lines? Can we get back to the best parts of the lost world that made Colin Powell?"[1]

I contend that, yes, we are still making their kind—I have worked for and with them. There are leaders who possess character and competence, but we don't have enough of them. As General Martin Dempsey so profoundly put it, "This is no time for spectators!" I often ask the complainers who seem to whine about every problem under the sun, "What are you doing about it? You need to lead, follow, or get out of the way. If you choose the latter two, then quit complaining!" They need to have the courage of their loud convictions to do something about whatever they're complaining about. In every walk of life and at every level, demand for leaders of character and competence is high, but supply is low.

If you haven't already, I urge you to pick up the torch and be a leader. It doesn't matter where. We face grave challenges in every corner of our lives: in the halls of government, in corporate offices, on the shop floor, in our neighborhoods, and in our families. Who leads matters![2] Commit to becoming a leader of consequence. More than ever, we need leaders willing to do what it takes to solve the ever-increasing problems and overwhelming challenges we face. The belief that an individual can make a difference is the first step.[3] The next is believing that you can be that individual. Leading with character and competence changes the lives of everyone you touch. That's no small thing. I urge you to do what it takes to be a leader. Nobody said it better than Teddy Roosevelt:

"It is not the critic who counts. The credit belongs to the man who is actually in the arena; whose face is marred by dust and sweat and blood; who strives valiantly; who spends himself in a worthy cause; who at the best knows in the end the triumph of high achievement, and who at the worst, if he fails, at least fails while daring greatly, so that his place shall never be with those cold and timid souls who neither know victory nor defeat."

It's a Beautiful Thing to See

We need more men and women who are willing to get into that arena. Leaders who make a real difference in our lives are a dying breed. Now is the time to get out of the foxhole and move to the sound of the guns. Build yourself into someone whose example influences others to be successful professionals and better people. Build yourself into a leader of uncompromising character and undeniable competence. As Plato put it, "Leaders touch the soul of those they lead, turning the souls toward a good purpose." We need and want leaders who can stir our souls a little. Be one!

Leading is an exhilarating burden for those strong enough to bear it and can

> **"What you leave behind is not engraved in the stone monuments but what is woven into the lives of others."**
> **—Pericles, Greek politician**

be one of life's most rewarding experiences.[4] It's a privilege, just like the responsibility of parenting, entrusted with the safety, nurturing, and development of children into moral, ethical, and productive adults.[5] The sense of pride derived from knowing you've been a catalyst to your organization's prosperity and instrumental in influencing those you lead to grow, thrive, and be better versions of themselves is personally rewarding beyond explanation. It's an indescribable but palpable sense of gratification, fulfillment, and personal and professional satisfaction when a collective success can be attributed to your leadership. The most important legacy you leave behind as a leader isn't the sum of your professional accomplishments but the people you've touched. When you achieve a level of leadership success where your character and competence lives on in others, that legacy can never be taken away from you. When someone tells you, "You made a difference in my life," you have left the woodpile higher. That's not nothing!

If not you, who? If not now, when? Why not you, NOW?

ACKNOWLEDGMENTS

I HAVE MANY people to thank for inspiring me to write this book. My parents, both charter members of the Greatest Generation, profoundly influenced who I am today. My father, who started his Army career as a private landing on Omaha Beach on D-Day and ended it as a colonel thirty-four years later, taught me that no matter what you do in life, you have to do it with character. My mother, a British war bride who spent many nights during WWII in her backyard air-raid shelter as bombs dropped around her house, taught me that no matter how tough things are, you have to keep a stiff upper lip and carry on. From them, I first learned that leadership isn't about what you say but what you do—your deeds not your words. You are known for what you do, not what you say you're going to do.

I am forever grateful for the soldiers I had the privilege of serving with and leading during my Army career. The soldiers and noncommissioned officers I had the honor to command taught me more about leadership than any other source. They were a constant and reliable barometer who let me know if I was leading or merely presiding. They didn't suffer fools lightly, and they didn't suffer foolish leadership lightly. I have learned powerful leadership lessons from the Army's noncommissioned officers corps, those humble professionals who lead without pretense or fanfare. I owe a special debt to my first platoon sergeant, Sergeant First Class Earnie Reeves, who taught this still-wet-behind-the-ears second lieutenant that those you lead don't care how much you know until they know how much you care.

It was my great fortune early in my Army career to have served with some exceptional role models of junior leadership. In my first unit, The Old Guard, 1st Lieutenant Robert Gussoni (Gus) and Captain David (Dave) Rivers were exceptional leaders who maintained exceedingly high standards while simultaneously winning the strong admiration of the soldiers they led. They say that imitation is the highest form of flattery. I have tried to emulate their leadership since I met them.

I would be remiss if I didn't mention my gratitude to the many leaders whom I have served and who have strongly influenced me as a person and leader. These leaders exemplify the characteristics of character and competence I have written about in this book. Exceptional among those were Colonels Bob Carroll, Hal Darden, Walt Mather, and Warner D. Stanley. Generals John Abrams, Rob Goff, George Joulwan, Jim Noles, and Gerry Rutherford were my senior leadership role models of character and competence. I owe a great debt to these exceptional leaders whom I have had the privilege of serving.

Men in uniform don't have a monopoly on good leadership. I have had the good fortune of learning from several impressive private-sector leaders. They include Walter Dunn and John Walsh at Coca-Cola; Frank Gren, the founder of ViaGlobal; and Jack Yeager, who introduced me to the consulting world.

I am also indebted and grateful to the many people who read the draft of my book and provided feedback. All were candid and did not hold back, which was a great help: Richard Aston, Tony Campbell, Bob Carroll, Mike Cloy, Dr. Dale Elliott, Larry Fussner, French MacLean, Roger McDonald, Warren Mills, Mike Ross, Dr. Bill Ruud, Jeff Decker, and Tom Sittnick. I owe a special thanks to General Marty Dempsey who pushed me toward the finish line on several occasions.

Finally, I'm indebted to two extraordinary people for inspiring me to cross the finish line with *What It Takes to Be a Leader*. First is my wife, Vicki, for convincing me that what I have to say is worth saying. She has given me the strength and support to focus on not quitting the project. Her relentless encouragement to complete this book was indefatigable. Without her, it would never have seen the finish line. For over forty-five years, I have watched her easily influence those around her with an undeniable humility and sincerity that has endeared her to everyone whose life she touches. No other person has taught me more about what it is to be a person of character than Vicki. She is my best friend and toughest critic. Second, my son, Drew. Every time I replied no when he asked if the book was done, he threw back at me my own preaching: "A person is measured by his deeds, not his words." I will be forever grateful for his help in pulling me into the 21st century in many aspects of life. I am so proud of the leader of character and competence he has become. Vicki and Drew's perpetual encouragement and unwavering support mean more to me than I can express. I love them both dearly.

NOTES

Preface

1 John C. McManus, *The Dead and Those About to Die, D-Day: The Big Red One at Omaha Beach* (New York: Penguin Publishing Group, 2015), 181.

Introduction

1 Martin E. Dempsey, *No Time For Spectators, The Lessons that Mattered Most from West Point to the West Wing* (Missionday, 2020).
2 Jim Mattis and Bing West, *Call Sign Chaos: Learning to Lead* (New York: Random House, 2019), 237.
3 Douglas Adams and Mark Carwardine, *Last Chance to See* (New York: Ballantine Books, 1992).

PART ONE: LEADERSHIP

Chapter 1
Be a Leader, Not a Spectator!

1 Mike Myatt, "Why You're Not a Leader," *Forbes* magazine newsletter (Jan 28, 2013) https://www.forbes.com/sites/mikemyatt/2013/01/23/why-youre-not-a-leader/?sh=908e3c06fb85.
2 John P. Kotter, "What Leaders Really Do" (Harvard Business Review Press, 2001), 2.
3 James M. Kouzes and Barry Z. Posner, *The Leadership Challenge, Third Edition* (San Francisco, CA: Jossey-Bass, 2003), xviii.
4 Robert F. Hurley, "The Decision to Trust" (Harvard Business Review, Sept 2006).
5 IBID.
6 Anne Fisher, "Turning Clock-Watchers into Stars" (*Fortune Magazine*, March 22, 2004), 60.
7 Chris Brady and Orrin Woodward, *Launching a Leadership Revolution: Mastering the Five Levels of Influence* (New York, Business Plus, 2005), xii.
8 Bill George, *Discover Your True North* (New Jersey: Wiley, 2015), vii.
9 Timothy R. Clark, *Leading with Character and Competence: Moving

Beyond Title, Position, and Authority (Oakland, CA: Berrett-Koehler Publishers, 2016), 9.

10 Ram Charan, *The High Potential Leader: How to Grow Fast, Take on New Responsibilities, and Make an Impact* (New Jersey: Wiley & Sons, 2017), 168.

11 Warren Bennis, *On Becoming A Leader* (Cambridge, MA: Perseus Books, 2003), xxvii.

12 DeMille, Nelson, *The Cuban Affair* (New York: Simon & Schuster, 2017), 386.

13 Myatt, "Why You're Not a Leader."

14 John W. Gardner, *On Leadership* (New York: The Free Press, 1990), xix.

15 Charan, *The High Potential Leader*, 1.

Chapter 2
Dictators — Maintainers — Leaders

1 John C. Maxwell, *Good Leaders Ask Great Questions: Your Foundation for Successful Leadership* (New York: Center Street Press, 2014), 4.

2 Thomas E. Cronin, "Thinking and Learning about Leadership." *Presidential Studies Quarterly 14*, (Winter, 1984), 22-24, 33-34.

3 John C. Maxwell, *The 21 Irrefutable Laws of Leadership, Follow Them and People Will Follow You* (Nashville: Thomas Nelson, 1998), 14-21.

4 Alan Axelrod, *When the Buck Stops With You: Harry S. Truman on Leadership* (New York: Portfolio, 2004), 184.

5 Clark, *Leading with Character and Competence*, ix.

6 Robert M. Gates, *A Passion for Leadership, Lessons on Change and Reform from Fifty Years of Public Service* (New York: Vintage, 2017), 104.

7 Colonel George E. Reed, "Toxic Leadership," *Military Review*, Jul-Aug 2004.

8 Stanley Bing, "Why Crazy Works." *The Wall Street Journal*, (Sept 1, 2010), 108.

9 Dr. Gene Klann, "The Application of Power and the Influence in Organizational Leadership." Fort Leavenworth, KS USACGSC, Aug 2013; reprinted in US Army Command and General Staff College L100 Book of Readings, 10.

10 Bennis, *On Becoming a Leader*, 147.

11 Harold S. Kushner, *Living a Life That Matters* (New York, Anchor, 2002), 91.

12 Kotter, "What Leaders Really Do," 37.

13 Jared Sandberg, "Been Here 25 Years and All I Got Was This Lousy T-Shirt," *The Wall Street Journal* (Jan 28, 2004).

14 Fisher, "Turning Clock-Watchers into Stars," 60.

15 Gates, *A Passion for Leadership*, 24.

16 Henry Kissinger, *Leadership: Six Studies in World Strategy* (USA, Penguin Press, 2022), xi.

17 Gary Yukl, *Leadership In Organizations, Sixth Edition* (Upper Saddle River, NJ: Pearson Education, 2006), 147.

18 Klann, "The Application of Power and the Influence in Organizational Leadership," 1.

19 Franklin Miller, *Reflections of a Warrior* (Novato, CA: Pocket Books, 1992).

20 Peter M. Senge, *The Fifth Discipline: The Art & Practice of the Learning Organization* (New York: Random House Business, 2006), 128.

21 James MacGregor Burns, *Leadership* (New York: Harper Torchbooks, 1978), 4.

22 Callum Borchers, *"Employers Strike Back at 'Quitters,'"* *The Wall Street Journal* (Sept 29, 2022), A12.

23 R.E. Quinn, *Deep Change: Discovering the Leader Within* (San Francisco: Jossey-Bass, 1996), 151.

24 James C. Rees with Stephen Spignesi, *George Washington's Leadership Lessons, What the Father of our Country Can Teach Us about Effective Leadership and Character* (Hoboken, New Jersey: Wiley, 2007), xxiii.

25 Gus Lee with Diane Elliott-Lee, *Courage: The Backbone of Leadership* (San Francisco: Jossey-Bass, 2006), 31.

26 Christopher Kolenda, *Leadership: The Warrior's Art* (Carlisle, PA: Army War College Foundation Press, 2001), 19.

27 David Foster Wallace, "The Weasel, Twelve Monkeys, and the Shrub: Seven Days in the Life of the Late, Great John McCain," *Rolling Stone* magazine (April 13, 2000).

28 Gardner, *On Leadership*, 1.

29 Quinn, *Deep Change: Discovering the Leader Within*, xii.

30 John Brubaker, "Why You Should Run Your Business Like Bill Belichick," *Entrepreneur* magazine (Feb 4, 2015).

31 Nicholas Pearce, "The Patriot's Bill Belichick Inspires His Team By Calling Them This," *Fortune* magazine (Feb 3, 2017).

32 Burns, *Leadership*, 36.

33 Bob Seger & The Silver Bullet Band, "Against the Wind" (Capital Records, 1980).

34 Jordan B. Peterson, *12 Rules for Life: An Antidote to Chaos* (Toronto: Random House Canada, 2018), 11.

35 Daniel Goleman, *"Harvard Business Review's 10 Must Reads on Leadership: '*What Makes a Leader?'" (Boston: Harvard Business Review Press, 2011), 20.

Chapter 3
The Value of Commitment

1 Many times in the course of this book I use my experiences in and out of uniform to make a point. I attempt to keep the moral of my points intact while disguising the details enough to protect the privacy of those involved. The executive who gave me this advice was not reflective of the other senior leaders in the company.

2 Jim Collins, *Good to Great: Why Some Companies Make the Leap. . .and Others Don't* (New York: Harper Business, 2001).

3 Tracy Maylett and Paul Warner, *Magic: Five Keys to Unlock the Power of Employee Engagement* (Austin, TX: Greenleaf Book Group, 2014), 3.

4 Gallup, *The State of the American Workplace: Employee Engagement Insights for US Business Leaders (2013).*

Chapter 4
The Leadership Equation

1 Chris Westfall, "Leadership Development Is a $366 Billion Industry: Here's Why Most Programs Don't Work," *Forbes* (June 20, 2019).

2 *Herodotus: The Histories* (New York: Penguin Classics, 1954 Translation).

3 David Brooks, *The Road to Character* (New York: Random House, 2015), xi.

4 Brooks, *The Road to Character*, xi.

5 Patrick O'Brian, *Master and Commander* (New York: William Collins, Sons & Co., 1970), 134.

6 Stephen R. Covey, *The 7 Habits of Highly Effective People: Powerful Lessons in Personal Change (*New York: Fireside, 1989), 95.

7 Brady, *Launching a Leadership Revolution,* 173.

8 John Maxwell, *Leadership 101: What Every Leader Needs to Know* (Nashville, TN, Thomas Nelson Publishers, 2002) 64.

9 Maxwell, *Leadership 101*, 64.

19 John Baldoni, *Lead by Example: 50 Ways Great Leaders Inspire Results* (New York: Amacom, 2008), 60.

11 Karen Twaronite, A Global Survey on the Ambiguous State of Employee Trust, *Harvard Business Review* (July 22, 2016), https://hbr.org/2016/07/a-global-survey-on-the-ambiguous-state-of-employee-trust.

12 Gerald Baker, *American Breakdown: Why We No Longer Trust Our Leaders and Institutions and How We Can Rebuild Confidence (New York, Twelve, 2023),* xii.

13 Gallup, *Confidence in Institutions* survey (2023). https://news.gallup.com/poll/1597/confidence-instituions.aspx.

14 Baker, *American Breakdown*, 6.

15 James M. Kouzes and Barry Z. Posner, *The Truth About Leadership: The No-Fads, Heart-of-the-Matter Facts You Need to Know* (San Francisco: Jossey-Bass, 2010), 77.

16 General Martin Dempsey, personal conversation.

17 Mark Brouker, *Lessons From The Navy: How to Earn Trust, Lead Teams, and Achieve Organizational Excellence (*Lanham, MD: Rowman & Littlefield, 2020), 178.

18 David Stuart and Todd Nordstrom, "10 Shocking Workplace Stats You Need to Know." *Forbes.* (March 8, 2018).

19 Bennis, *On Becoming a Leader*, 148.

20 Clark, *Leading with Character and Competence*, 7.

Chapter 5
Your Leadership Philosophy

1 Gallup, *Re-engineering Performance Management* (2019) https://www.gallup.com/workplace/238064/re-engineering-performance-management.aspx.

2 Full Disclosure: In my consulting life, I do 360s with senior managers and supervisors. The 360s give the manager a good view of his leadership, strengths and weaknesses. The sad truth is that most of the participants in these formal programs claim to want to learn to be better leaders and commit to do what it takes to improve their weak areas, but very few do.

3 Bennis, *On Becoming a Leader*, xx.

4 Edith Hall, *Aristotle's Way:The Ancient Greek's; Ten Ways They Shaped the Modern World* (New York: Penguin Press, 2019), 23.

5 Clark, *Leading with Character and Competence*, 7.

6 Richard Aston, *Views from Gold Mountain: History, Memory, Voices* (San Francisco: Sixth Avenue Books, 2019), xi.

7 Harold S. Kushner, *Living a Life That Matters* (New York: Anchor Books, 2002), 66.

8 George, *Discover Your True North*, 1.

9 Kouzes and Posner, *The Leadership Challenge*, 50.

10 Maryam Kouchaki and Isaac H. Smith, "Building an Ethical Career," *Harvard Business Review* (Jan 1, 2020), 135.

11 Richard Brookhiser, *George Washington on Leadership* (New York, Basic Books, 2008), 213.

12 Kolenda, *Leadership: The Warrior's Art*, 16.

13 General (USMC) Charles G. Krulak, "Character," *Leatherneck* magazine (Dec 1996), 14

14 Robert C. Carroll, *Building Your Leadership Legacy: It's All About Character* (Sarasota, FL: Suncoast Digital Press, 2017), 108.

15 Walter Isaacson, *Benjamin Franklin: An American Life* (New York: Simon & Schuster, 2003), 89.

16 Alden Mills, *Unstoppable Teams: The Four Essential Actions of High-Performing Leadership* (New York: Harper Business, 2019), 33.

17 Kouchaki and Smith, "Building an Ethical Career," 135.

18 These honest assessments of leader character are only provided when respondents are insured and have complete confidence that their feedback will be anonymous and confidential. In other words, they get to hide their honest opinions in a cloak of anonymity, which gives them the courage to state the truth.

19 George, *Discover Your True North*, 15.

20 Peterson, *12 Rules for Life*, 156.

21 Christian B. Miller, *The Character Gap: How Good Are We?* (Oxford, UK: Oxford University Press, 2019), 6.

22 Hall, *Aristotle's Way*, 197.

23 George, *Discover Your True North*, 48.

24 Carroll, *Building Your Leadership Legacy*, 48.

25 Kolenda, *Leadership: The Warrior's Art*, 12.
26 Kouzes and Posner, *The Leadership Challenge*, 77.

Chapter 6
Your Organization's Culture

1 Bret Baier, *Three Days in January: Dwight Eisenhower's Final Mission* (New York: William Morrow, 2017), 168.
2 Mike Ettore, *Trust-Based Leadership: Marine Corps Leadership Concepts for Today's Business Leaders* (Fidelis Leadership Group, 2019), 392.
3 Clark, *Leading with Character and Competence*, 32.
4 Thomas J. Peters and Robert H. Waterman Jr., *In Search of Excellence: Lessons from Amercia's Best-Run Companies* (New York: Harper Collins, 2004).
5 Robert K. Greenleaf, *Servant Leadership: A Journey into the Nature of Legitimate Power and Greatness* (Mahwah, NJ: Paulist Press, 1977).
6 Bobby Jindal, "The Roots of Political Polarization: Our Politics Seem to Be Degenerating Because We No Longer Understand Each Other's Priorities," *The Wall Street Journal* (Nov 1, 2018), A15.

PART TWO: CHARACTER—WHO LEADERS ARE

Chapter 7
The Power of Character

1 Kissinger, *Leadership: Six Studies in World Strategy*, xxii.
2 Bennis, *On Becoming a Leader*, xxii and 32.
3 Clark, *Leading with Character and Competence*, ix.
4 Joseph J. Ellis, *His Excellency: George Washington* (New York: Alfred A Knopf, 2004), 74.
5 Ellis, *His Excellency George Washington*, xiv.
6 Ron Chernow, *Washington, A Life* (New York: Penguin Press, 2010), 324.
7 James Thomas Flexner, *George Washington, The Forge of Experience (1732-1775), Vol 1.* (Canada: Little, Brown and Company Limited, 1965), 5.
8 Glen Beck, *Being George Washington: The Indispensable Man, As You've Never Seen Him* (New York: Threshold Editions, 2011), xi.
9 Chernow, *Washington: A Life*, 324.
10 John E. Ferling, *The Ascent of George Washington: The Hidden Political Genius of an American Icon* (New York: Bloomsbury Press, 2009), 246.
11 Peter Cozzens, "'Valley Forge' Review: In the Bleak Midwinter," *The Wall Street Journal* (Dec 21, 2018), C7.
12 Brady and Woodward, *Launching a Leadership Revolution*, 186.
13 Chernow, *Washington: A Life*, 293.
14 Beck, *Being George Washington*, 46.
15 Chernow, *Washington: A Life*, 329.

16 Cozzens, "'Valley Forge Review," C7.

17 Chernow, Washington: A Life, 454.

18 IBID 457.

19 Beck, Being George Washington, 136.

20 Bill O'Reilly and Martin Dugard, Killing England: The Brutal Struggle for Independence (New York: Henry Holt and Company, 2017), 23.

21 Robert Middlekauff, Washington's Revolution: The Making of America's First Leader (New York: Alfred A. Knopf, 2015), xx.

22 Beck, Being George Washington, 168.

23 Flexner, George Washington: The Forge of Experience (1732-1775), Vol 1, 5.

24 James Merritt, Character Still Counts (Eugene, Oregon: Harvest House Publishers, 2020), 183.

25 Brookhiser, George Washington on Leadership, 213.

Chapter 8
Integrity

1 Carroll, Building Your Leadership Legacy, 108.

2 Kouchaki and Smith, "Building an Ethical Career,"135.

3 EduBirdie survey (April 16, 2019), https://www.yahoo.com/video/survey-reveals-majority-company-executives-173033472.html.

4 EduBirdie survey.

5 Martin Dempsey with Ori Brafman, Radical Inclusion: What the Post-9/11 World Should Have Taught Us About Leadership (USA: Missionday, 2018), 3.

6 Warren Bennis, "The Seven Ages of the Leader," Harvard Business Review (January 2004), 49.

7 Rob Goffee and Gareth Jones, "Managing Authenticity: The Paradox of Great Leadership." Harvard Business Review (Dec 2005).

8 George, Discover Your True North, 3.

9 Fawn M. Brodie, The Devil Drives: A Life of Sir Richard Burton (New York: Norton Press, 1967), 187.

10 Patrick Lencioni, "The No-Cost Way to Motivate." Businessweek (Sept 24, 2009), 84.

11 Kouzes and Posner, The Truth about Leadership, 27.

12 Dale Carnegie, How to Win Friends and Influence People (New York: Simon & Schuster, 1936), 36.

13 Rick Atkinson, The Day of Battle: The War in Sicily & Italy 1943-1944, Vol II (Picador Press, , 2007, 95.

14 Erin White, "'Authentic' Ways of Leading: George's 'True North' Shares Some Insights from 125 Interviews," The Wall Street Journal (Dec 3, 2007), B3.

15 Boris Johnson, The Churchill Factor: How One Man Made History (New York: Riverhead Books, 2014), 90.

16 Gates, A Passion for Leadership, 99.

17 Baldoni, Lead by Example, 184.

18 Greenleaf, *Servant Leadership*.
19 George, *Discover Your True North*, 134.
20 Aristotle's "Golden Mean" or "Golden Middle Way": This terms refers to the Greek philosopher's discussion in his Nicomachean Ethics of the desirable middle between two extremes, one of excess and the other of deficiency. Example: Courage is a virtue, but if taken to excess would manifest as recklessness, and, in deficiency, cowardice. With his Golden Mean, anger is not a vice and patience is not a virtue. In the right situation, at the right time and toward the right people, anger is a virtue. Without anger, we would not stand up for our core values.
21 Goffee, "Managing Authenticity."
22 Hyacinth, Brigette, "Why a Good Boss is the Best Incentive of All!" *LinkedIn* (March 1, 2018), https://www.linkedin.com/pulse/why-good-boss-best-incentive-all-brigette-hyacinth/.

Chapter 9
Humility

1 Merritt, *Character Still Counts*, 72.
2 Brooks, *The Road to Character*, 6.
3 Tom Brokaw, *The Greatest Generation* (New York: Random House, 1998).
4 James Bradley with Ron Powers, *Flags of Our Fathers* (New York: Bantam Books, 2000).
5 John C. Maxwell, "Are You an Effective Leader?" (*Success* magazine (April 2010), 16.
6 Brooks, *The Road to Character*, xiii.
7 Collins, *Good to Great*, 22.
8 IBID, 39.
9 Patrick O'Brian, *Master and Commander*, 448.
10 Brooks, *The Road to Character*, 8.
11 John Ortberg, *Life-Changing Love: Moving God's Love from Your Head to Your Heart* (Grand Rapids, MI: Zondervan, 1998), 141-142.

Chapter 10
Grit

1 From William Ernest Henley's (1849-1903) poem *Invictus* (Latin for "Unconquered"): Henley was an English poet who wrote *Invictus* during a several-year stay in the hospital while suffering from tuberculosis. It is said that he wrote the poem shortly after he had a leg amputated due to complications from the disease.
2 George, *Discover Your True North*, 157.
3 Atkinson, *The Day of Battle*, 121.
4 Robert O'Connell, *Team America: Patton, MacArthur, Marshall, Eisenhower, and the World They Forged* (New York: Harper Collins, 2022), 304.
5 Kissinger, Henry, *Leadership: Six Studies in World Strategy*, xvii.
6 Ram Charan, *Know-How, The 8 Skills That Separate People Who Perform*

from Those Who Don't (New York: Crown Business, 2007), 40.

7 Joshua D. Margolis and Paul G. Stoltz, "How to Bounce Back from Adversity," *Harvard Business Review* (Jan-Feb 2010), 87.

8 Viktor Frankl, *Man's Search for Meaning* (Boston: Beacon Press, 1959), x.

9 Doris Kearns Goodwin, *Leadership In Turbulent Times (New York:* Simon & Schuster, 2018), xiii.

10 David Margolick, "*Unbeaten* Review: Forty-nine Wins and No Losses," *The Wall Street Journal,* (July 19, 2018), 21-22.

11 Margolis and Stolz, "How to Bounce Back from Adversity," 87.

12 In an interview on Fox News, October 28, 2018, Charles Krauthammer said the irony of the incident was that, at the time of the accident, he was studying the spinal cord in school. "There were two books on the side of the pool when they picked up my effects, one was *The Anatomy of the Spinal Cord* and the other was *Man's Fate* by Andre Malraux."

13 Collins, *Good to Great,* 30.

14 Women were allowed to attend Ranger school beginning in 2018 with two graduating from the first class attended by women.

15 *Ranger Training Brigade Brief (Nov 29, 2021),* https://www.moore.army. mil/INFANTRY/ARTB/History.html.

17 Geoff Colvin, *Talent Is Overrated – What Really Separates World-Class Performers from Everybody Else* (New York: Portfolio, 2008).

18 Edward Kosner, "*The Right Call* Review: The Sheep from the GOATs," *The Wall Street Journal* (Aug 1, 2023), A15.

19 Andrew J. Bacevich, *The Limits of Power: The End of American Exceptionalism* (New York: Metropolitan Books, 2008), 6.

Chapter 11
Courage

1 David Brooks, *The Road to Character,* 46.

2 Andrew Roberts, *Churchill: Walking with Destiny* (Viking, 2018), 970.

3 Lee, *Courage,* dust cover front flap.

4 Brooks, *The Second Mountain,* 194.

5 Benjamin Shull, "*How to Think Like a Roman Emperor* Review: Meditations for the Masses," *The Wall Street Journal,* (April 4, 2019), A13.

6 Rick Atkinson, *The Guns at Last Light: The War in Western Europe, 1944 – 1945, Vol III (New York:* Picador, 2014), 267.

7 Paulo Coelho, *The Alchemist* (Rio de Janeiro: Harper Collins, 1993), 130.

8 Clark, *Leading with Character and Competence,* 74.

9 Brookhiser, *George Washington on Leadership,* 81.

10 Robert Steven Kaplan, "The Tests of a Leader: What to Ask the Person in the Mirror," *Harvard Business Review* (Jan 2007), 128.

11 Winston Churchill, *My Early Life* (London, Odhams Press Limited, 1930), 27.

12 Bennis, *On Becoming a Leader,* 136.

13 Brady, *Launching a Leadership Revolution,* 50.

14 The rest of the story: Because of the huge turnout of 770 big and little civil-

ian boats and 200 naval ships, and the fact that for some reason Hitler chose not to attack the beached force, over 331,000 British and French troops were successfully evacuated from Dunkirk, including the 13,000 wounded.

15 Roberts, *Churchill: Walking with Destiny,* 214.

16 Baldoni, *Lead by Example,* xv.

17 Lt. Gen. Robert F. Foley, *Standing Tall: Leadership Lessons in the Life of a Soldier* (Havertown, PA, Casement, 2022), 44.

18 Atkinson, *The Day of Battle,* 201.

19 Brady, *Launching a Leadership Revolution,* 72.

20 Atkinson, *The Day of Battle, Vol II,* 201.

21 Mattis and West, *Call Sign Chaos,* 233.

22 Kissinger, *Leadership: Six Studies in World Strategy,* 403.

23 Baldoni, *Lead by Example,* 52.

24 Roberts, *Churchill: Walking with Destiny,* 165.

25 Gates, *A Passion for Leadership,* 108.

Chapter 12
Passion

1 Thoreau famously stated in his book *Walden* that "The mass of men lead lives of quiet desperation." He went on to state that misplaced value is the cause: We feel a void in our lives, and we attempt to fill it with things like money, possessions, and accolades.

2 George, *Discover Your True North,* 123.

3 Merritt, *Character Still Counts,* 182.

4 Source: The New England/Employee Equation Survey, Harris Interactive Inc., 7,718 American employees.

5 Jason Gay, "Shock Claim: Bill Belichick Not a Barrel of Laughs," *The Wall Street Journal* (June 3, 2018).

PART THREE: COMPETENCE—WHAT LEADERS DO

Chapter 13
The Power of Competence

1 Clark, *Leading with Character and Competence,* 87.

2 Alfred Lansing, *Endurance: Shackleton's Incredible Voyage* (New York: Carroll & Graf Publishers, 2002), 13.

3 IBID, 12.

4 Lansing, *Endurance,* 39.

5 Lansing, *Endura nce,* 102.

6 Nancy Koehn, *Forged In Crisis: The Power of Courageous Leaders in Turbulent Times* (New York: Scribner, 2017), 47.

7 Lansing, *Endurance,* 46.

8 IBID,128.

9 Koehn, *Forged in Crisis.*

10 Lansing, *Endurance,* 258.

11 Lansing, *Endurance,* 90.

12 Nancy F. Koehn, "Leadership Lessons From the Shackleton Expedition," *New York Times* (Dec 24, 2011).

Chapter 14
Charting the Course

1 Bennis, *On Becoming a Leader,* 31.

2 Clark, *Leading with Character and Competence,* 153.

3 Kolenda, *Leadership: The Warrior's Art,* 346.

4 The Human Era @ Work website, 2014, http://uli.org/wp-content/uploads/ULI-Documents/The-Human-Era-at-Work.pdf.

5 Clark, *Leading with Character and Competence,* 162.

6 Kotter, *What Leaders Really Do,* 82.

7 Oren Harari, *The Leadership Secrets of Colin Powell* (New York: McGraw-Hill, 2002), 119.

8 Kouzes and Posner, *The Leadership Challenge,* 28.

9 Brady, *Launching a Leadership Revolution,* 59.

10 Robert M. Galford and Regina Fazio Maruca, *Your Leadership Legacy: Why Looking Toward the Future Will Make You a Better Leader Today* (Boston: Harvard Business School Publishing, 2006), 5.

11 Quinn, *Deep Change,* 197.

12 Quinn, *Deep Change,* 19.

13 George Joulwan with David Chanoff, *Watchman at the Gates: A Soldier's Journey from Berlin to Bosnia* (Lexington, KY: University Press of Kentucky, 2021), 83.

14 Frankl, *Man's Search for Meaning.*

15 Anton Myrer, *Once an Eagle: A Novel (New York:* Holt, Rinehart and Winston, 1968), 387.

16 Shawn Achor, *The Happiness Advantage: The Seven Principles of Positive Psychology That Fuel Success and Performance at Work* (New York: Crown Business, 2010), 80.

17 Lauren Weber, "As Pandemic Slows Business, Workers Fret: Is My Job Relevant?" *The Wall Street Journal,* (June 22, 2020), A9.

18 Dempsey, *Radical Inclusion,* 89.

19 Lauren Weber, "At Kimberly-Clark, 'Dead-Wood' Workers Have Nowhere to Hide," *The Wall Street Journal,* (Aug 22, 2016), A10.

20 W.C.H. Prentice, *Understanding Leadership, Harvard Business Review* (Jan 2004), 103.

21 Prentice, *Understanding Leadership,* 104.

22 Ettore, *Trust-Based Leadership,* 54.

23 John Wooden with Steve Jamison, Wooden: *A Lifetime of Observations and Reflections On and Off the Court* (New York: McGraw-Hill, 1997).

Chapter 15
Actively Leading

1 Larry Bossidy and Ram Charan, *Execution: The Discipline of Getting Things Done* (New York: Crown Business, 2002), 29.
2 US Bureau of Labor Statistics, 2010-2019, "Percentage of Businesses That Fail and How to Boost Chances of Success," https://www.lendingtree.com/business/small/failure-rate/#percentageofbusinessesthatfail.
3 Lou Gerstner, "The Culture Ate Our Corporate Reputation," *The Wall Street Journal*, (Oct 2, 2016).
4 Larry Bossidy, *Execution*, 5.
5 Bossidy, *Execution*, 6.
6 Peter F. Drucker, *Classic Drucker: From the Pages of Harvard Business Review* (Boston: Harvard Business Review Press, 2006), 83.
7 2002 study by Bruce Tulgan and Rainmaker Thinking Inc. of 500 managers, https://rainmakerthinking.com/wp-content/uploads/2018/05/Underman-agement-Epidemic-WP1.pdf)

Chapter 16
Situationally Aware

1 Memorandum: Full Transcript: Aircraft Accident, AWE 1549, NYC, NY, Jan. 152009, FAA (June 19, 2009), P.4.
2 Associated Press, NTSB: Wayward pilots were working on laptops (Oct 26, 2009).
3 FAA letter revoking Captain Cheney's license (Oct 27, 2009).
4 Fox News, "Coakley Risks Offending Red Sox Nation, Calls Schilling 'Another Yankee Fan'" (Dec 23, 2015).
5 Daniel Goleman, *Emotional Intelligence: Why It Can Matter More Than IQ* (New York: Bantam Dell, Tenth Anniversary Edition, 2006).
6 Chip Cutter, "Rich Lesser, CEO Whisperer, on His Toughest Moments," *The Wall Street Journal* (June 25, 2021).
7 Gates, *A Passion for Leadership*, 170.

Chapter 17
Teaching — Coaching — Mentoring

1 Vernon Carter, *The Forbes Scrapbook of Thoughts on the Business of Life* (New York: Forbes Inc., 1976), 238.
2 Herminia Ibarra and Anne Scoular, "The Leader as Coach: How to Unleash Innovation, Energy, and Commitment," *Harvard Business Review* (Nov-Dec 2019), 113.

Chapter 18
Leading by Example

1 Baldoni, *Lead by Example*, 1.
2 Michael Lane Smith, "How Chesty Puller Earned His 5 Navy Crosses," (Sept 22, 2015).
3 Alan Deutschman, *Walk the Walk: The #1 Rule For Real Leaders* (London: Portfolio, 2009), 157.
4 Chesty Puller is the most decorated Marine in American history with five Navy Crosses, a Distinguished Service Cross, a Silver Star, two Legion of Merit for valor, a Bronze Star for valor, three Air Medals and a Purple Heart.
5 Deutschman, *Walk the Walk,* 66.
6 IBID, 65.
7 Peggy Noonan, "We Must Improve Our Trust in American Institutions," *The Wall Street Journal* (May 31, 2018)
8 Jeffrey M. Jones, "Confidence In US Institutions Down; Average at New Low," Gallup (July 5, 2022)
9 Kolenda, *Leadership: The Warrior's Art,* 4.
10 Simon Sinek, *Leaders Eat Last: Why Some Teams Pull Together and Others Don't (New York:* Portfolio, 2017), 85.
11 Deutschman, *Walk the Walk,* 62.
12 IBID, 63.
13 Abha Bhattarai and Daniela Santamaria, "Bonuses before bankruptcy: Companies doled out millions to executives before filing for Chapter 11" *The Washington Post* (Oct 26, 2020), Business Section.
14 Abha Bhattarai and Daniela Santamaria, "Bonuses Before bankruptcy."
15 Dempsey, *Radical Inclusion*, 129.
16 Jeffrey A. Krames, (2002). *The Rumsfeld Way-Leadership Wisdom of a Battle-Hardened Maverick* (New York: McGraw-Hill, 2002), 48.

Chapter 19
Decision-Making

1 Noel M. Tichy and Warren G. Bennis, *Judgment: How Winning Leaders Make Great Calls (New York:* Portfolio, 2007), 4.
2 Hall, *Aristotle's Way,* 62.
3 Tichy and Bennis, *Judgment: How Winning Leaders Make Great Calls,* 4.
4 Warren E. Buffet, *The Berkshire Hathaway Inc. 2008 Annual Report.*
5 Mattis and West, *Call Sign Chaos,* 165.
6 IBID, 141.
7 Dexter Filkins, "Colin Powell's Fateful Moment," *The New Yorker* (Oct 18, 2021).
8 Krames, *The Rumsfeld Way,* 153.
9 Kissinger, *Leadership: Six Studies in World Strategy,* xvi.
10 IBID, 338

Chapter 20
Succeeding

1 Stanley McChrystal, *Team of Teams: New Rules of Engagement for a Complex World (New York:* Portfolio, 2015), 8.
2 Mattis and West, *Call Sign Chaos*, 6.
3 Mike Ettore, "Why Most New Executives Fail–and Four Things Companies Can Do About It," *Forbes* (March 13, 2020).

Chapter 21
The Final Afterthought

1 Peggy Noonan, "Colin Powell's Great American Journey," *The Wall Street Journal* (Oct 21, 2021).
2 Peggy Noonan, "Kamala Harris Needs to Get Serious," *The Wall Street Journal* (Dec 9, 2021).
3 Ryan Holiday, *Courage Is Calling: Fortune Favors the Brave* (New York: Penguin Press, 2021), 140.
4 John W. Gardner, *Morale (*New York: W.W. Norton & Co., 1980*)*, 66.
5 Ettore, *Trust-Based Leadership*, 34.

BIBLIOGRAPHY

Achor, S. (2010). *The Happiness Advantage: The Seven Principles of Positive Psychology That Fuel Success and Performance at Work.* New York: Crown Business.

Adams, D.; Carwardine M. (1992). *Last Chance to See.* New York: Ballantine Books.

Addison, J. (2016). *Real Leadership: 9 Simple Practices for Leading and Living with Purpose.* NY, NY: McGraw-Hill.

Air Command and Staff College, C.M. (2013). ACSC. *Leadership Competencies, Lesson 2.* Maxwell AFB, Alabama.

Army, U. (1999). *Army Leadership: Be, Know, Do Field Manual 22-100.* Washington, DC: USA.

Aston, R. (2019). *View From Gold Mountain: History, Memory, Voices.* San Francisco: Sixth Avenue Books.

Atkinson, R. (2007). *The Day of Battle: The War in Sicily and Italy, 1943-1944, Vol II.* New York: Picador.

Atkinson, R. (2013). *The Guns At Last Light: The War in Western Europe, 1944-1945, Vol III.* New York: Picador.

Axelrod, A. (2004). *When the Buck Stops With You: Harry S. Truman on Leadership.* New York: Portfolio.

Bacevich, A.J. (2008). *The Limits of Power: The End of American Exceptionalism.* New York: Metropolitan Books.

Baier, B. (2017). *Three Days in January: Dwight Einhower's Final Mission.* New York: William Morrow.

Baker, G. (Feb 21, 2020). "A Man For All Seasons at 100." *The Wall Street Journal.*

Baker, G. (2023). *American Breakdown: Why We No Longer Trust Our Leaders and Institutions and How We Can Rebuild Confidence.* New York: Twelve.

Baldoni, J. (2008). *Lead By Example: 50 Ways Great Leaders Inspire Results.* New York: Amacom.

Barber, J.D. (1977). *The Presidential Character: Predicting Performance in the White House.* Englewood Cliffs, NJ: Prentice-Hall.

Beck, G. (2011). *Being George Washington: The Indispensable Man, As You've Never Seen Him.* New York: Threshold Editions.

Bender, T.B. (1992). *Don't Squat With Yer Spurs On! A Cowboy's Guide To Life.* Layton, UT: Gibs Smith.

Bennett, W. (1993). *The Book of Virtues: Treasury of Great Moral Stories.* New York: Simon & Schuster.

Bennis, W.G.; Tichy N.M. (2007). *Judgment: How Winning Leaders Make Great Calls.* New York: Penguin Publishing Group.

Bennis, W.G.; Tichy N.M. (2007). "Making Judgment Calls:-*Harvard Business Review.*

Bennis, W.G. (2003). *On Becoming a Leader.* Cambridge, MA: Perseus Publishing.

Bennis, W.G. (Jan 2004). "The Seven Ages of the Leader." *Harvard Business Review.*

Bennis, W.; Thomas, R.J. (2002). Crucibles of Leadership. *Harvard Business Review.*

Berra, Y. (2001). *When You Come to a Fork in the Road, Take It! Inspiration and Wisdom from One of Baseball's Greatest Heroes.* New York: Hyperion.

Bhattarai, A.; Santamariña, D. (Oct 27, 2020). Bonuses Before Bankruptcy: Companies doled out millions to executives before filing for Chapter 11. *Washington Post.*

Bing, S. (Sept 1, 2016). Why Crazy Works. *The Wall Street Journal.*

Blanchard, K.; Johnson, S. (2001). *The One Minute Manager.* New York: Simon & Schuster.

Blanchard, Muchnick, M. (2003). *The Leadership Pill: The Missing Ingredient in Motivating People Today.* New York: Free Press.

Borchers, C. (Sept 19, 2022). "Employees Strike Back at 'Quitters,'" *The Wall Street Journal.*

Bossidy, L.; Charon, R. (2002). *Execution: The Discipline of Getting Things Done.* New York: Crown Business.

Boyle, M. (Oct 3, 2006). "Why Costco Is so Damn Addictive." *Fortune magazine.*

Brady, C.; Orrin, W. (2007). *Launching a Leadership Revolution: Mastering the Five Levels of Influence.* New York: Business Plus.

Bersin, J. (Feb 4, 2014). Spending on Corporate Training Soars: Employee Capability Now a Priority. *Forbes.*

Brodie, F.M. (1967). *The Devil Drives: A Life of Sir Richard Burton.* New York: Norton Press.

Brokaw, T. (1998). *The Greatest Generation.* New York: Random House.

Brookhiser, R. (2008). *George Washington on Leadership*. New York: Basic Books.

Brooks, D. (2015). *The Road to Character*. New York: Random House.

Brooks, D. (2019). *The Second Mountain: The Quest for a Moral Life*. New York: Random House .

Brouker, M. (2020). *Lessons from The Navy: How to Earn Trust, Lead Teams, and Achieve Organizational Excellence* . Lanham, MD: Rowman & Littlefield.

Brown, D. J. (2014). *The Boys in the Boat: Nine Americans and Their Epic Quest for Gold at the 1936 Berlin Olympics*. New York: Penguin Books.

Brown, S. M. (2021). *https://www.militry.com/marine-corps/5-reasons-why-chesty-puller-marine-corps-legend.html*. Retrieved from Military.com.

Brubaker, J. (Feb 4, 2015). Why You Should Run Your Business Like Bill Belichick. *Entrepreneur*.

Buckingham, M. (April 30, 2022). Annual Reviews Are a Terrible Way to Evaluate Employees. *The Wall Street Journal*.

Buffet, W.E. (2008). *Berkshire Hathaway Inc., 2008 Annual Report*. Omaha, Nebraska.

Burns, J.M. (1978). *Leadership*. New York: Harper Colophon.

Calpan, R.S. (Jan 2007). "What to Ask the Person in the Mirror." *Harvard Business Review*.

Carnegie, D. (n.d.). *How to Win Friends and Influence People*.

Carroll, R.C. (2017). *Building Your Leadership Legacy: It's All About Character*. Sarasota, FL: Suncoast Digital Press.

Charan, R.; Bossidy, L. (2002). *Execution: The Discipline of Getting Things Done*. New York: Crown Business.

Charan, R. (2007). *Know-How: The 8 Skills That Separate People Who Perform from Those Who Don't*. New York: Crown Business.

Charan, R. (2017). *The High Potential Leader: How to Grow Fast, Take on New Responsibilities, and Make an Impact*. Hoboken, New Jersey: Wiley.

Chernow, R. (2010). *Washington: A Life* (Vol. Vol I). New York: Penguin Books.

Churchill, W. (1930). *My Early Life*. London: Odhams Press Limited.

Citrin, J. (May 21, 2016). "The Life-Changing Power of Small Things." Commencement Address at Wesleyan College.

Clark, T.R. (2016). *Leading with Character and Competence: Moving Beyond Title, Position and Authority*. Oakland, CA: Berrett-Koehler Publishers.

Coelho, P. (1993). *The Alchemist.* Rio de Janeiro: Harper Collins.

College, A.W. (2010). USAF Leadership in Warfare Course. *Lesson 2 Leadership Competencies.* Maxwell Air Force Base, Alabama: USAF.

Collier, P. (2005). *Medal of Honor: Portraits of Valor Beyond the Call of Duty.* New York: Artisan.

Collins, J. (2001). *Good to Great: Why Some Companies Make the Leap...and Others Don't.* New York: Harper Business.

Colvin, G. (2008). *Talent Is Overrated: What Really Separates World-Class Performers from Everybody Else.* New York: Portfolio.

Covey, S.R. (1989,). *The 7 Habits of Highly Effective People,.* New York: Simon and Schuster.

Cozzens, P. (Dec 21, 2018). "*Valley Forge* Review: In the Bleak Midwinter." *The Wall Street Journal.*

Cronin, T.E. (Winter 1984). "Thinking and Learning about Leadership." *Presidential Studies Quarterly.*

Cutter, C. (June 25, 2021). Rich Lesser, CIO Whisperer, on His Toughest Moments. *The Wall Street Journal.*

Dalio, R. (2017). *Principles.* New York: Simon & Schuster.

Daniel, T.A. (2015). *Crossing the Line: An Examination of Toxic Leadership in the U.S. Army.* Louisville, KY: Sullivan University IRB Ref # 05212014-01.

Gay, J. (June 3, 2018). Shock Claim: Bill Belichick Not Barrel of Laughs. *The Wall Street Journal.*

Delfino, D.; Shepard, D. (April 8, 2024) "Percentage of Businesses That Fail—and How to Boost Chances of Success." Lending Tree blog.

DeMarco, C.J. (Dec 15, 2020). "Leadership Philosophy 101: Who Are You?" Retrieved from Applied Leadership and Command Seminar, Air University: https://m100group.com/2020/12/16/leadership-philosophy-git-u-some-demarco-banter/

DeMille, N. (2017). *The Cuban Affair.* New York: Simon & Schuster.

Dempsey, M.E.; Brafman, O. (2018). *Radical Inclusion: What the Post-9/11 World Should Have Taught Us About Leadership.* USA: Missionday.

Dempsey, M.E. (2020). *No Time For Spectators: The Lessons That Mattered Most from West Point to the West Wing.* USA: Missionday.

Deutschman, A. (2009). *Walk the Walk: The #1 Rule For Real Leaders.* New York: Portfolio.

Drucker, P.F. (2006). *Classic Drucker: Wisdom from Peter Drucker from the Pages of Harvard Business Review.* Boston: Harvard Business School Publishing.

Duckworth, A. (2016). *Grit: The Power of Passion and Perseverance.* New York: Scribner.

Duckworth, A. (June 23, 2017). "Is There Anything Grit Can't Do?" *The Wall Street Journal.*

Ellis, J. (2004). *His Excellency: George Washington.* New York: Alfred A Knopf.

Ettore, M. (2019). *Trust-Based Leadership: Marine Corps Leadership Concepts for Today's Business Leaders.* Fidelis Press.

Ettore, M. (March 13, 2020). Why Most New Executives Fail—and Four Things Companies Can Do About It. *Forbes.*

Ferling, J. (2009). *The Ascent of George Washington: The Hidden Political Genius of an American Icon.* New York: Bloomsbury Press.

Filkins, D. (Oct 18, 2021). Colin Powell's Fateful Moment. *The New Yorker.*

Fisher, A. (March 22, 2004). Turning Clock-Watchers into Stars. *Fortune magazine.*

Fleming, T. (December 24, 2007). Washinton's Gift. *The Wall Street Journal,* A11.

Flexner, J.T. (1965). *George Washington, The Forge of Experience (1732-1775).* Little, Brown & Company Limited .

Foley, R.F. (2022). *Standing Tall: Leadership Lessons in the Life of a Soldier.* Havertown, PA: Casemate Publishers.

Forbes. (1976). *The Forbes Scrapbook of Thoughts on the Business of Life.* New York: B.C. Forbes & Sons Publishing.

Frankl, V.E. (1959). *Man's Search For Meaning.* Boston, MA: Beacon Press.

Gallup Poll (July 14, 2021). Gallup Poll. Retrieved from news.gallup.com

Gallup. (2013). *The State of the American Workplace: Employee Engagement Insights for US Business Leaders.* Gallup Inc.

Gardner, J.W. (1978). *Morale.* New York: W.W. Norton & Co.

Gardner, J.W. (1990). *On Leadership.* New York: The Free Press.

Gates, R.M. (2017). *A Passion for Leadership: Lessons on Change and Reform from Fifty Years of Public Service.* New York: Penguin Random House.

George, B.; Sims, P.; McClean, A.N.; Mayer, D. (Feb 2007). "Discovering Your Authentic Leadership." *Harvard Business Review.*

George, B. (2015). *Discover Your True North.* Hoboken, NJ: Wiley.

Gerstner, L. (Oct 2, 2016). "The Culture Ate Our Corporate Reputation." *The Wall Street Journal.*

Goffee, R.; Jones, G. (Dec 2005). "Managing Authenticity: The Paradox of Great Leadership." *Harvard Business Review.*

Goleman, D. (2004). "What Makes a Leader?" *Harvard Business Review*.

Goleman, D. (Tenth Anniversary Edition 2006). *Emotional Intelligence: Why It Can Matter More Than IQ*. New York: Bantam.

Goodwin, D K. (2005). *Team of Rivals: The Political Genius of Abraham Lincoln*. New York: Simon & Schuster.

Goodwin, D.K. (2013). *Bully Pulpit: Theodore Roosevelt and the Golden Age of Journalism*. New York: Simon & Schuster.

Goodwin, D.K. (2018). *Leadership in Turbulent Times*. New York: Simon & Schuster.

Graham, S. (2019). *Identity Leadership: To Lead Others You Must First Lead Yourself*. New York: Center Street.

Greenleaf, R.K. (1977). *Servant Leadership: A Journey into the Nature of Legitimate Power & Greatness*. Mahwah, New Jersey: Paulist Press.

Hall, E. (2019). *Aristotle's Way, The Ancient Greeks; Ten Ways They Shaped the Modern World*. New York: Penguin Press.

Harari, O. (2002). *The Leadership Secrets of Colin Powell*. New York: McGraw-Hill.

Herodotus. (1954 Translation). *The Histories*. New York: Penguin Classics.

Holiday, R.; Hanselman, S. *The Daily Stoic: 366 Meditations on Wisdom, Perservance and the Art of Living*. New York: Portfolio

Holiday, R. (2021). *Courage Is Calling: Fortune Favors the Brave*. New York: Portfolio.

Hurley, R. (Dec 12, 2006). Prof Hurley article. *Executive Leadership, Vol. 21*.

Hurley, F. (Spring 2006). "The Decision to Trust." *Harvard Business Review OnPoint*.

Hyacinth, B. (March 1, 2018). "A Good Boss Is the Best Incentive of All!" *https://www.linkedin.com/pulse/why-good-boss-best-incentive-all-brigette-hyacinth/*. Retrieved from LinkedIn.

Isaacson, W. (2003). *Benjamin Franklin: An American Life*. New York: Simon & Schuster.

Jindal, B. (Nov 2, 2018). "The Roots of Political Polarization." *The Wall Street Journal*.

Johnson, B. (2014). *The Churchill Factor: How One Man Made History*. New York: Riverhead Books.

Jones, G.; Goffee, Ro. (2005). "Managing Authenticity: The Paradox of Great Leadership." *Harvard Business Review*

Joulwan, G. (2021). *Watchman at the Gates: A Soldier's Journey from Berlin to Bosnia*. Lexington, KY: The University Press of Kentucky.

Kissinger, H. (2022). *Leadership: Six Studies in World Strategy*. New York: Penguin Books.

Klann, D.G. (Aug 2013). *The Application of Power and the Influence in Organizational Leadership*. Fort Leavenworth, KS USACGSC: reprinted in US Army Command and General Staff College L100 Book of Readings.

Klay, P. (Feb 10, 2017). "What We're Fighting For." *The New York Times*.

Koehn, N. (Dec 24, 2011). *Leadership Lessons from the Shackleton Expedition. The New York Times*.

Koehn, N. (2017). *Forged In Crisis: The Power of Courageous Leadership in Turbulent Times*. New York: Scribner.

Kolenda, C. (2001). *Leadership: The Warrior's Art*. Carlisle, PA: The Army War College Foundation Press.

Kosner, E. (Aug 2, 2023). "*The Right Call* Review: The Sheep from the GOATs." *The Wall Street Journal*.

Kotter, J.P. (1999) *John P. Kotter on What Leaders Really Do*. Harvard Business Review Press.

Kouchaki, M.; Smith, I.H. (Jan 1, 2020). Building an Ethical Career. *Harvard Business Review*.

Kouzes, J.M.; Posner, B.Z. (2012). *The Leadership Challenge: How to Make Extraordinary Things Happen in Organizations, 5th Edition*. San Francisco, CA: Jossey-Bass.

Kouzes, J. M.; Posner, B.Z. (Oct 8, 2003). "Challenge Is the Opportunity for Greatness." *Leader to Leader Newsletter*.

Kouzes, J.M.; Posner, B.Z. (2003). *The Leadership Challenge, 3rd Edition*. San Francisco, CA: Jossey-Bass.

Krulak, C.G. (Dec 1996). Character. *Leatherneck* magazine, 14.

Kushner, H.S. (1959). Forward in Viktor E. Frankl's *Man's Search for Meaning*. Boston, MA: Beacon Press.

Kushner, H.S. (2002). *Living a Life That Matters*. New York: Anchor Books.

Lansing, A. (2002). *Endurance: Shackleton Incredible Voyage, 6th Edition*. New York: Carroll & Graf Publishers.

Lee, G. (2006). *Courage: The Backbone of Leadership*. San Francisco, CA: Jossey-Bass .

Leinwand, P.; Blount, S. (Nov-Dec 2019). "Why Are We Here?" *Harvard Business Review*.

Lencioni, P. (Sept 24, 2009). "The No-Cost Way to Motivate." *Businessweek*.

Lewis, C.S. (1943). *Mere Christianity*. New York: Touchstone.

Margolis, J.D.; Stolz, P. (Jan-Feb 2010). "How to Bounce Back from Adversity." *Harvard Business Review*.

Maruca, R.F.; Galford, R.M. (2006). *Your Leadership Legacy: Why*

Looking Toward the Future Will Make You a Better Leader To-day. Boston: Harvard Business School Press.

Mattis, J.; West, B.. (2019). *Call Sign Chaos: Learning to Lead*. New York: Random House.

Maxwell, J.C. (2002). *Leadership 101: What Every Leader Needs to Know*. Nashville, TN: Thomas Nelson Publishers.

Maxwell, J.C. (1998). *The 21 Irrefutable Laws of Leadership: Follow Them and People Will Follow You*. Nashville, TN: Thomas Nelson.

Maxwell, J.C. (April 2010). "Are You an Effective Leader?" *Success* magazine.

Maxwell, J.C. (2014). *Good Leaders Ask Great Questions: Your Foundation for Successful Leadership*. New York: Center Street Press.

Maylett, T.; Warner, P. (2014). *Magic: Five Keys to Unlock the Power of Employee Engagement*. Austin, TX: Greenleaf Book Group.

McCain, J.; Salter, M. (2007). *Hard Call: Great Decisions and the Extraordinary People Who Made Them*. New York: Twelve, Hatchett Book Group.

McChrystal, S. (2015). *Team of Teams: New Rules of Engagement for a Complex World*. New York: Portfolio.

McLean, B.; Elkind, P. (2003). *The Smartest Guys In The Room: The Amazing Rise and Scandalous Fall of Enron*. New York: Portfolio.

McManus, J.C. (2015). *The Dead and Those About to Die: D-Day: The Big Red One at Omaha Beach*. New York: Penguin Publishing Group.

Melton, T. (May 26, 2018). *Understanding the Say-Do Gap*. Melton Leadership website. https://meltonleadership.org/understanding-the-say-do-gap/.

Merritt, J. (2019). *Character Still Counts: It Is Time to Restore Our Lasting Values*. Eugene, Oregon: Harvest House Publishers.

Middlekauff, R. (2015). *Washington's Revolution: The Making of America's First Leader*. New York: Alfred A. Knopf.

Miller, C. (Jan 5, 2018). *The Character Gap: How Good Are We?* Oxford, UK: Oxford University Press.

Miller, J. (1992). *Reflections of a Warrior: Six Years as a Green Beret in Vietnam*. Novato, CA: Pocket Books .

Mills, A. (2019). *Unstoppable Teams: The Four Essential Actions of High-Performance Leadership*. New York: Harper Business.

Montini, L. (March 21, 2014). "The Positive Power of Your Team's Darkest Days." *Inc.* magazine. https://www.inc.com/laura-montini/how-you-can-actually-boost-morale-in-your-companys-darkest-days.html.

Myatt, M. (Jan 23, 2013). *Why You're Not a Leader.* Retrieved from Forbes blog.

Myrer, A. (1968). *Once An Eagle.* Canada: Holt, Rinehart and Winston of Canada.

News, F. (Jan 16, 2010). "Coakley Risks Offending Red Sox Nation, Calls Schilling 'Another Yankee Fan'." Fox News.

Noonan, P. (Oct 21, 2021). "Colin Powell's Great American Journey." *The Wall Street Journal.*

Noonan, P. (Dec 9, 2021). "Kamala Harris Needs to Get Serious." *The Wall Street Journal.*

Obodaru, O.; Ibarra, H. (Jan 2009). "Women and the Vision Thing." *Harvard Business Review.*

O'Brian, P. (1970). *Master and Commander.* New York: William Collins Sons & Co. Ltd.

O'Connell, R.L. (2022). *Team America: Patton, MacArthur, Marshall, Eisenhower, and the World They Forged.* New York: Harper Collins.

Oppenheimer, M. (July 30, 2021). "The Power of Purpose-Driven Schools." *The Wall Street Journal.*

O'Reilly, B.; Dugard, M. (2017). *Killing England: The Brutal Struggle for American Independence.* New York: Henry Holt and Co.

Ortberg, J. (1998). *Life-Changing Love: Moving God's Love from Your Head to Your Heart.* Grand Rapids, MI: Zondervan.

Pearce, N. (Feb 3, 2017). The Patriot's Bill Belichick Inspires His Team By Calling Them This. *Fortune.*

Peters, T.J.; Waterman Jr., R.H. (2004). *In Search of Excellence.* New York: Harper Collins .

Peterson, J. (2016). *The 10 Laws of Trust: Building the Bonds That Make a Company Great.* New York: Amacom.

Peterson, J.B. (2018). *12 Rules For Life: An Antidote to Chaos.* Toronto: Random House Canada.

Pew Research Center. (2021). *Pew Research Center.* Retrieved from https://www.pewresearch.org/politics/2024/06/24/public-trust-in-government-1958-2024/

Posner B.; Kouzes, J. (2010). *The Truth About Leadership: The No-Fads, Heart-of-the-Matter Facts You Need to Know.* San Francisco: Jossey-Bass.

Posner, J. M. (Jan 2009). "To Lead, Create a Shared Vision." *Harvard Business Review.*

Powers, J.B. (2000). *Flags of Our Fathers.* New York: Bantam Books.

Prentice, W.H. (Jan 2004). "Understanding Leadership." *Harvard Business Review.*

Quinn, R.E. (1996). *Deep Change: Discovering the Leader Within.* San Francisco: Jossey-Bass.

Ranger Training Brigade Brief, R. (Nov 29, 2021), https://www.moore.army.mil/INFANTRY/ARTB/History.html

Reed, G.E. (Jul-August 2004). "Toxic Leadership." *Military Review*.

Rees, J.C. (2007). *George Washington's Leadership Lessons: What the Father of our Country Can Teach Us about Effective Leadership and Character*. Hoboken, New Jersey: Wiley

Rennie, J. (Aug 2, 2017). "Chick-fil-A Generates Most Revenue Per Restaurant in US." The Daily Caller.

Robert F. Foley, L. U. (2022). *Standing Tall: Leadership Lessons in the Life of a Soldier*. Havertown, PA: Casemate Publishers.

Roberts, A. (2018). *Churchill: Walking with Destiny*. Viking.

Shull, B. (April 4, 2019). "*How to Think Like a Roman Emperor* Review": Meditations for the Masses." *The Wall Street Journal*.

Krames, J.. (2002). *The Rumsfeld Way: Leadership Wisdom of a Battle-Hardened Maverick*. McGraw-Hill.

Sandberg, J. (Jan 28, 2004). "Been Here 25 Years and All I Got Was This Lousy T-Shirt." *The Wall Street Journal*.

Santamarina, D.; Bhattarai, A.. (Oct 26, 2020). "Bonuses before bankruptcy: Companies doled out millions to executives before filing for Chapter 11." *The Washington Post*.

Scoular, I. (Nov-Dec 2019). "The Leader as Coach." *Harvard Business Review*.

Senge, P.M. (2006). *The Fifth Discipline: The Art & Practice of the Learning Organization*. New York: Doubleday.

Sibley, G. (May 24, 2013). *Van Gogh and the Self-portrait— Who Knew He Painted So Many?* Gail Sibley website. https://www.gailsibley.com/2013/05/24/van-gogh-and-the-self-portrait/#:~:text=Vincent%20Van%20Gogh%20(1853%2D1890,died%20%E2%80%93%20four%20years%20in%20total!

Simons, T. (2008). *The Integrity Dividend: Leading by the Power of Your Word*. San Francisco, CA: Josey-Bass.

Sinek, S. (2017). *Leaders Eat Last: Why Some Teams Pull Together and Others Don't*. New York: Portfolio.

Smith, I.H.; Kouchaki, M. (Jan-Feb 2020). "Building an Ethical Career." *Harvard Business Review*.

Smith, M.L. (Sept 22, 2015). "How Chesty Puller Earned His 5 Navy Crosses." Task & Purpose. https://www.bloomberg.com/news/articles/2007-10-31/win-smith-on-the-exit-of-merrills-ceobusinessweek-business-news-stock-market-and-financial-advice?embedded-checkout=true

Smith, W. (Nov 11, 2011). Exit of Merrill CEO Stan O'Neal. *Businessweek*.

Margolick, D. (July 19, 2018). "*Unbeaten* Review: Forty-nine Wins and No Losses." *The Wall Street Journal*.

Stephens, B. (Aug 29, 2016). "Who Did This to Us?" *The Wall Street Journal*.

Sturt, D.; Nordstrom, T. (March 8, 2018). "10 Shocking Workplace Stats You Need to Know." *Forbes*.

The Human Era @ Work. (2014). *Harvard Business Review*. *http://uli.org/wp-content/uploads/ULI-Documents/The-Human-Era-at-Work.pdf*.

Thoreau, H.D. (1854). *Walden: Life in the Woods*. Boston, MA: Ticknor and Fields.

Walker, S. (Aug 11, 2018). "Why the Future Belongs to Challenge-Driven Leaders." *The Wall Street Journal*, Living Section.

Wallace, D.F. (2000). "David Foster Wallace on John McCain: The Weasel, Twelve Monkeys and the Shrub." *Rolling Stone*.

Warren, R. (2002). *The Purpose Driven Life: What On Earth Am I Here For?* Grand Rapids, MI: Zondervan.

Weber, L. (Aug 21, 2016). "At Kimberly-Clark, 'Dead Wood' Workers Have Nowhere to Hide." *The Wall Street Journal*.

Weber, L. (June 21, 2020). "As Pandemic Slows Business, Workers Fret: Is My Job Relevant". *The Wall Street Journal*.

Welch, S. (Feb 11, 2009). "Finding Your Inner Courage." *Businessweek*.

Westfall, C. (June 20, 2019). "Leadership Development Is a $366 Billion Industry: Here's Why Most Programs Don't Work." *Forbes*.

White, E. (Dec 3, 2007). "Authentic Ways of Leading." *The Wall Street Journal*.

Wooden, J. (1997). *Wooden: A Lifetime of Observations and Reflections On and Off the Court*. New York: McGraw-Hill.

Worther, M. (Oct 18, 1915). Lecture Me - Please. *The Wall Street Journal*,https://www.nytimes.com/2015/10/18/opinion/sunday/lecture-me-really.html

Yeager, D.S. (Oct 2014). "Boring But Important: A Self-Transcendent Purpose for Learning Fosters Academic Self-Regulation." *Journal of Personality and Social Psychology*.

Yukl, G.A. (2002). "Leadership in Organizations, *Sixth Edition.*" Upper Saddle River, NJ: Pearson Education, Inc.

ABOUT THE AUTHOR

GEORGE ALDRIDGE'S LIFELONG interest in leadership was inspired during his youth as an Army brat growing up in the shadows of two charter members of the Greatest Generation, his father a WWII, Korea, and Vietnam veteran, and his mother, a British War Bride. His father instilled in George a philosophy that being a leader is about selflessness, doing what is best for the greater good, even if it comes at a personal expense. From his English mother, who as a teenager, had to climb into bomb shelters during German air raids most nights during WWII, he learned how to keep a stiff upper lip, keep calm, and carry on in tough times.

George was commissioned a second lieutenant of infantry through the North Georgia College ROTC program and served thirty years in the Army retiring as a colonel. He is a graduate of the Army's Airborne and Ranger schools and commanded infantry units at the platoon, company, battalion, and brigade level.

After retiring from the Army, George entered the corporate world serving in leadership positions at The Coca-Cola Co. and IMI Cornelius. He ended his corporate life as president of Via-Global. Since leaving the corporate world, George has been an adjunct professor teaching graduate-level leadership courses for the US Air Force Air University and a leadership consultant and coach for mid- to large-size companies.

Along with a bachelor's degree in history from North Georgia College, George holds a master's degree in psychology from Purdue University. He is also a graduate of the National War College.

He and his wife, Vicki, have been married for over forty years and have one son and one granddaughter.